WOMEN, PRISON, & CRIME

Illinois Central College
Learning Resources Center

Contemporary Issues in Crime and Justice Series
Roy Roberg, San Jose State University: Series Editor

Crime and Justice: Issues and Ideas (1984)
Philip Jenkins, Pennsylvania State University

Hard Time: Understanding and Reforming the Prison (1987)
Robert Johnson, The American University

The Myth of a Racist Criminal Justice System (1987)
William Wilbanks, Florida International University

Gambling Without Guilt: The Legitimation of an American Pastime (1988)
John Rosecrance, University of Nevada at Reno

Ethics in Crime and Justice: Dilemmas and Decisions (1989)
Joycelyn M. Pollock-Byrne, University of Houston

Sense and Nonsense about Crime: A Policy Guide, Second Edition (1989)
Samuel Walker, University of Nebraska at Omaha

Crime Victims: An Introduction to Victimology, Second Edition (1990)
Andrew Karmen, John Jay College of Criminal Justice

Death Work: A Study of the Modern Execution Process (1990)
Robert Johnson, The American University

Lawlessness and Reform: The FBI in Transition (1990)
Tony G. Poveda, State University of New York at Plattsburg

Women, Prison, and Crime (1990)
Joycelyn M. Pollock-Byrne, University of Houston

WOMEN, PRISON, & CRIME

Joycelyn M. Pollock-Byrne
University of Houston-Downtown

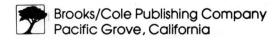 Brooks/Cole Publishing Company
Pacific Grove, California

Consulting Editor: Roy R. Roberg

Brooks/Cole Publishing Company
A Division of Wadsworth, Inc.

Printed in the United States of America

10   9   8   7   6   5   4   3   2   1

Library of Congress Cataloging in Publication Data
Pollock-Byrne, Joycelyn M., [date]
Women, prison, and crime / Joycelyn M. Pollock-Byrne.
        p.   cm.
Includes bibliographical references.
ISBN 0-534-12888-2
1. Women prisoners—United States.   2. Reformatories for women—
United States.   I. Title.
HV9471.P65   1990
365'.43'0973--dc20   89-25164
                                                                              CIP

Sponsoring Editor: Cynthia C. Stormer
Marketing Representative: Ragu Raghavan
Editorial Assistant: Cathleen Sue Collins
Production Editor: Linda Loba
Manuscript Editor: Catherine Cambron
Permissions Editor: Carline Haga
Interior Design: Linda Loba
Cover Design and Illustration: Erin Mauterer, Bluewater A & D
Printing and Binding: Malloy Lithographing, Inc.

To Tony

Foreword

Through the Contemporary Issues in Crime and Justice Series, students are introduced to important topics that until now have been neglected or inadequately covered and that are relevant to criminal justice, criminology, law, political science, psychology, and sociology. The authors address philosophical and theoretical issues and analyze the most recent research findings and their implications for practice. Consequently, each volume will stimulate further thinking and debate on the topics it covers, in addition to providing direction for the development and implementation of policy.

Women, Prison, and Crime is an attempt to increase our understanding of female criminality and women's prisons. The need for such knowledge is evidenced by the fact that most current and past research on criminal and institutional behavior has been directed at males. This lack of attention to women's prisons is all the more disconcerting when one considers that female incarceration rates continue to increase. Joy Pollock-Byrne has used this work to bring the available research findings together in a comprehensive and informative format, providing a much needed treatise on female criminality, prisons, and prison behavior.

Discussion focuses on the development of female criminality, the history of women's prisons, an analysis of women prisoners and how they are treated, correctional staff and their roles, legal issues confronting incarcerated women, and future directions in the field. A bevy of prison life stories and quotes are provided, which adds realism and depth to our understanding of what life is like inside a women's institution. The author has further added to the scope of her work by comparing female inmates and prison settings with their male counterparts, and by utilizing a cross-cultural perspective.

From this analysis, several important findings are evident, including: the existence of competing paradigms in research on women offenders; the possibility that women suffer more in prison than men, despite the appearance of "softer" treatment; the inappropriateness of using programs designed for men in women's facilities; the likelihood that recent higher rates of female incarceration are due more to sentencing practices than increased levels of crime; the development of a unique subculture among women inmates, and finally, the importance of children in the majority of women inmate's lives. Through her comprehensive review, Pollock-Byrne has done an admirable job of clarifying these findings, and providing sensible alternatives to a very complex set of circumstances. This work will provide valuable guidance to both students and practitioners in the development of future policies with respect to women's prisons and the treatment of women prisoners.

Roy Roberg

Preface

Some readers may be asking, "Why another book on women's prisons?" Although there are still relatively few works in this area compared to the available sources on prisons for men, in the last several years we have seen the early works of Giallombardo and Ward and Kassebaum joined by a number of other studies. Researchers have looked at female homosexuality, leadership, the history of reformatories for women, and other topics. One of the purposes of this text is to gather in all these threads and weave them together to create a cohesive, comprehensive tapestry describing women's prisons today and the women who live and work within their walls. Some thoughts on the history of female institutions serve as a preface to a discussion of current facilities. Current information on the female criminal and theories of criminality are used to make sense of what happens to the female offender in prison.

An author must always choose whether to write for the uniniti-ated or for those already familiar with the works discussed. I have chosen to assume the reader has no knowledge of the literature on female institutions. This choice may mean that the knowledgeable will be told what they already know; for that I apologize. But I hope even those familiar with the works presented will find something of value in these pages.

Prison is like the elephant in the fable: several people may describe different parts of it and their descriptions will sound wildly inconsistent. Further, authors usually choose to describe that with which they are familiar. My work has been with correctional officers. I believe they are, for the most part, sensitive observers of the prison experience and of women prisoners. I also feel that they have been overlooked in many of the writings on prisons for women. For better or worse, the influence of correctional officers pervades the living environment of women's prisons and is one of the elements making them uniquely different from men's prisons. The correctional officer will be included in the portrait painted in this work.

Because this field is one that changes constantly, it is impossible to be completely up to date. However, I have tried to include all current works on the subject, including governmental reports and published writings. Even as I write, the Bureau of Justice Statistics is announcing that the number of female prisoners has risen dramatically in federal and state prisons and that their increase exceeds that for males. It is a sad fact of today's correctional environment that we are incarcerating more and more people; some of these people, indeed more than ever before, are women. For this reason, we must attempt to understand the woman in prison and her experience there. Only then can we hope to reduce the numbers of women in prison.

Every author has the pleasure of acknowledging those who have helped in the creation and production of a book. I would like to thank the staff at the University of Houston, Downtown, library for their cheerful assistance. A relatively small library might have posed a problem, but the skill and diligence of the staff—including Laura Olejnik, Henri Achee, and Anita Garza—and their astute use of computer searches and interlibrary loans made the task painless. I also thank Barbara Rivers, who improved rough drafts; Hans Toch, for reading and commenting on an early version; and the three reviewers provided by Brooks/Cole: Professor Meda Chesney-Lind, University of Hawaii; Professor Mary E. Gilfus, University of Wis-consin; and Professor Roslyn Muraskin, Long Island University. Of course, Roy Roberg and Cindy Stormer and her staff deserve praise, as always, for their efficient and enthusiastic support.

Joycelyn M. Pollock-Byrne

CONTENTS

1 Introduction

Three basic facts characterize women's institutions. First, they are smaller than most prisons for males. Second, there are fewer of them. Third, they are different from prisons for males. The first two elements affect the third, but other factors also contribute to make women's prisons unique.

In the past we have incarcerated women reluctantly, hesitantly, and with no very clear mandate for what to do with them once incarcerated. The percentage of women in prison is still miniscule compared to the large numbers of men behind bars; however, there has been a dramatic increase in the number of women incarcerated. The Bureau of Justice Statistics recently reported that the number of inmates in federal and state prison populations increased by 4 percent in the first six months of 1988 to a record 604,824 inmates,

1

but the number of female prisoners increased at a far higher rate than the number of males, increasing 6.7 percent compared to an increase of 3.9 percent for males. This follows an even larger 15.1 percent increase for females incarcerated in 1986. In fact, the number of women in prisons has increased at a faster rate than men every year since 1981 (Bureau of Justice Statistics, 1989). Since 1980 the number of female prisoners has increased 130 percent, compared to a male increase of 81 percent. The relatively small number of women imprisoned—6,269 in 1972, 8,580 in 1975—has increased to 30,834 in state or federal prisons as of June 1988. However, this figure is dwarfed by a total number of 573,990 incarcerated men; women still account for only a little more than 5 percent of the total prisoner population (Bureau of Justice Statistics, 1988).

These 5 percent can be found in types of institutions different from those that house men. Women's institutions range from Bedford Hills' turn-of-the-century brick buildings, situated in affluent Westchester County, New York, to the college-like "campus" of Purdy Treatment Center for Women, surrounded by towering trees and overlooking picturesque Gig Harbor in Washington state. Some states did not have separate institutions for women until very recently. States without a women's prison usually housed female felons in jails or contracted with another state to take their female offenders; for example, Hawaii sent its female prisoners to California for many years before building its own facility in the 1970s.

States typically have only one or two institutions for women, however, so whether women prisoners are housed in cottages or a Gothic castle, they are likely to include all custody grades and to be imprisoned for a variety of crimes, from murder to welfare fraud. Women's institutions have been described as being found in "pastoral areas," with well-kept buildings and few signs of strict security (Baunach, 1977). They typically are described as more pleasant and much less violent than male institutions; however, the women incarcerated in these prisons complain of oppressive supervision and staff attempts to "play with their minds." Women also usually have fewer programs that might make their stay productive. Training programs are usually few in number and often traditionally sex-stereotyped. Although most institutions for women have programs in cosmetology, office skills, and homemaking, few have programs that can help a woman achieve economic self-sufficiency upon release. Yet studies show most female prisoners have children, and most will be the primary economic providers for these children upon release (Baunach, 1977: 17).

In one way, women's prisons are like prisons for men. Like men's prisons, women's prisons also house a disproportionate number of minorities and poor. In 1982, the population of women's prisons was 50 percent black, although blacks comprised only 11 percent of the total population in this country; 9 percent Hispanic, when Hispanics were only 5 percent of the total population; and 3 percent Native American, although this group comprised only .4 percent of the total population (Flowers, 1987: 150). Women in prison, like men in prison, are likely to come from impoverished backgrounds. Very often, the female prisoner is a single mother, either divorced, separated, or never married. An American Correctional Association study reported that in 1983, 75 percent of women in prison were between the ages of twenty-five and thirty-four and were single mothers unemployed at the time of commitment (Dobash, Dobash, and Gutteridge, 1986: 1). While the woman criminal serves her prison term, the children left behind are cared for most often by relatives or by the state in foster homes and institutions.

Women in prison were most often sentenced for property crimes (51 percent), and the percentage of women incarcerated for violent crimes (10 to 11 percent) hasn't changed much for twenty years (Dobash et al., 1986: 1; Crawford, 1988). Early in the century, women were often incarcerated for public-order crimes, such as prostitution and other forms of vice. Today, female crime is likely to be minor property crime, often drug-related. Although women's participation in violent crime has not changed much over the years, the percentage of women incarcerated for violent crime is higher than the figure for men. This disparity may be due to sentencing practices: women are more likely to be imprisoned for less serious crimes. This so-called chivalry may be changing, however, and many suggest that increases in the numbers of women in prison may be partly due to more egalitarian sentencing practices rather than to an increase in female crime. These issues are covered in more detail in subsequent chapters.

The history of women's prisons, described more fully in the next chapter, indicates that the treatment of women has always been different from that of men. While men and women were incarcerated together, there was little official difference in their treatment; but during that period, women were preyed upon by male prisoners and guardians and suffered or participated in sexual exploitation. When women were separated into wings and separate buildings, they were only marginally more secure. They often were still exploited by male guards and suffered from neglect due to their small numbers and the perception that they were irredeemable. In the later part of the nineteenth century, northeastern states began building separate institutions for women. Some of these new facilities were built in response to a reformatory ideal and sought to make over the woman inmate into what was perceived to be "a lady." Those who ran the reformatories only accepted inmates thought to be susceptible to their influence; a great number of women offenders still lived out their incarceration in dank, poorly supervised, harsh penitentiaries. Today, women's institutions still carry the legacy of their reformatory history, partly because many are still in the original buildings designed for women and partly because the ideas regarding what should be done with female prisoners have only gradually changed. Consequently, institutions for women of the 1990s are often still very similar to the institutions of the 1890s.

The correctional field has virtually ignored women in prison. The needs of the small number of female inmates are low on the correctional priority scale. What is more, information on women's prisons and the women incarcerated within them has not been available until fairly recently. For instance, the study of crime by the President's Commission on Law Enforcement and Administration of Justice in the 1960s contained no information on women criminals or prisoners. It wasn't until the 1970s that any comprehensive descriptive studies were published, including those of Glick and Neto (1977) and the Government Accounting Office (1979). Crawford's (1988a, 1988b) recent surveys, conducted under the auspices of the American Correctional Association, will provide updated information on women prisoners and the prisons that house them throughout this text.

Recently, the National Institute of Corrections created a Task Force on Women Offenders, which recommended allocating funds in the coming years to studies surveying the needs of female jail prisoners, development of a resource guide for programs in jails, and technical assistance for jail managers interested in developing programs for female prisoners. The task force also suggested that funds be allocated to state prisons, to be spent on such projects as improving the design of women's prisons, improving classification and training, and providing technical assistance for vocational training programs and service programs. The task force also recommended allocating funds to improve parole for women and develop other community programs (National Institute of Corrections, 1988). The increasing and long overdue interest in women prisoners is no doubt influenced by the rapid escalation in their numbers. With any luck, this attention will fill gaps in the available information and provide much needed resources for improving women's prisons and prison programs.

Academic researchers also ignored prisons for women until fairly recently. The writings on prisons have been almost exclusively concerned with prisons for men. This field has a rich and extensive tradition, starting in the 1940s, with works by Sykes (1958) and Clemmer (1940) on the prisoner subculture, and continuing through the 1970s and 1980s, with descriptions of the prison experience by Johnson (1987), Jacobs (1977), and Toch (1975, 1977). Other writers have chosen to document other aspects of prison life, such as victimization (Bowker, 1980), staff (Crouch, 1980), racial issues (Carroll, 1974; Davidson, 1974), or philosophical issues of imprisonment (Hawkins, 1976). However, few of these writers have chosen to explore the world of female prisoners. The few exceptions include Bowker (1978) and Fox (1975).

The literature on women's prisons has a separate and much truncated history, which began almost 30 years after research started to be conducted in prisons for men. Apart from a single history and description published in 1931 (Lekkerkerker, 1931), Giallombardo (1966) and Ward and Kassebaum (1965) pioneered the line of works describing women's prisons. These initial works were followed several years later by other studies that further explored female prison homosexuality (Propper, 1976) and a few that looked at other aspects of the female prisoner subculture (Heffernan, 1972; Mitchell, 1975). Finally, books have recently been published on the history of women's prisons (Freedman, 1981; Rafter, 1985).

A few books have also been published that describe female prisons in Great Britain (Dobash et al., 1986; Smith, 1962). The history and current conditions of British female prisoners appear very similar to those of their sisters in the States. Women prisoners in Great Britain are also disproportionately black and poor, are incarcerated mostly for property crimes, and comprise a very small portion (3 to 4 percent) of the total incarcerated population (Dobash et al., 1986: 2). These women are housed in eight closed and three open institutions for adult women in England and Wales and one prison in Scotland (Dobash et al., 1986: 4).

Many questions are still unanswered. Aspects of the prisoner subculture other than homosexuality either have yet to be explored or could be explored more fully. Questions include: What methods do women use to distribute contraband goods? What forms of leadership exist among women? What sanctions are imposed against those who violate the norms and what is the general adherence to an inmate code by the female population? What subcultural groupings exist in different types of prisons? What is the level of drug and alcohol abuse in prison? What forms and level of aggressiveness and violence are displayed in prisons for women? And what is the nature and effect of the interaction between staff and inmates? Some of these questions are addressed in this work; others are still left to be explored.

Even more important, however, are the questions concerning the present alarming increase in the number of women being incarcerated. Does this increase parallel an increase in female crime, or is it due to a change in sentencing practices? Are prison sentences needed for these women or are community placements more efficacious and appropriate? Are programs for women improving in number and quality, and are they serving the needs of women prisoners who must support themselves and their children upon release? Has current litigation, focused on equal protection, served the best interests of female prisoners, or has it endangered the few beneficial aspects of the different philosophy that seems uniquely to characterize the prison for women?

Unfortunately, most of these pressing issues are beyond the scope of this work. Little information is available, although a great deal of activity is happening across the country. Any generalizations based on survey results are suspect, and a more detailed research effort is sorely needed. For instance, a later chapter discusses current programs; but programs start and close weekly. Surveys may provide information on the numbers of programs but shed no light on quality or what is really happening in these programs. Many of the most beneficial programs are often run by private groups that volunteer their time in prisons. These efforts are largely uncounted and unrecognized except within the local area. Although numbers may give the age, marital status, race, and background characteristics of the female felon, only her own voice can describe who she is and what she is experiencing in prison. Except for a few collections of narratives, the phenomenological research needed to provide that voice has not been undertaken. However, by examining the history of the institutions and the theories that rationalize confinement, and by beginning to understand who these women are, we may come to understand the problems better and make more enlightened choices for the future.

IIIII References

Baunach, P. (1977) "Women Offenders: A Commentary—Current Conceptions on Women in Crime." *Quarterly Journal of Corrections* 1, 4: 14–18.

Bowker, L. (1978) *Women, Crime and the Criminal Justice System*. Lexington, Mass.: Lexington Books.

Bowker, L. (1980) *Prison Victimization*. New York: Elsevier Press.

Bureau of Justice Statistics. (1989) "Prisoners in 1988." Washington, D.C.: U.S. Government Printing Office.

Carroll, L. (1974) *Hacks, Blacks and Cons*. Lexington, Mass.: Lexington Press.

Clemmer, D. (1940) *The Prison Community*. New York: Holt, Rinehart & Winston.

Crawford, J. (1988a) "Tabulation of a Nationwide Survey of Female Offenders." College Park, Md.: American Correctional Association.

Crawford, J. (1988b) "Tabulation of a Nationwide Survey of State Correctional Facilities for Adult and Juvenile Female Offenders." College Park, Md.: American Correctional Association.

Crouch, B. (1980) *The Keepers: Prison Guards and Contemporary Corrections*. Springfield, Ill.: Charles C Thomas.

Davidson, T. (1974) *Chicano Prisoners: The Key to San Quentin*. New York: Holt, Rinehart & Winston.

Dobash, R., R. Dobash, and S. Gutteridge. (1986) *The Imprisonment of Women*. New York: Basil Blackwell.

Flowers, R. B. (1987) *Women and Criminality: The Woman as Victim, Offender and Practitioner*. Westport, Conn.: Greenwood Press.

Fox, J. (1975) "Women in Crisis." In H. Toch, *Men in Crisis*, pp. 181–205. Chicago: Aldine-Atherton.

Freedman, E. (1981) *Their Sister's Keepers: Women's Prison Reforms in America, 1830–1930*. Ann Arbor, Michigan: University of Michigan Press.

Giallombardo, R. (1966) *Society of Women: A Study of a Women's Prison*. New York: Wiley.

Glick, R., and V. Neto. (1977) *National Study of Women's Correctional Programs*. Washington, D.C.: U.S. Government Printing Office.

Government Accounting Office. (1979) *Who Are the Women in Prison and What Are the Problems Confronting Them?* Washington, D.C.: U.S. Government Printing Office.

Hawkins, G. (1976) *The Prison: Policy and Practice*. Chicago: University of Chicago Press.

Heffernan, R. (1972) *Making it in Prison: The Square, the Cool and the Life*. New York: Wiley.

Jacobs, J. (1977) *Statesville*. Chicago: University of Chicago Press.

Johnson, R. (1987) *Hard Time: Understanding and Reforming the Prison*. Pacific Grove, Calif.: Brooks/Cole.

Lekkerkerker, E. (1931) *Reformatories for Women in the U.S.* Gronigen, Netherlands: J.B. Wolters.

Mitchell, A. (1975) *Informal Inmate Social Structure in Prisons for Women: A Comparative Study*. San Francisco: R & E Research Associates.

National Institute of Corrections, Task Force on Women Offenders. (1988) "Final Report." Paper presented at Academy of Criminal Justice Sciences conference, San Francisco, 1988.

Propper, A. (1976) *Importation and Deprivation Perspectives on Homosexuality in Correctional Institutions: An Empirical Test of Their Relative Efficacy*. Ph.D. diss., University of Michigan, Ann Arbor.

Rafter, N. (1985) *Partial Justice: State Prisons and Their Inmates, 1800–1935*. Boston: Northeastern Press.

Smith, A. (1962) *Women in Prison: A Study in Penal Methods*. London: Stevens Publishers.

Sykes, G. (1958) *The Society of Captives*. Princeton, N.J.: Princeton University Press.

Toch, H. (1975) *Men in Crisis*. Chicago: Aldine-Atherton.

Toch, H. (1977) *Living in Prison*. New York: Free Press.

Ward, D., and G. Kassebaum. (1965) *Women's Prison: Sex and Social Structure*. Chicago: Aldine-Atherton.

2 ||||||||||||||||||||||||||||||||||||||||||||||||||||||||||
Female Criminality

Crime causation theories have a direct influence on the correctional treatment of female and male criminals. Before we begin to discuss prisons and their purposes, some explanations of crime causation must be analyzed. This chapter briefly describes the theories that have been developed to explain female criminality; both historical and current theories are presented. The chapter then presents female crime statistics and discusses some of the research analyzing these statistics. Finally, the chapter outlines how these theories and the reality of female criminality—or what we think is reality—affects what we do in the name of treatment and punishment.

Researchers must resolve the following questions with regard to women: Do women commit less crime than men, as evidenced by official statistics and self-reports? If so, why do they commit less crime than men? Are women committing crime more often today than in the past? If so, why? These questions are hotly debated among a small group of criminologists who currently study female criminality. Interestingly, despite the research and publications of these few, women have so far remained a non-issue for most researchers and writers in the field.

A sampling of criminology texts indicates the lack of interest in the female criminal. Most texts now have a few short paragraphs or pages devoted to a brief summary of Lombroso and the "female emancipation" theories discussed below. For instance, Barlow (1987) has one paragraph on female crime, discussing only the opportunity theory. Siegel (1986) has index entries for *The Female Offender* by Lombroso; under the entry for "women," two pages are devoted to a brief discussion of the "female emancipation" theories. Fox (1976) also devotes only two pages to female crime in a 400-page criminology text. Textbook writers who devote slightly more space to the female offender include Conklin (1986), who offers seven pages discussing differences in crime rates and two pages for biological differences; and Vetter and Silverman (1986), who win the prize in this small survey for producing an entire 21-page chapter on female crime statistics and theories of causation. This nearly complete silence regarding one-half of the population is explained partly by the fact that women criminals are so few in number and probably partly by the fact that male criminologists are so many in number as compared to female ones. Feminist criminologists propose that the problem of crime has been seen through male eyes and thus viewed as a male problem in a male society. At best women were seen as an interesting anomaly to the reality of maleness. Women, if mentioned at all, were compared to a male standard and analyzed under male perspectives; their behavior was explained largely through the use of stereotypes propagated by a male-dominated society and accepted by male theorists (Naffine, 1987; Morris, 1987; Heidensohn, 1985).

Theories of female criminality have ranged from biological to psychological, from economic to social. Two approaches may be observed in the literature. The first approach is taken by theories that attempt to explain female criminality individually, without recourse to theories of male criminality. These theories often used assumptions about the female psyche that were blatantly sexist and without empirical support. In the 1970s, the new theory explaining female criminality was that the women's movement had created a liberated, "tougher" class of female criminal. However, statistics did not support the assumption that females were engaging in more violent, male-type crime. Feminists objected to both the assumption that females were achieving any kind of parity with men in economic and social spheres and the stereotyping implicit in the premise that female criminals were somehow "liberated" when their behavior patterns showed more similarity to male patterns. The second approach is to apply traditional, "mainstream" theories of crime, developed to explain male criminality, to women. As will be seen later in this chapter, most of these theories are unable to explain the discrepancy in crime rates or explain the pattern of female crime commission. The dominant sexist stereotypes that influenced theories of crime were most prevalent in early writings. Early theories are important to review because they illustrate how women were seen as less than men and as possessing inborn traits of hysteria, passivity, and immaturity.

lllll Early Theories

Historically, the theories explaining female criminality were largely biological and psychological. The prevailing studies on women viewed females as ruled by their biology to a much greater extent and for a longer period of time than did similar theories regarding male criminality (Klein, 1973: 28). The biological school is best represented by Caesare Lombroso, but before Lombroso several other research efforts explored female criminality. Tarnowsky conducted a study on female criminals and contributed data on Polish murderesses to Lombroso's study (Pollak, 1950). In 1876, Pike explained that the sex differential was due to anthropological differences between the sexes, such as the smaller stature and weaker strength of females. Also, females' childbearing functions left them in a weakened and dependent state for long periods of time. In early days, when crime was always physical, women were incapable of being successful criminals; therefore they were not criminalistic. As society became urbanized and criminality without force became possible, women still were less involved due to the early anthropological differences (Pike, 1876). Other theories were more psychological, such as van de Warker's idea that women's entry into crime was determined by the (almost) biological requirement that each woman secure the permanent attentions of one man. This drive or instinct was so strong that the female would commit serious crime to achieve it. For instance, infanticide was explained by the social stigma and poor future an illegitimate birth would bring; the woman would kill the baby to improve her chances of getting a husband. Women also had "pride of adornment," which explained the domestic servant's propensity to steal (van de Warker, 1875–1876).

Lombroso and Ferrero published the first edition of *The Female Offender* in 1894. In this book, the authors employed the same methodology Lombroso had used for his work on criminal men. The authors compared criminal women, found in prisons for women and the courts, to noncriminal women. They recorded comparisons of physical features such as cranial capacities, facial anomalies, facial angles, and brain weights. It was believed that criminal women could be categorized by their physical features. For instance, prostitutes were said to have heavy lower jaws, large nasal spines, simple cranial sutures, deep frontal sinuses, and wormian bones (Lombroso and Ferrero, 1920: 28). All criminal women could be identified by the higher percentage of physical abnormalities or atavistic qualities they possessed. Mental and nervous abnormalities accompanied these physical defects. For instance, criminal women were believed to be deficient in moral sensibilities, to have unstable characters, and to possess excessive vanity, irritability, desire for revenge, and sexuality.

Lombroso believed that in the evolutionary scale, noncriminal men had evolved to the highest stage, followed by criminal men, then noncriminal women; criminal women were the least evolved of all groups. Lombroso explained the prevalence of prostitution among criminal women by the theory that all women were more primitive than men, and all primitive women were prostitutes (Lombroso and Ferrero, 1920: 29). Criminal women supposedly possessed more male characteristics, both physical and mental. Their masculinity suppressed the female maternal drives that kept other women law-abiding, and their female traits created a criminal "more vicious" than the worst criminal male.

Lombroso and Ferrero explained the fact of fewer women criminals by sexual selection. Because the atavistic qualities that all criminal women possessed made their appearance unattractive, they were not selected by males for sexual intercourse; thus they did not reproduce. Dobash, Dobash, and Gutteridge describe other early theorists' emphasis on the ugly and masculine characteristics of the female criminal. They quote Havelock Ellis as describing the criminal woman as "masculine, unsexed, ugly, abnormal women . . . most strongly marked with the signs of degeneration" (Dobash et al., 1986: 115).

Lombroso developed a typology for female criminals as he did for males. The "born criminal" was said to represent 14 percent of the total. The occasional criminal was said to be primarily a normal woman except that she was led into crime by a male. Another type of criminal was the hysterical offender, although this type was rare—only 3.9 percent of the total criminal population. This offender experienced rapid mood changes, delusions, and destructive behavior. Another type was the passion criminal who committed crimes because of an excess of strong feelings, whether the object was love or material riches. Suicide-prone individuals were a fourth criminal type. The last two were lunatics and epileptic delinquents; both of these types were also rare. Lombroso and Ferrero further believed that higher education for women increased crime by prolonging marriage and encouraging the woman to want more (1920: 204).

In brief, Lombroso postulated a biological theory of crime. The criminal was a primitive breed recognizable by physical, atavistic qualities. Women were, on the whole, less inclined to criminality because of constitutional and psychological factors. They were organically conservative. Atavistic qualities had been bred out by sexual selection and feminine qualities such as piety and maternal affection further worked against criminal tendencies. When criminality overcame these factors and "reared its ugly head," it was much worse than criminality as it appeared in the male. The predominate type of criminal was the less serious occasional offender. They only committed crime under the influence of a male or in a situation of extreme temptation (Pollock, 1978: 30–31).

Although Lombroso's theories regarding male criminality lost favor with criminologists fairly quickly as researchers identified social factors of crime causation, the biological theories regarding female crime causation were slower to be discarded. Lombroso, along with many other researchers, confused sex and gender. It is admittedly difficult to separate traits that are biological and inherent in the sex from traits that are socially induced (gender differences). Yet researchers from the days of Lombroso and even today consistently confuse socialized traits with biological traits. For instance, it is naive to believe that women are "more submissive" than men *biologically*, yet researchers may attribute their fewer numbers in crime to this so-called trait. Similarly, some researchers thought that women possessed other biological traits, such as deviousness, that made them criminal or influenced the type of crime they committed. The implications for treatment are obvious: if women are born criminal, little can be done but to hold them so they cannot hurt others. If a woman was corrupted and no longer bound by the feminine "virtues" of piety and passivity, she was incapable of redemption. Prisons for women at the time reflected this pessimism in the care and custody of female criminals. They were considered beyond hope and therefore beyond sympathy.

Other contemporaries of Lombroso looked to psychological causes of female crime. Puibaraud explained female crime as due to psychological motives, such as sexual repression, envy, jealousy, and vengeance (Pollak, 1950: 140). Griffiths also attributed psychological motives to female crime, especially "feminine rage," which evidently all women had but only some expressed in criminal behaviors (Griffiths, 1895: 145). Another researcher of this type was Adams, who spoke of female traits such as a lack of willpower and a tendency to excess (Adams, 1914). Gross postulated that deceit was a trait common to all women and was evident not only in the type of crime women committed but also in the methods they employed when they committed crime. For instance, it was written that women were more likely to use poison to kill victims and were very successful liars in a confidence game (Pollak, 1950: 9, 12).

Lombroso's work was replicated in American prisons, such as the Geneva Reform School, the Joliet Penitentiary, the Cincinnati Workhouse, the Ohio State Penitentiary, New York City's Blackwell's Island Workhouse and Penitentiary, and Bedford Hills. Frances Kellor was one American researcher who measured and tested physical qualities of female prisoners and compared them to a normal sample. She found that very few of Lombroso's findings could be replicated. In her comparisons, nativity proved to be a strong intervening factor, as did the social environment the criminal women came from. Kellor wisely attributed many of the criminal sample's lower scores in smell, hearing, pain, fatigue, and memory to poor physical health brought on by poor living conditions. Kellor found that workhouse women had even lower scores than penitentiary women on all physical tests and were more likely to come from backgrounds of poverty (1900a, 1900b).

Kellor, as well as others who studied women in prison in the late 1800s and early 1900s, believed that the women's life experiences and generally deprived backgrounds had much to do with their entry into criminality. For instance, Kellor wrote that many women criminals came from the ranks of domestic service. She found several explanations for this fact: proportionally, many women were employed in domestic service; inadequate salaries spurred women to steal; workers engaged in domestic service were typically unskilled and unable to do anything else; domestic service was an easy route to prostitution; and employment bureaus were often procurement places for prostitution (Kellor, 1900b: 676).

Jean Weidensall studied female prisoners and conducted research at Bedford Hills in the early 1900s. She compared reformatory inmates to working women and schoolgirls using a variety of tests that measured intelligence, skill, and mechanical ability. She also collected comparisons on height, weight, strength of grip, and visual acuity. The reformatory inmates generally did worse on all tests. Criminal women were found to be "dull," meaning they had lower intelligence and mechanical scores than average in a general population. They also were found to be easily frustrated, emotionally unstable, suspicious, and unthinking. Obviously, some of these observations must be understood in light of the times. Women were held to a strict standard of conduct, and criminal women's conduct did not fit into the ladylike mold. The women researchers were also a product of their time, and they no doubt were influenced by stereotypes of women that held that women were, or should be, more docile, compliant, and "nicer" than men. Weidensall believed that there were several types of female criminals. Some, she wrote, were intelligent but too lazy to work, some were truly criminal, and some were just so unintelligent that they drifted into crime. She believed that this latter type could be guided by moral training and turned around (Weidensall, 1916).

The Laboratory of Social Hygiene at Bedford Hills, the site of Weidensall's research, was funded by outside grants. This laboratory was housed in a separate building on the grounds of the prison; Weidensall was both the director of the laboratory and superintendent of the prison. As will be touched on in chapter 3, the reformatory experiment at Bedford Hills was eventually dropped and the laboratory was also discontinued, but for a time it was the locale for research that was in some ways ahead of mainstream (male) criminology in its approach and the amount of material collected.

One account of an experiment undertaken with "intractable and trouble-making" inmates at Bedford is interesting in its use of "innovative" methods for dealing with prisoners. Spaulding (1923) wrote about how a number of these prisoners were identified and moved to isolated patient cottages on the grounds of Bedford Hills. These "psychopathic" prisoners were then encouraged to create a type of self-government. Spaulding wrote that the research was not a success; the prisoners wore down the staff by the frequency and seriousness of their outbursts. Soon the self-government attempt was abandoned and institutional discipline reinstated, including wet packs and isolation.

Another group of women researchers collected large amounts of information from women prisoners in the State Prison for Women at Auburn, New York, the New York County Penitentiary, the New York City Workhouse, and the New York Magdalen Home. They collected case studies from many women prisoners and compared histories. Two general causal factors were identified: poor economic background, with its resulting impoverished home environment; and inferior mental ability. They found that almost half the women studied had "defective strains" within their families, such as alcoholism, feeblemindedness, neuroticism, or sexual irregularities (Fernald, Hayes, and Dawley, 1920). This identification of genetic strains paralleled earlier research on families of male criminals, such as the research by Dugdale (1895), and reflected a Darwinian influence in criminology.

Hahn (1979) called these studies "cacogenic," explaining that they identified the woman as a breeder of criminals and elevated her to the status of "social menace." According to Hahn, researchers such as Dugdale believed harlotry was hereditary and that the bad woman was inevitably the mother of children who would grow up to be criminals and degenerates.

> The old imagery of the bad woman thus underwent considerable modification and embellishment in the Social Darwinist family studies. They showed her promiscuity to be a matter far more serious than mere personal immorality: the loose woman became a prolific breeder of harlots and a criminal type in her own right (Hahn, 1979: 8).

Freedman found that there were two competing theories of female criminality during the early 1900s (1981: 40). The social determinism implicit in the family studies and studies conducted at the Laboratory for Social Hygiene at Bedford Hills encouraged such policies as sterilization and the incarceration of women for long periods of time in reformatories and penitentiaries (Hahn, 1979: 15). Another train of thought was slightly more feminist and pointed out the "bad influence" of men in the women's histories. However, this approach refused to view women as more than hapless victims of males; these researchers were either unwilling or unable to see women as individuals in their own right. Freedman wrote, "The economic explanation predominated in women's rights movement literature; it constituted a minor theme for prison reformers, who launched their major attack on the sexual victimization of women by men" (1981: 41). Thus, women's criminality was explained by either biological or social causes. Some women were still thought to be born criminal, either because of defective strains they inherited (and could pass on to their children) or because of mental defectiveness or stupidity, which created a propensity to commit crime. Social causes involved the environment women were raised in. If a woman had poor parental models, or if she was corrupted by evil males, then she was only weak and not inherently defective. These women could be saved. Separate institutions for women were supported by both trains of thought.

Those researchers that emphasized the social factors in female crime causation believed that training and moral uplifting offered the best chance of rehabilitation. As a man may have caused the woman offender's downfall, a good man could also be her salvation (Healy and Bronner, 1926). Consequently, theories regarding crime and treatment solutions were oriented to isolating and teaching her better moral habits in the hope that she could attract a suitable marriage partner. Women in prison were taught domestic skills to prepare them for this goal. The facts that these women would probably need to support themselves as they had before prison and that what they needed were the skills to do so were ignored.

The 1930s marked the beginning of "modern" studies exploring male criminality, but very few gave any attention to females. Articles on women offenders were either statistical explorations of a specific subtopic of female crime, such as infanticide or abortion; statistical reports similar to earlier studies; or articles proposing psychological theories. The Gluecks studied criminal women as well as delinquents; their research, done in the tradition of the earlier researchers at Bedford Hills, concentrated on the case study (Glueck and Glueck, 1934). They collected data on the offenders' personal, family, reformatory, parole, and post-parole histories. Court records, school records, personal interviews, physical examinations, parole reports, and arrest records were some of the documents used

to develop these case histories. The Gluecks, like the earlier researchers, identified both social and hereditary factors. For instance, they reported that mental disease was present in 58 percent
of the women's backgrounds, and only 33 percent were not psy-
chotic, psychopathic, epileptic, alcoholic, addicted to drugs, psycho-
neurotic, or of marked unstable personality; but they also reported
that 78 percent of the women had come from "marginal" economic
circumstances (1934: 64–67). Like early researchers, the Gluecks
focused on the sexual histories of their women subjects. They
concluded that 86.4 percent of the women had "bad" sex habits,
which might have meant that a woman was involved in prostitution,
was merely promiscuous, or even simply lived with a man without
the benefit of marriage. Prostitution was broken into categories from
the professional prostitute to the "doubtful good girl." Most of the
women identified as prostitutes fell into the "occasional" category.
The Gluecks also found that 67 percent of their subjects had
venereal disease.

The combination of environmental and genetic factors affected
the implications for treatment. The Gluecks believed that some of
the women should be kept indeterminately or sterilized in order to
prevent them from reproducing. Promiscuous urges would also
decline with age, thus allowing the release of older offenders. Those
without biologically caused degeneracy could be retrained and their
delinquency could be prevented by education and social work.

W. I. Thomas (1937) published a psychological theory late in the
1930s that paralleled some of the early psychological theories
discussed previously. In this work, Thomas described the female as
a passive opposite to the active male. All humans sought excitement
and response, but women sought excitement and response through
sexual means—that is, prostitution. Thomas, as did most other
researchers who looked at female criminals, defined women's criminality solely in terms of sexuality. Hence, the morality of the woman
was just as important, if not more so, than the crime that she
committed. In fact, most women in the criminal justice system were
there for sexual, not economic, crimes. An early researcher who
noticed this was Tappan (1947), who found that wayward girls were
given harsher sentences in New York City than those who committed
more serious crimes but were found morally superior.

Thus we see that in the 1930s, when attention had shifted to
social structure theories to explain male criminality, the few researchers interested in female criminals continued to resort to
psychological or biological explanations.

The Chicago School identified crime as an ecological phenomenon that could be pinpointed as taking place within certain areas
of the community, with certain similarities among all areas showing
high levels of criminality (Shaw and McKay, 1942). This shift to

social structure was not represented at all in the literature on female criminals. Further, this theory of crime made no attempt to explain why women who live in high-crime areas are not affected by the same factors said to influence male criminality. Women were again excluded from analysis in Sutherland's theory of differential association. According to this theory, crime occurred when antisocial definitions, which came from associations with those who had criminal value systems, outweighed pro-social definitions. Sutherland made no attempt to explain why women, who might also have had criminal associations, did not engage in actions consistent with the definitions with which they were surrounded (Sutherland, 1939).

Pollak's study in 1950 comprehensively summarized all earlier studies and offered some additional theorizing on female criminality. Pollak believed a substantial body of crime committed by females did not find its way into official statistics. Female crime was difficult to detect because of both the type of crime and the methodology. For instance, women would shoplift rather than commit armed robbery; they would use poison rather than use a weapon; and they would kill a family member rather than a stranger. The woman, according to Pollak, was more likely to be the instigator than the actor; she was likely to be behind a male, urging and enticing him into criminal action. Pollak attributed this deceit to biological and social factors. He wrote that the relative weakness of the female made deceit necessary as a defense and observed that subversion was a common tactic among all oppressed classes (interestingly and uncharacteristically, considering his largely sexist analysis, Pollak did identify women as an oppressed class). He also believed that the biology of a female allowed her to deceive, pointing out that women could use deception in sex by pretending orgasm or enjoyment, whereas men could not, and that women were trained from birth to hide such natural processes as menstruation, sexual desire, and frustration.

Pollak believed that if the true amount of all female crime were counted, especially shoplifting, the numbers would exceed figures for male crime. Even if hidden male crime were added, the differential would be much less than official figures indicate. Furthermore, male victims would supposedly be less likely to report a female offender and male police officers would be less likely to arrest. Even when she was arrested, chivalry would intervene, and the charge would be dismissed, she would be acquitted, or she would be given probation rather than a prison sentence (Pollak, 1950: 4). Later studies have completely discounted these ideas; there seems to be no support whatsoever for the notion of hidden female crime. Self-report and victimization studies do not indicate large numbers of uncounted female criminals, and any undetected female crime is probably more than matched by uncounted male crimes. These issues are explored in greater detail in a later section on female crime statistics.

Pollak was an early proponent of the female liberation theory. He offered a prophecy that as women gained greater equality, they would also become more involved in crime. As proof, he pointed out that during the war years women entered the mainstream of work and also engaged in greater amounts of crime or at least were prosecuted for more crimes (Pollak, 1950: 64). But later studies have cautioned that these figures may have misrepresented the greater involvement of women by not adjusting for a smaller number of men at risk.

In the 1970s several reviews of early theories criticized misconceptions and stereotypes. Smart (1977), Crites (1976), and Klein (1973) were among those who criticized the early theories discussed in this section. Their reviews pointed out the flaws in attributing socialized differences to biological factors, identified methodological inconsistencies, and criticized formal treatment of women by the criminal justice system as discriminatory.

In conclusion, early theories on female criminality tended to concentrate on biological or psychological theories and continued to do so long after theories on male criminality moved on to look at social factors or social structure. The early theories tended to see women primarily as sexual beings, ruled by biological and psychological drives and needs that explained their criminal activities and the relatively small amount of crime they participated in. In the early 1900s social factors were identified, but women's vulnerability to "evil males" and temptations continued to be explained by female traits such as passivity and the need for male response. Implications for treatment were obvious: women must be isolated and prevented from passing on degenerate traits, and those who could be retrained and morally uplifted needed the firm but gentle hand of other women. Thus we will see that theory and practice were consistent.

IIIII "Male Theories"

A review of the major theories in criminology, such as the Chicago School, differential association, strain theory, and subcultural deviance, will show that they either do not help explain or are inconsistent with what we know about female criminality (Leonard, 1982; Morris, 1987; Naffine, 1987). Most of these traditional theories not only did not attempt to explain this differential but totally ignored female criminals. Often only males were used in samples, and the language describing causation referred only to male development, male values, and male motivations. Feminist criminologists have provided excellent and comprehensive critiques of these theories; thus there is no need to perform the same task here (Leonard, 1982; Morris, 1987; Heidensohn, 1985). However, some generalizations are in order.

The male theorists who saw criminals as a product of their environment—be it a subculture (subcultural deviance theory), a criminogenic zone (Chicago School), or influential friends and primary "others" with criminal definitions of society (differential association)—neglected to explain how females could be a part of this same environment and not commit as much crime. Further, these writers viewed delinquency and crime as an essentially male activity with certain favorable features; criminality was at least creative, active, and daring. Women, of course, could not be expected to be involved in such activity, and thus their absence made sense (Heidensohn, 1985). If the male theorists recognized the presence of females at all, they attributed to the female a different culture or made simplistic conclusions about the greater control of the family over the female. Thus it was left for psychologists, such as the ones soon to be discussed, to explain that females became deviant as a result of dysfunctional family life or trauma. In other words, it was "natural" for certain boys to turn to delinquency and crime, but it was "unnatural" for females; therefore, any female delinquent was individually deviant, and it was appropriate to look for individual dysfunction.

Strain theory proposed that delinquents and criminals were innovators who were blocked from the legitimate means to achieve the societal goals of money and material success (Merton, 1949). This theory is most problematic for females, since they are arguably more blocked than males and should "innovate"—commit crime—more often. Strain theorists either did not have much to say about women or concluded that they were motivated by different goals (Cohen, 1955). Evidently, whereas men desire and strive for material success, women desire and strive for marriage. Since marriage is easier to accomplish, women are not forced to innovate to reach their goal. This supposition, of course, fails to recognize that marriage is not nor ever was the goal of all women; it also does not explain why those women who do turn to crime do so.

Only labeling and control theory might explain the male–female crime differential. However, the theorists who proposed these explanations did not direct them to female criminality. Labeling theory might be consistent with the lower crime rates for women, since it postulates that any formal stigmatization is likely to create secondary deviance. If one assumes that women are less likely to be formally prosecuted, then their small arrest figures may be explained by the idea that women are less subject to stigmatization. However, this explanation ignores the findings summarized next that at least juvenile females may be more, not less, likely to be stigmatized by formal intervention from the juvenile system.

Control theory (Hirschi, 1969) explains that those who have stronger bonds to society—attachment, commitment, involvement, and belief—are less likely to be delinquent. Bonds may involve personal relationships with family and friends; activities such as school or work; and aspirations—goals and beliefs. Although Hirschi did not originally use the females in his sample to develop control theory, later replications have lent fairly strong support to the idea that the theory applies to females as well as males (Naffine, 1987: 64–71). To explain the female's lower rate of criminality, one might point to the greater involvement of females with family responsibilities and their greater success at school in early years.

Radical theorists have used Marxist theory to explain criminality, but again the principles and applications of this theory have largely ignored women. This neglect is all the more strange when one assumes that Marxist theorists would accept the fact of women's oppression and male domination in society (Morris, 1987: 11–12; Heidensohn, 1985). Marxist feminists have used the theory and its analysis of capitalism to explain how women enter into crime and also how they are treated by the system. Capitalism and paternalism are combined in this analysis, both contributing to the woman's powerlessness (Mann, 1984: 266). This use of Marxist analysis, however, was not offered by the male theorists, who devoted little attention to the economic subjugation of women.

Perhaps because of the absence of women in these major theories of crime, criminologists concerned with female criminality continue to develop new theories to explain female crime rates. Although understanding the women's criminal motivations is important, it is obviously a weak theory that can explain criminality for only one-half of the population. No theory will ever explain all crime, but any theorist who seeks validity must develop a theory that can help explain the behavior of both men and women in crime.

IIIII Current Theories

It is fairly well accepted that women do commit less crime than men; exactly how much will be discussed in a later section. Thus, any current theory must explain not only why women commit crime but also why they commit less crime.

Very few criminologists concentrated directly on female criminals during the long gap between Pollak and current theorists. During the 1950s and 1960s, explanations continued to concentrate on the background of the female criminal and her particularly "feminine" traits. More research was conducted on female delinquents than on adult criminals; thus, many of the sources mentioned here are directed toward explaining delinquency rather than criminality. Female delinquents were said to be prone to psychiatric abnormality much more often than male delinquents (in a continuation of the psychological/physiological tradition) and to come from more disturbed backgrounds (Cowie, Cowie, and Slater, 1968). Parental deprivation was thought by some to be more detrimental to the female, resulting in her seeking male attention through promiscuity (Vedder and Somerville, 1970: 153). This deprivation of affection was also thought to be the cause of pseudofamilies and homosexuality in institutions (Halleck and Herski, 1962). These theories are consistent with the general notion that women are more prone to mental disorder than are males. Many writers have noticed how the mental health profession is male-dominated in its definitions of normality and in its paternalistic treatment of women. Women's "traits" (emotionality, passivity, excitability) are first defined as far removed from "mental health"; then women who lack these traits are defined as abnormal (Chesler, 1972). Thus, it is not surprising that women and women criminals were long believed to have more psychiatric problems than their male counterparts; this belief is reflected in the psychological theories discussed here (Morris, 1987: 52–57).

Earlier theories that pointed out the relationship between crime and women's biological processes, such as lactation, menstruation, and menopause, continued to be presented. For instance, the new version of older theories identifying menstruation as a causal factor in crime is the premenstrual syndrome (PMS) defense of today. According to some, women may commit crime while suffering from mood changes brought on by menstruation. This explanation has been used successfully as a legal defense to homicide in Great Britain (Dalton, 1964). Evidence supposedly has been gathered showing that females are more prone to violent acting-out behavior and other types of deviance in relation to their menstrual cycle. However, critics contend that the use of self-reports seriously weakens these research findings, because the women subjects accept the common societal perception that women do act differently because of their menstruation. What is being measured is thus more likely to be women's perception of different behavior patterns. Moreover, menstruation is proposed as an influence on criminal acts that occur during premenstrual, menstrual, and postmenstrual time periods. Since these periods cover at least half of every month, chance would put women criminals somewhere within this time period at least half the time. Finally, these theories have been criticized for assuming a 28-day cycle when it is known that many women do not follow such a pattern (Morris, 1987: 46–52).

Today opportunity and socialization seem to be the two strongest factors in explanations of female criminality. Socialization theories propose that women are socialized in ways that prevent their entry into crime. A popular stereotype historically was that women criminals were likely to be more "masculine" than their law-abiding counterparts. Some research purported to show this connection by measuring self-perceived masculine traits and self-reported delinquency (Cullen et al., 1979). However, more often studies found no relationship between "masculinity" and female delinquency.

Hoffman-Bustamante (1973) provided a more sophisticated theory of female criminality that takes into account socialization factors and opportunity theory. According to her theory, five major factors affect the differential involvement of females in crime: (1) differential role expectations for men and women; (2) sex differences in socialization patterns and application of social control; (3) structurally determined differences in opportunity to commit particular offenses; (4) differential access or pressure toward criminally oriented subcultures and careers; and (5) sex differences built into crime categories. Her explanation points to the different childhood experiences of boys and girls. Whereas males are allowed a great deal of free time and are exposed during their wanderings to various opportunities for delinquency, females tend to have greater responsibilities at home. They are more controlled by social rules to be "ladylike" and demure. They are less exposed to skills and training useful in criminal operations, such as auto mechanics (car theft), firearms (robbery), and mechanical ability (burglary). They are also less likely to develop useful physical skills, such as running, lifting, climbing, or fighting. The combination of social rules and the limitations on skills and opportunity combine to create a situation where women are unlikely to enter crime at any age. To illustrate this point, the crime women do tend to engage in most often is the type most appropriate to women's social role—specifically, consumer crime, such as shoplifting, forgery, and passing bad checks.

IIIII The "New" Female Criminal and Feminist Criminology

An increase in female crime in the 1960s and 1970s spurred theories relating to liberation and female criminality. Seemingly, women were entering crime in alarmingly high numbers and in rates that far surpassed their male counterparts. Between 1960 and 1975, arrests of adult females were up 60.2 percent and juvenile females' arrest rates increased by 253.9 percent (Chesney-Lind, 1982). Although the popular press and law enforcement first made the connection, the academic community followed with its own version. Adler's *Sisters in Crime* (1975) and Simon's *Women and Crime* (1975) elaborated on the theory that the women's movement would encourage liberation into criminal as well as legitimate occupations. Adler proposed that women were increasing their numbers of violent crimes, which had traditionally been the bastion of males. Extremely high percentage increases for female violent crime compared to male violent crime were used to bolster the theory.

Simon (1975) attributed a rise in women's involvement in property crime to the women's movement. According to her, as women entered previously male occupations, such as banking and business, they would be exposed to the opportunities previously held only by men. Thus, it would be expected that women would increase their representation in crimes such as embezzling and theft. Simon noted, contrary to Adler, that this newfound freedom might alleviate frustration and could lead in turn to a reduction in violent crime by women.

It wasn't long before critics presented evidence to controvert the female liberation theory. Smart (1979) criticized Adler's use of FBI percentage increases:

> There are two very elementary fallacies in these propositions, however; first, the comparison between two sets of percentage increases can be entirely misleading and, secondly, the assumption that juvenile delinquency of today sets the pattern of adult crime for tomorrow is quite unwarranted (1979: 51).

The use of percentage increases is misleading, of course, because the base figures for female crime are so low. Any increase in raw numbers will appear to be very large. Smart looked at statistics for Great Britain and discovered that the years in which the women's movement should have had its greatest effect on crime did not experience great increases:

> So although every decade except 1946 to 1955 shows women offenders to be increasing more rapidly than men this was much more the case between 1935 and 1946; 1955 and 1965, than between 1965 and 1975, the years during which the women's movement in Britain was revived (1979: 54).

Furthermore, females in the USA and Britain had not increased their representation in violent crime much at all. In fact, females have represented roughly 10 percent of arrests for violent crime consistently for well over a decade.

Steffensmeir (1980), using arrest data for 1965–1977, concluded that females were increasing their numbers in crime but were doing so largely in traditionally feminine areas, such as shoplifting, prostitution, and check forgery. A second study found that the same pattern characterized female delinquents. The large increases apparent in official statistics were primarily in areas such as larceny, liquor law violations, and drugs (Steffensmeir and Steffensmeir, 1980). Self-report studies of juveniles also show that, although the differential between males and females in crime was much smaller than reported by official statistics, it did not decrease during the years that it "should" have, when the women's movement was strongest (Chesney-Lind, 1982).

In fact, studies were unable to find a connection between "liberated attitudes" and delinquency or criminality among women sample groups. Giordana and Cernkovich (1979), for example, found no relationship between delinquency and "liberated" attitudes toward work and family; however, they did find a relationship between attitudes toward what was considered appropriate behavior for a woman and delinquency, indicating that female delinquents are traditional in their outlook.

Bowker (1981) disputes the theory as applied on an international basis. After comparing rates of industrialization, liberation, and female criminality, he found little support for the view that females become more violent criminals as they gain social equality.

> In summary, there is only very modest support for the idea that the increasing liberation of women results in the rise of the "violence-prone new female criminal." Economic need and economic opportunity notions about female crime receive considerably stronger support, but the available evidence does not allow a clear case to be made between these two economic theories about female crime. . . . Female participation in the economic institution seems to be most influential in women's choices to engage in criminal behavior, with the family and political institutions being only slightly less influential, and the educational being substantially less influential (Bowker, 1981: 25).

Nor has the opportunity hypothesis garnered much empirical support. Supposedly, as women leave the house and enter the world outside, they should find more opportunities for crime; however, only weak relationships have been found between women's entry into the work force and greater involvement in crime (Weishet, 1984: 569). In any event, women's entry into the work force has not necessarily enabled them to commit the "power crimes" Simon envisioned. Women account for disproportionate numbers of service and clerical workers, and large numbers of them are not in financial positions that could offer opportunities for embezzlement and high-finance crimes.

Chapman (1980) postulates almost the reverse of the liberation theory in her economic explanation of female crime. Because women, especially single women with children, are a growing percentage of the poor in this society, it is predicted that the numbers of women in property crimes will increase. This increase will be due, however, not to liberation but to need. Further, she predicts that women's crime will continue to be sex-specific, involving forgery, welfare fraud, and shoplifting. Another study that partly supports this concept found that women's recidivism rates were negatively correlated with the receipt of unemployment checks or employment, indicating an economic motivation for crime (Jurik, 1983). A British study also supports a correlation between economic distress and crime for women (Box and Hale, 1983).

Feminist writers have contributed a great deal to the understanding and analysis of how criminology has systematically ignored or stereotyped criminal women. Sexism, according to Price and Sokoloff, comprises the "socially organized cultural beliefs, practices and institutions that result in systematic male superiority and male domination over women as a group" (1982: xiii). We have seen how early theories used stereotypes to explain female criminals, how traditional criminology has ignored women, and how this treatment has resulted in a situation where we are still attempted to construct a unified theory that can account for both male and female behavior.

Smart (1976), Crites (1976), Klein (1973), and Pollock (1978) focused on the early theories of criminality, exposing the stereotypes and methodological inconsistencies between the study of male and female criminals. Later, Leonard (1982), Heidensohn (1985), Morris (1987), and Naffine (1987) critiqued the traditional theories and their weaknesses. There is disagreement over what exactly feminist criminology comprises—for instance, some would call Adler a feminist criminologist and some would not. There is no disagreement, however, on the basic principles of feminist analysis: first, that females have largely been invisible or marginal in theories of crime; and second, that when women are studied, "special" theories, often stereotypical and distorted, are used to explain their behavior (Heidensohn, 1985: 146). Unfortunately feminist criminology has not offered any comprehensive theory to supplant those it has criticized. The attempts have either emphasized women's domination and their control in and by domestic structures of society (Heidensohn, 1985: 161–178), emphasized economic factors and the women's greater poverty (Carlen, 1988), or only offered "suggestions" toward the construction of a theory (Naffine, 1987). The first alternative seems not too different from earlier theories such as control theory and Hoffman-Bustamante's opportunity theory; the second suffers from the same criticisms with which all economic theories must contend—namely, how to account for the large numbers of poor people who do not steal.

One contribution of feminist analysis has been to make linkages between female victims and criminals. For instance, using a phenomenological approach we have discovered that many female criminals have been victims in their past—victims of sexual and physical abuse as children and adults. Women are often victimized by an economic system that undervalues women's labor and makes it impossible for them to support themselves if they have small children to care for. These issues, although relevant for all women, impact the woman criminal and must be addressed for a full understanding of how women end up in prison.

IIIII Theory and Practice

What we do in the name of treatment is influenced in large measure by our theories regarding crime causation. If Chapman (1980) and Carlen (1988) are correct, the incarcerated woman is desperately in need of vocational and educational skills that will enable her to support herself and her children in legitimate ways. If Hoffman-Bustamante and others who postulate a role-opportunity theory are correct, the sex stereotyping and different socialization that women experience prevent women's criminal development. For those few who did not receive the proper socialization and did learn criminality, treatment may then take the form of resocialization, in effect, teaching the female criminal to be a woman, which means to be law-abiding. If women are increasing their numbers in crime because of social equality and more liberated attitudes, is the implication for treatment that we should squelch liberated attitudes toward women's role in society?

As we have discussed, facts don't support this supposition. Women in prison are a notably poor audience for liberation sentiments. They typically hold very traditional stereotypes of female and male roles and their goals tend to focus on home and family. Women in prison have been "properly" socialized in that they subscribe to the dominant male concept and their criminality is often appropriately "feminine" (Morris, 1987: 39). Some argue, in fact, that women in prison *need* to be liberated—from their poverty, from their typically dysfunctional relationships with men, and from their tendencies to get involved in relationships that lead to criminal involvement.

Women's prisons today have no clear mandate for treatment. Attempts to increase the number of programs available to women tend to continue to be traditional. Attempts to encourage women to seek further education run into cost-benefit problems. Continuing ad hoc programs encourage the women to strengthen and improve ties with family, especially children; these are consistent with early versions of the women's role. It may be that the traditional role of wife and mother did insulate the woman from criminal opportunity, at least as long as she accepted that role and was provided for. However, through the ages, women who have had to survive on their own or who have little to care about in legitimate society have resorted, as have males, to crime.

IIIII Is Chivalry Dead, or Did It Ever Exist?

There is a recurring belief that the numbers presented in official statistics do not represent the true statistics on female crime. The rationale for this belief is that the male system of criminal justice protects and excuses women from their actions and punishments. Several attempts have been made to discover whether this belief is myth or reality.

Steffensmeir (1980) found that preferential treatment consistently showed up at each stage of the criminal justice process, although it was of a small magnitude. He postulates that chivalry contributes to this differential treatment but that the perceived unlikelihood of future criminality on the part of women offenders and the absence of perceived danger may be more important factors. The offender's naivete is also factored in. All these elements create a situation in which women are more likely to receive probation than prison. Steffensmeir further proposes that determinate sentencing and increased bureaucratization and professionalism will decrease this differential in sentencing.

Tjaden and Tjaden (1981) found that in a sample of Colorado offenders, the male–female differential in sentencing was substantially reduced when controlled for previous crimes. A differential between who received arrest as opposed to a summons, and who received probation as opposed to imprisonment, was still present; but this differential was slight. Kruttschnitt and Green (1984) used court records from 1965 to 1980 and found that pretrial release status explained the prison or probation sentence to the point of completely eliminating the effect of gender. Gender did seem to influence the pretrial release decision, but a closer analysis uncovered factors such as economic dependency and single parenthood which impacted the decision more than sex. Farrington and Morris also found that judges were influenced by factors for women, such as marital status, family background, and the involvement of other offenders, that did not influence their decision making for male offenders (1983). Interestingly, these studies show that judicial decision making has not been affected by perceptions of liberation per se, in that females are still given differential treatment according to their economic dependence or the presence of children. In other words, this study neither supports the chivalry hypothesis nor the theory that chivalry has been overtaken by an egalitarian viewpoint sweeping the judicial bench.

Wilbanks (1986) reported that females in the California court system experienced leniency but not consistently, and in some crime categories they received even harsher treatment than males. The treatment seemed to have no relationship to the seriousness of the crime or sex stereotyping of crimes. The greatest differential between the treatment received by males and females occurred at sentencing. A possible factor in differential sentencing may be whether or not the woman offender has other social controls. Kruttschnitt (1982) pointed out a relationship between the severity of the disposition of a female's case in criminal courts and her dependency; for instance, if she is dependent on a male as daughter or wife, she is more likely to receive probation. The suggestion is made that consciously or unconsciously, the court system allows informal social control systems to operate if they are present. Thus, if a woman is under the control of another authority figure she is left to that person's informal control; if she is free from informal social controls, then the state steps in to take control. The strength of this theory is that it could apply equally well to both sexes.

Chesney-Lind (1982) pointed out that female delinquents have always received differential treatment, but in a negative way. Even if adult women may be less likely to receive prison sentences, female juveniles are (or at least were) more likely to receive institutionalization than their male counterparts. They were also more likely to be drawn into the juvenile justice system because of status offenses such as incorrigibility rather than delinquent offenses, despite the fact that self-reports show that boys and girls are fairly similar in the commission of their delinquencies. The reasons for this may be found in the prevalent theories regarding the female delinquent—for instance, that she is more psychologically disturbed than the male delinquent or that her home life is more disrupted. Chesney-Lind wrote that those who developed the theories regarding female delinquency were in the treatment business themselves, so it is not surprising that they justified the differential treatment females received. An example of such a justification is the following: "When you train a man you train one individual; when you train a woman, you train a family" (Vedder and Somerville, 1970: viii). Females were dealt with harshly when they challenged the double standard of behavior for males and females and when they threatened social norms by their sexual activities.

> Indeed physical examinations of young women often conducted in search of venereal disease, pregnancy or other substances are routine in many jurisdictions regardless of the nature of the charge against them. It is clear that these examinations are not only degrading but also serve to remind all women that any form of deviance will be defined as evidence of sexual laxity (Chesney-Lind, 1982: 93).

Thus, the treatment of female delinquents in the 1960s, 1970s, and probably into the 1980s still emphasizes the woman's sexual role and her sexual morality much more than her criminality, as was the case almost a hundred years earlier during the reformatory movement. Current efforts at deinstitutionalizing juvenile offenders have led to a decrease in the practice of differential sentencing; however, Chesney-Lind believes that the new hard-line emphasis on juvenile delinquency and adult criminality and the right-wing emphasis on family may well continue the discriminatory treatment of young girls (1982).

At least one research effort has postulated that the treatment of women in the criminal justice system has to do with the sex ratio of males to females in society. According to South and Messner (1986), the sex ratio influences not only women's victimization rates but also their treatment as offenders in the system. When men outnumber women, the female is highly valued, crimes against women such as rape are harshly punished, and the traditional domestic role is emphasized. The woman offender is protected from the system and treated more leniently and her rate of offending is also less. When there are more women in a society, they are not as highly valued; consequently, violence directed against them is only moderately punished, and the female offender is treated harshly by the system. Although this theory is interesting, it seems unable to explain the relatively harsh treatment of women in the late 1800s.

IIIII Female Crime

Today, female criminal activities continue to be largely in the area of larceny, primarily shoplifting and forgery. The latest figures from the Uniform Crime Reports show that females' crime activities, as measured by arrests, have increased in every major category but murder and nonnegligent manslaughter between 1978 and 1987. Male crime, on the other hand, has increased in every category but arson. The largest increases for women occurred in the crime categories of embezzlement (135.2 percent increase) and curfew/loitering laws (130.9 percent increase). Other large increases occurred in "other assaults" (80.8 percent), "offenses against family and children" (82.4 percent), and liquor laws (85.4 percent). No increases for males even approached these percentage increases. On the other hand, these increases are small in real numbers. For instance, whereas the 80.8 percent increase in arrests of women for "other assaults" translates to 40,194 arrests, the 67.8 percent increase of males translates to 203,310! Thus, the "explosion" that has taken place in female crime means little in terms of real numbers.

In other crimes, males and females seem to be reaching parity; for instance, women now represent 38 percent of all arrests for embezzlement and 43.5 percent of all arrests for fraud. Women's involvement in violent crime has remained stable for many years around 10–12 percent of the total number of arrests. Smith and Visher (1980) collapsed fifty-four studies into one data set and then analyzed the differential in crime rates between men and women. These authors found that the gap has narrowed for juveniles and in minor deviant acts, but not in serious criminal behavior. There seems to be greater convergence among nonwhites than among whites.

Table 2-1 Women's involvement in crime by category

Crime	Percent of Total Arrests
Murder and nonnegligent manslaughter	12.5%
Forcible rape	1.2%
Robbery	8.1%
Aggravated assault	13.3%
Burglary	7.9%
Larceny/theft	31.1%
Motor vehicle theft	9.7%
Arson	13.7%
Other assaults	15.1%
Forgery and counterfeiting	34.4%
Fraud	43.5%
Embezzlement	38.1%
Stolen property	11.6%
Prostitution	64.8%
Drug abuse violations	14.9%
Offenses against family and children	17.4%
(Other crime categories excluded)	

Source: Uniform Crime Report, U.S. Department of Justice; release date: July 1988.

Although women still represent only a small fraction of those arrested for drugs, their involvement may be increasing. In a recent survey of female inmates, it was discovered that about a third of the women used heroin and about half used cocaine (Crawford, 1988a: 20). More than 20 percent of the women were incarcerated for drug offenses, and 25 percent of the women said they committed the crime they were sentenced for to get money to buy drugs (Crawford, 1988a: 32). Other studies have noted the relationship between crime and drug addiction. A review of past literature offered by Anglin and Hser indicates that drug addiction for women seems to be correlated mostly with three types of crimes—prostitution, reselling narcotics or assisting male drug dealers, and property crimes such as larceny (1987: 361). Studies previously reported that between 40 and 70 percent of female drug users supported their habit through prostitution. However, female addicts also report participation in a relatively wide range of other criminal activity. In fact, in Anglin and Hser's study with 328 white and Chicana methadone maintenance clients, they found that the women addicts did use prostitution but did not depend on it and committed other types of crimes, primarily burglary, theft, and forgery, to support their habits. Anglos favored theft and Chicanas favored burglary and theft. One-third of the Anglo and 49 percent of the Chicana women were first arrested before becoming addicted; however, these first arrests were often for such things as curfew violations, incorrigibility, trespassing, and vandalism. Arrests became more common and frequent after addiction, and crime commission was correlated with high drug use. Treatment and low drug use were correlated with lower rates of crime. The authors compared these findings to studies of male addicts and concluded that women are slightly more likely to have never been arrested; women are less likely than men (except Chicanas) to have extensive arrest records before addiction; for both men and women robbery seems to occur only at high levels of drug use; women differ greatly from men in the level and type of criminal activity (1987: 392–393). Personalized accounts also illustrate how predominant drugs and alcohol are in the lives of women criminals (Carlen, 1988: 24).

Table 2-1 illustrates the involvement of women in all crime categories.

IIIII Conclusion

In this chapter, we have seen how theories of female criminality have been more or less consistent with the treatment women have received from the criminal justice system. During the late 1800s and early 1900s, theories tended to be either biologically deterministic or socially deterministic. Both sorts were consistent with the reformatory experiment, sterilization, and resocialization efforts. Later, during the middle part of the 1900s, psychological theories of female crime predominated, and practices followed this line of reasoning; for instance, females were more likely to be institutionalized. Today, we have more or less discredited the notion that female "liberation" has had any effect on female crime. Further, the much written-about explosion of female crime is more a statistical anomaly than the reality. However, despite the relatively small increases in the percentage of total arrests of females, their rate of imprisonment is going up, contributing to a terrible problem of overcrowding (Kempinen, 1984). This increase in female imprisonment may be a result of a general increase in severity of sentencing, an effect of determinate sentencing, or an effect of the faulty perception that female criminality and especially violent crime has tremendously increased, which may influence judicial sentencing.

The most comprehensive theories of female criminality include socialization, opportunity, and economic factors; each has different implications for treatment. It is not surprising, then, that what is occurring in prisons for women tends to be disorganized, fragmented, and without clear direction. Before we address what is occurring in women's prisons today, however, it is necessary to go back to the late 1800s when these prisons were first created in order to understand their original purpose and rationale.

References

Adams, H. (1914) *Women and Crime*. London: T. Warner Laurie.

Adler, F. (1975) *Sisters in Crime: The Rise of the New Female Criminal*. New York: McGraw-Hill.

Anglin, M., and Y. Hser (1987) "Addicted Women and Crime." *Criminology* 25, 2: 359–394.

Barlow, H. (1987) *Introduction to Criminology*. Boston: Little, Brown.

Bowker, L. (1979) *Women, Crime and the Criminal Justice System*. Lexington, Mass.: Lexington Books.

Bowker, L. (1981) "The Institutional Determinants of International Female Crime." *International Journal of Comparative and Applied Criminal Justice* 5, 1: 11–28.

Box, S., and C. Hale. (1983) "Liberation and Female Criminality in England and Wales." *British Journal of Criminology* 23, 1: 35.

Carlen, P. (1988) *Women, Crime and Poverty*. Philadelphia: Open University Press.

Chapman, J. (1980) *Economic Realities and Female Crime*. Lexington, Mass.: Lexington Books.

Chesler, P. (1972) *Women and Madness*. New York: Avon.

Chesney-Lind, M. (1982) "Guilty by Reason of Sex: Young Women and the Juvenile Justice System." In B. Price and N. Sokoloff, *The Criminal Justice System and Women*, pp. 77–105. New York: Clark Boardman.

Cohen, A. (1955) *Delinquent Boys*. Glencoe: The Free Press.

Conklin, J. (1986) *Criminology*. New York: Macmillan.

Cowie, J., J. Cowie, and E. Slater. (1968) *Delinquency in Girls*. Cambridge, Mass.: Humanities Press.

Crawford, J. (1988a) "Tabulation of a Nationwide Survey of Female Offenders." College Park, Md.: American Correctional Association.

Crawford, J. (1988b) "Tabulation of a Nationwide Survey of State Correctional Facilities for Adult and Juvenile Female Offenders." College Park, Md.: American Correctional Association.

Crites, L. (1976) *The Female Offender*. Lexington, Mass.: Lexington Books.

Cullen, F., et al. (1979) "Sex and Delinquency: A Partial Test of the Masculinity Hypothesis." *Criminology* 17, 3: 301–311.

Dalton, K. (1964) *The Premenstrual Syndrome*. Springfield, Ill.: Charles C Thomas.

Dobash, R., R. Dobash, and S. Gutteridge. (1986) *The Imprisonment of Women*. New York: Basil Blackwell.

Dugdale, R. (1895) *The Jukes: A Study in Crime, Pauperism, Disease and Heredity*. New York: Putnam.

Farrington, D., and A. Morris. (1983) "Sex, Sentencing and Reconvictions." *British Journal of Criminology* 23, 3: 229.

Fernald, M., M. Hayes, and A. Dawley. (1920) *A Study of Women Delinquents in New York State*. New York: Century.

Fox, V. (1976) *Introduction to Criminology*. Englewood Cliffs, N.J.: Prentice-Hall.

Freedman, E. (1974) "Their Sister's Keepers: A Historical Perspective of Female Correctional Institutions in the U.S." *Feminist Studies* 2: 77–95.

Giordana, P., and S. Cernkovich. (1979) "On Complicating the Relationship Between Liberation and Delinquency." *Social Problems* 26, 4: 467–481.

Glueck, S., and E. Glueck. (1934) *Five Hundred Delinquent Women*. New York: Knopf.

Gora, J. (1982) *The New Female Criminal*. New York: Praeger.

Griffiths, A. (1895) "Female Criminals." *The North American Review* CLXI: 141–152.

Hahn, N. (1979) "Too Dumb to Know Better: Cacogenic Family Studies and the Criminology of Women." Paper presented at the American Society of Criminology Meeting, Philadelphia.

Halleck, S., and M. Herski. (1962) "Homosexual Behavior in a Correctional Institution for Adolescent Girls." *American Journal of Orthopsychiatry* 32: 911–917.

Healy, W., and A. Bronner. (1926) *Delinquents and Their Children: Their Making and Unmaking*. New York: Macmillan.

Heidensohn, F. (1985) *Women and Crime*. New York: New York University Press.

Hirschi, T. (1969) *Causes of Delinquency*. Berkeley: University of California Press.

Hoffman-Bustamante, D. (1973) "The Nature of Female Criminality." *Issues in Criminology* 8, 2: 117–123.

Jurik, N. (1983) "The Economics of Female Recidivism." *Criminology* 21, 4: 3–12.

Kellor, F. (1900a) "Psychological and Environmental Study of Women Criminals." *The American Journal of Sociology* 5: 527–543.

Kellor, F. (1900b) "Criminal Sociology: Criminality Among Women." *Arena* 23: 516–524.

Kempinen, C. (1984) "Changes in the Sentencing Patterns of Male and Female Criminal Defendants." *The Prison Journal* 64, 2: 3–12.

Klein, D. (1973) "The Etiology of Female Crime: A Review of the Literature." *Issues in Criminology* 8: 3–29.

Kruttschnitt, C. (1982) "Women, Crime and Dependency." *Criminology* 19, 4: 495–513.

Kruttschnitt, C. and D. Green. (1984) "The Sex Sanctioning Issue: Is It History?" *American Sociology Review* 49: 541–551.

Leonard, E. (1982) *Women, Crime and Society.* New York: Longman.

Lombroso, C., and W. Ferrero (1920 [1894]) *The Female Offender.* New York: Appleton.

Mann, C. (1984) *Female Crime and Deliquency.* Birmingham: University of Alabama Press.

Merton, R. (1949) *Social Theory and Social Structure.* New York: Free Press.

Morris, A. (1987) *Women, Crime and Criminal Justice.* London: Basil Blackwell.

Naffine, N. (1987) *Female Crime: The Construction of Women in Criminology.* Sydney, Australia: Allen & Unwin.

Pike, L. (1876) *A History of Crime in England.* London: Smith, Edler.

Pollak, O. (1950) *The Criminality of Women.* Philadelphia: University of Pennsylvania Press.

Pollock, J. (1978) "Early Theories of Female Criminality." In L. Bowker, *Women, Crime and the Criminal Justice System,* pp. 25–50. Lexington, Mass.: Lexington Books.

Price, B. and N. Sokoloff (1982) *The Criminal Justice System and Women.* New York: Clark Boardman.

Rasche, C. (1975) "The Female Offender as an Object of Criminological Research." In A. Brodsky, ed., *The Female Offender,* pp. 9–28. Newbury Park, Calif.: Sage.

Schwendinger, H., and J. Schwendinger. (1973) "The Founding Fathers: Sexists to a Man." In H. Schwendinger and J. Schwendinger, *Sociologists of the Chair,* pp. 290–334. New York: Basic Books.

Shaw, C. R., and H. D. McKay. (1942) *Juvenile Delinquency and Urban Areas.* Chicago: Chicago Press.

Siegel, L. (1986) *Criminology.* St. Paul, Minn.: West.

Simon, R. (1975) *Women and Crime.* Lexington, Mass.: Lexington Books.

Smart, C. (1976) *Women, Crime and Criminology: A Feminist Critique.* London: Routledge & Kegan Paul.

Smart, C. (1979) "The New Female Criminal: Reality or Myth?" *British Journal of Criminology* 19, 1: 50–57.

Smith, D., and C. Visher. (1980) "Sex and Involvement in Deviance/Crime: A Quantitative Review of the Empirical Literature." *American Sociological Review* 45: 691–701.

South, S., and S. Messner. (1986) "The Sex Ratio and Women's Involvement in Crime: A Cross-National Analysis." *The Sociological Quarterly* 28, 2: 171–188.

Spaulding, E. (1923) *An Experimental Study of Psychopathic Delinquent Women.* New York: Rand McNally.

Steffensmeier, D. (1980) "Assessing the Impact of the Women's Movement on Sex-Based Differences in the Handling of Adult Criminal Defendants." *Crime and Delinquency* 26: 344–357.

Steffensmeir, D., and R. Steffensmeier. (1980) "Trends in Female Delinquency." *Criminology* 18: 62–85.

Sutherland, E. H. (1939) *Principles of Criminology*. Philadelphia: Lippincott.

Tappan, P. (1947) *Delinquent Girls in Court*. New York: Columbia University Press.

Thomas, W. I. (1937) *The Unadjusted Girl*. Boston: Little, Brown.

Tjaden, P., and C. Tjaden. (1981) "Differential Treatment of the Female Felon: Myth or Reality?" In M. Warren, ed., *Comparing Male and Female Offenders*, pp. 73–89. Newbury Park, Calif.: Sage.

van de Warker, E. (1875–1876) "The Relations of Women to Crime." *Popular Science Monthly* 8: 1–16.

Vedder, C., and D. Somerville. (1970) *The Delinquent Girl*. Springfield, Ill.: Charles C Thomas.

Vetter, H., and I. Silverman. (1986) *Criminology and Crime: An Introduction*. New York: Harper & Row.

Weidensall, J. (1916) *The Mentality of the Criminal Woman*. Baltimore: Warwick and York.

Weishet, R. (1984) "Women and Crime: Issues and Perspectives." *Sex Roles* 11, 7/8: 567–580.

Wilbanks, W. (1986) "Are Female Felons Treated More Leniently by the Criminal Justice System?" *Justice Quarterly* 3, 4: 517–529.

3 The History of Women's Prisons

The history of women's institutions reflects the history of women. Because women have long been thought to hold a special place in society, deviant women have been treated differently not only from their more law-abiding sisters but also from their male counterparts. In short, women offenders have been a class of people perceived as not wholly feminine but definitely not masculine either. Dobash, Dobash, and Gutteridge wrote, "From the very beginning, women in prison were treated differently from men, considered more morally depraved and corrupt and in need of special, closer forms of control and confinement" (1986: 1). Some have described these women as "lost," and indeed in both physical surroundings and attitudes toward their redemption, female prisoners have been either brutalized or ignored for the greater part of this country's history.

This chapter relies extensively on two major works in the area of history. Estelle Freedman published an extensive exploration of the reformatory movement in the late 1800s and early 1900s, which proposed an environment designed to help deviant women become "ladies" in the model of their female administrators and advocates (1974, 1981). Nicole Rafter provided a more complete picture of the historical treatment of women, which shows that only a small proportion of women were ever "treated" in reformatories while the vast majority continued to spend sentences in harsh penitentiaries, or in work camps and agricultural prisons in the South and West (1985). Dobash, Dobash, and Gutteridge (1986) also offer unique contributions to the history of prisons for women; and Lekkerkerker published a description in 1931 of the history of women's reformatories and the state of reformatories in the early 1900s.

Although primarily concerned with prisons for women in Great Britain, Dobash, Dobash, and Gutteridge offered the following summary of women's treatment in the United States:

> In the first decades of nineteenth century America, women were predominantly confined in separate wings of prisons for men, usually provided with poorer living conditions and sometimes subjected to physical and sexual abuse by male warders. By the end of the century, wider social and ideological forces produced strong pressures to change the conditions of confinement for these women. Reformatories for women emerged in the context of growing concern for the regulation of youth, public morals and domestic training. The American reformatory movement was the answer to the neglect and repression experienced by women. Reformatories were not built in every state. They spread primarily in the north and northeast. These institutions were the epitome of progressive ideals. According to their creators women would be diagnosed and assessed by a group of professionals who would then be able to apply the best individualized treatment (1986: 1).

From Dobash's history, we can see that the differential treatment of women offenders has its roots in English common law, and the United States merely continued a tradition of legal and social sexual discrimination started in England. Indeed, the histories are parallel and overlap at times, since many of the reformers who advocated separate institutions for women in England were influential in this country as well.

IIIII Early Punishments and Places of Confinement

Early English law made it very clear that women and men were different and possessed different rights under the law. Some behavior, for instance, was not considered criminal when committed by men or was punished much less severely, such as adultery. For other crimes, however, women may have been punished less often or less severely than men who committed the identical activity (Dobash et al., 1986: 17). The social order was a male hierarchy; several public-order crimes were directed toward those who violated this social order. For instance, women who were too vocal or too critical of men were punished, as were those who were not monogamous. Men who let their wives dominate them or who allowed themselves to be "cuckolded" were also punished.

> Men, for example, might be subjected to a "cuckold's court" or forced to ride backward on a donkey for allowing their wives to cuckold or dominate them. They might also provoke community sanction for overstepping the bounds of appropriate patriarchal domination, when, for example, they beat their wives to excess. It is important to note that it was only when a man grossly overstepped the bounds of appropriate chastisement by mutilation or by nearly killing his wife, that he might be sanctioned by the community through the performance of a misrule or a charivari" (Dobash et al., 1986: 18).

Women who violated the social order were subject to the ducking stool or more serious punishments.

> The branks was an iron cage placed over the head, and most examples incorporated a spike or pointed wheel that was inserted into the offender's mouth in order to "pin the tongue and silence the noisiest brawler." This spiked cage was intended to punish women adjudged quarrelsome or not under the proper control of their husbands (Dobash et al., 1986: 19).

Thus, women were firmly under the control of men and their behavior judged against the male model of female submissiveness. First fathers, then husbands had almost total legal control over their daughters and wives. Punishment could be imposed whenever the wife or daughter was considered disobedient or unchaste. Women were sent to monasteries when out of control, and husbands turned their errant wives over to bridewells or poorhouses (Dobash et al., 1986: 22–23).

Wives had some legal recourse against brutal or improvident husbands, but very little. Thus, if a woman was married to a drunk who did not give her money to buy food, there was little she could do to provide for herself and her children. Consequently, many of the early imprisoned women were committed for theft or begging. Many succumbed to the only other way females could obtain money—prostitution. Women criminals, when sentenced to bridewells, often received substantially longer sentences than men (Fox, 1984: 16).

When incarcerated, women did not escape their female duties. Women in poorhouses and bridewells were expected to do the cooking and cleaning, spinning and sewing required for the institution (Dobash et al., 1986: 24–25). Other uses of incarcerated women involved their sexual role. The following quote describes what awaited women who were transported to Australia in the early 1800s.

> In 1812, the Committee on Transportation observed that women were ". . . indiscriminately given to such of the inhabitants as demanded them, and were in general received rather as prostitutes than as servants. . . ." The British Government transported women for the purpose of preventing unrest among the free and convict male population by providing convict women as sexual commodities (Dobash et al., 1986: 33).

Those in bridewells in England found that prostitution was one of the few ways to better their living conditions in the prison (Fox, 1984: 16).

Feinman described the treatment of women in this country as basically egalitarian during the colonial period, when women were needed on farms and were considered equal partners. Both men and women were likely subjected to physical punishments and treated similarly by the courts (Feinman, 1984: 12). However, with increasing urbanization and industrialization after the American Revolution, the cult of "True Womanhood" developed in the East: women were expected to be "pure, submissive, and pious." Those who did not fit this mold were considered more deviant than criminal men since they went against a natural order (Feinman, 1984: 13). Freedman explains that the cult of "True Womanhood" created a model of female virtue that was hard to live up to. According to this theme, women provided the moral boundaries of society and controlled social disorder. Thus, the female deviant, whether a prostitute, vagrant, murderess, or thief, "threatened social order doubly, both by sinning and by removing the moral constraints on men." Further, "they justified harsher treatment of female criminals by the argument that women convicts were more depraved than men since, having been born pure, they had fallen further than had their male counterparts in crime" (Freedman, 1974: 78).

Descriptions of early places of confinement for women indicate that there was little regard for the safety or health of female prisoners. Before classification of the sexes in Europe and the United States, men and women were housed together in large rooms where the strong preyed upon the weak and each individual's life was made bearable only by the resources each received from his or her family or could acquire by begging, bartering, or stealing from other prisoners. After the separation of the sexes, women's lives in prison were only marginally better.

Freedman describes early institutions for women as over-crowded and filthy. In the 1820s, a Philadelphia jail had seven women in a cellar with only two blankets among them; and in Albany, a jail placed fifteen women in one room (Freedman, 1974: 78). Freedman also describes the New York City Tombs jail as having forty-two cells to hold seventy women in 1838 (Freedman, 1981: 16). Women were found only in jails because prisons were built solely for male prisoners at this time (Strickland, 1976: 40). In 1825, separate quarters for women were built at a Baltimore prison, and in 1835 officials at Ossining State Penitentiary (Sing Sing) built a separate unit for women (Strickland, 1976: 40).

Feinman described Sing Sing Penitentiary in 1843 as a place where mothers and other women were housed in a room eighteen feet square and where the "hot, crowded, and unsanitary conditions during the summer led to the death of one baby" (Feinman, 1984: 15). Further, floggings and harsh physical punishments led to miscarriages and even death (Feinman, 1984: 15). Women were subject to forced prostitution by male warders (Freedman, 1981: 17). Freedman reports that a young male prisoner in Indiana State Prison at Jeffersonville revealed that younger female prisoners were "subjected to the worst of debasement at the hands of prison officials and guards," while the older ones were "obliged to do the work of all." In this prison, the warden established concubinage and there were "sadistic beatings," "rape," and "illegitimate births" (Freedman, 1981: 60). This terrible treatment was rationalized by a belief that the women were beyond any redemption or reformation.

More often than not, women were simply left alone in the wing or building that comprised the women's portion of the institution. Rafter writes that women prisoners experienced lower levels of surveillance, discipline, and care. For instance, she writes that women held in Auburn Prison in 1825 were housed in an attic and visited only once a day when a steward came to deliver food and remove waste (Rafter, 1985: 6).

Before the mid-1800s, the use of imprisonment for female criminals was very limited. In 1831 an average of only one in twelve prisoners was female, and in 1850 women comprised only 3.6 percent of the incarcerated in thirty-four states (Freedman, 1981: 11). Shortly after 1840, however, female prisoners' numbers began to rise. Indeed, in 1864, females represented 37.2 percent of all commitments to prisons and jails in Massachusetts (Freedman, 1981: 13). By the end of the nineteenth century, nearly every state had some place to confine women criminals; however, women's quarters were usually within the walls of male prisons, and the few that were in separate buildings were typically run by the male warden (Rafter, 1985: xxi).

lllll Early Reformers

In the late nineteenth century, the perception of female criminals changed somewhat: they began to be seen as not so much evil as misguided. The female deviant was seen to be affected by poverty and a poor home environment, and her descent into depravity was attributed more often than not to an evil male (Freedman, 1974: 84). With this change in perception came a number of reformers who sought to improve the prison conditions of women.

Elizabeth Fry in England and several reformers in this country advocated not only separate housing but also female supervision of women in prison. Women were marginally protected from male inmates in their separate quarters, but there was still the possibility of exploitation from male warders as long as female prisoners were administratively and physically located in male institutions.

Dobash, Dobash, and Gutteridge wrote that Elizabeth Fry was the first penal reformer to devote her attention solely to the plight of imprisoned women. Fry visited Newgate in 1813 and was "shocked and sickened" by the "blaspheming, fighting, dram-drinking, half-naked women" found there. In her words: "All I tell thee is a faint picture of reality; the filth, the closeness of the rooms, the furious manner and expressions of the women towards each other, and the abandoned wickedness, which everything bespoke, are quite inde-scribable" (Dobash et al., 1986: 43). Fry went on to visit northern jails and bridewells and wrote and spoke on the terrible conditions she found there. Her *Observations on the Siting, Superintendence and Government of Female Prisoners,* published in 1825, advocated work, training, religion, routine, manners, and continuous surveil-lance for female prisoners.

Further, Fry proposed that female prisoners should be super-vised by women, not men. "Since female felons were of 'light and abandoned character' it was impossible and unreasonable to 'place them under the care of men . . .' because it 'seldom fails to be injurious to both parties'" (Dobash et al., 1986: 51). Elizabeth Fry advocated women warders for three reasons: first, they would prevent sexual abuse by male guards; second, they would set moral examples of "true womanhood" for their female charges; and third, they could provide a sympathetic ear for female inmates (Freedman, 1974: 79). Primarily through her efforts, a separate system for female inmates developed in England long before the United States undertook the same reforms.

> By mid-century, the British had created unique and austere institutions that usually provided secure, sanitary conditions for prisoners. . . . In contrast to the United States where women were

held in cramped, unsanitary gaols and often subjected to sexual assaults by warders, it seems that women in British prisons had been granted a fair degree of security and protection by this time (Dobash et al., 1986: 61).

In this country reformers such as Dorothea Dix, Mary Wister, Sarah Doremus, and Abby Hopper Gibbons advocated female warders in the 1820s. In 1845, Doremus and Gibbons established a Ladies Association within the New York Prison Association, which became autonomous several years later as the Women's Prison Association of New York. This organization also opened the Isaac Hopper Home for released women (Freedman, 1974: 80).

Private institutions for female deviants were created when public agencies were recalcitrant. In 1825, a House of Refuge was established in New York City. In 1833 the Magdalen Home for wayward women was created to inculcate virtue through education, religious instruction, and work. The House of Shelter was run by a woman in Indiana in 1869; the Home for the Friendless had female managers in 1870 in New York; and homes for women opened in Dedham, Springfield, Richmond, and other cities in the 1870s and 1890s. These homes emphasized religion, education, discipline, reading, and sewing (Freedman, 1981: 52, 55).

The goal of the reformers, however, was to establish separate state penal institutions for women prisoners, run by women and with the purpose of instilling feminine values in the female residents. The reformers felt that only women could be successful in pursuing this goal. The female reformers encountered strong resistance to the notion of a female institution run by females. Primary among the reasons such an idea was so abhorrent to those in charge was that the place for women was considered to be in the home, not in public service. Moreover, women were seen as incapable of controlling female prisoners; the institution run by women would lack a normal, family atmosphere if men were excluded; and, women's institutions would reduce male dominance in society and destroy femininity (Freedman, 1974: 86).

Rafter wrote that those who championed the cause of separate women's facilities can be divided into several groups.

> Those who campaigned for women's reformatories can be separated, for analytical purposes, into three groups. First and most influential were the women who spearheaded state campaigns and those superintendents who became prominent advocates of the reformatory cause. A second group comprised supporters with positions on prison and welfare boards. At first these were nearly all men, but as women recognized their need for political leverage, they found ways to join men on these state boards. The third and most peripheral group consisted of loose confederations of individ-

uals and organizations that, in the various states, helped lobby for separate women's prisons (Rafter, 1985: 41).

Gradually the resistance gave way, and women were hired to run the separate buildings or wings that housed women offenders. In 1822, Maryland became the first state to hire a female jail keeper (Freedman, 1974: 80). In 1827, Connecticut hired a woman to oversee the female department of the state prison. In 1828, a separate building for women was built at Ossining, New York (euphemistically called Mt. Pleasant) (Rafter, 1985: 17). In 1830, Maine and Ohio also opened separate buildings for women prisoners (Freedman, 1974: 80).

Elizabeth Farnham, appointed in 1844 as matron of Mt. Pleasant, was very influenced by Elizabeth Fry. She made many changes in the institutional surroundings, designed to "feminize" the women prisoners there. For instance, she allowed female prisoners to decorate their rooms with curtains and flowers. She brought in a piano and instituted educational classes and readings. Her tenure lasted only two years, however, because of harsh critics who objected to her "atheism" and lack of discipline (Freedman, 1981: 46; Feinman, 1984: 17).

The women who championed the cause of female prisoners were not the equivalent of women's rights advocates. Rather, they believed that women had a special and unique ability to help their "fallen sisters" achieve the purity that all women should possess. Freedman explains the difference between these reformers and suffragists.

> An important distinction must be drawn between the prison reformers' appeal to sisterhood and the demand of the women's rights movement for political equality. Most antebellum prison reformers did not support women's rights. Like more vehement opponents, such as Catharine Beecher or the vocal antisuffragists of the late 19th century, benevolent reformers assumed that women's power emanated from the moral influence of their separate sphere. In contrast to radical feminists, they did not seek equality in the public sphere; many even prided themselves on remaining outside of politics (1981: 34).

Freedman further explains:

> Like temperance advocates, social purity leaders, and settlement house founders, the postwar prison reformers believed in women's separate sphere and superior morality. Even as they entered the public sphere and gained valuable skills by building separate women's organizations, social feminists continued to argue that women had unique, feminine virtues that should be embodied in social policy (1981: 39).

lllll Reformatories for Women

The pressure exerted by female reformers for the separation of women prisoners from men, control over women's prisons by female staff and management, and provision of different feminine care, finally led to the establishment of completely separate institutions.

> Male prejudices, male exploitation, and male-dominated institutions, the reformers believed, denied justice to female criminals. Thus, they reasoned, if male influence were removed by placing the female criminal solely in the hands of her sisters, virtue might be restored. Female officers would provide the salutary influences of education, religion, and love to redeem the female criminal class (Freedman, 1974: 86).

In the late 1800s, the female reformers were finally successful in their drives to establish separate female institutions run by women. In the 1870s, separate institutions in Indiana and Massachusetts were built, which employed female staff. In 1881, the New York House of Refuge for female misdemeanants was created, and in 1900, Bedford Hills was built (Freedman, 1974: 80). Houses of refuge were designed for young women (as young as twelve or fifteen) who had been convicted of minor crimes, such as "petit larceny, habitual drunkenness, or being a common prostitute, of frequenting disorderly houses or houses of prostitution or of any misdemeanor," and who were "not insane or mentally or physically incapable of being substantially benefitted" by the discipline found there (Lekkerkerker, 1931: 102).

Four factors contributed to the women's prison movement: first, an apparent increase in female criminality during the 1860s, from prostitution and abortion associated with the Civil War; second, women's Civil War social service experience; third, the development of the charities organization movement and of a prison reform movement which emphasized the investigation of criminality and the reformatory ideal; and fourth, an embryonic feminist analysis of women's place in U.S. society (Freedman, 1974: 82).

Ironically, the first completely separate institution for women run by women did not follow the reformatory ideal. In 1874, the Female Prison and Reformatory Institution for Girls and Women was opened in Indiana. Here, the reformatory concept was only partially followed. The institution received only felons; it did not originally use indeterminate sentencing; it made no attempt to reform through education; and its architecture did not follow the cottage system (Rafter, 1985: 33). In fact, the first prisons for women in Indiana and Massachusetts were described as castle-like—"grim, dark, 'bastille-like' structure[s]" (Freedman, 1981: 70). However, the women in Indiana did have separate rooms and wore gingham dresses instead of prison uniforms (Lekkerkerker, 1931: 99).

The Massachusetts prison, opened after a long delay, had three hundred individual cells and two fifty-bed dormitories. Run by a woman with an entirely female staff, this institution, like others, was under the authority of a male.

> At first men maintained ultimate authority over the Indiana and Massachusetts prisons, and male physicians served in New York and Indiana. Their presence contradicted the theory that women's problems, whether medical or emotional, could best be treated by members of the same sex. Other men worked at each institution, not only to calm fears that inmates would overrun their too-gentle female keepers, but also to perform engineering, firefighting, and carpentry tasks for which there were few women available (Freedman, 1981: 71).

It was a struggle to retain female supervisors once they were in place. For instance, Freedman wrote that Clara Barton was superintendent of Framingham for nine months in order to prevent the governor from appointing a man in 1882 (Freedman, 1981: 74). Low pay, uncomfortable living conditions, and questionable status made qualified women difficult to find and keep (Freedman, 1981: 75).

Male reformers of the late 1800s who advocated reformatories for males agreed that females would be useful in the care and treatment of female prisoners. Brockway, for instance, advocated using women to supervise women because of their "sisterly care, counsel and sympathy." He advocated the use of "family life, where they shall receive intellectual, moral, domestic, and industrial training, under the influence, example and sympathy of refined and virtuous women" (Rafter, 1985: 26). Brockway had himself dealt with female prisoners and had developed his ideas of grading and limited freedom with female prisoners in a House of Shelter at the Detroit House of Correction during the period from 1865 to 1869. He later implemented these ideas at Elmira with male prisoners (Strickland, 1976: 41).

Other institutions were opened and some of these followed strictly the ideals of the women reformers. These institutions followed a pattern more similar to the private homes and shelters described earlier. Institutions like the Hudson House of Refuge, which opened in New York in 1887, were built on the cottage system and were staffed almost entirely by women. The Hudson House of Refuge and institutions like it followed a domestic routine. In 1893, Albion followed the Hudson model, and then in 1901, Bedford Hills was opened (Freedman, 1981: 57). Although primarily for misdemeanants, these facilities also accepted some felony offenders by 1900 (Strickland, 1976: 47).

Rafter's historical study explained that women's prisons evolved into two distinct types: the reformatory and the custodial institution. The reformatory model was followed least often in new construction after 1930.

> The women's reformatory movement gathered momentum slowly. From its inception about 1870 to the century's close, it produced only four institutions. But this was a period of germination during which reformers experimented, venturing ever further from traditional concepts of the prison as they evolved their own model. . . . Between 1900 and 1935, seventeen states opened women's reformatories. . . . By 1935, the women's reformatory movement had exhausted itself (Rafter, 1985: xxiii).

Freedman began her history of the reformatory movement in the following way:

> A century ago, women reformers championed the creation of separate correctional institutions in order to protect female prisoners from widespread abuses of the male-dominated prison system. They revolutionized the treatment of "fallen" women by rejecting harsh punishment in favor of reform programs administered by their "more fortunate sisters" (Freedman, 1974: 78).

Lekkerkerker viewed the female reformatories as entirely different from reformatories for men and unique in the world (Lekkerkerker, 1931: 4). Part of the reason for their difference was the vague line drawn between crime and sexual immorality. According to Lekkerkerker, women's deviance took place primarily in the sexual area, and thus the institution used to control females, the reformatory, was concerned with the women's morality rather than their criminality (Lekkerkerker, 1931: 9).

Freedman described the early reformatories as "benevolent matriarchies," which offered a homelike atmosphere free "from the contaminating influences of men" (Freedman, 1974: 88). Training consisted of household work, including sewing, knitting, cooking, washing and ironing clothes, gardening, and farming. So, for instance, the Massachusetts Reformatory Prison for Women at Framingham, built in 1877, had private rooms, each with its own "iron bedsteads and white linen" (Freedman, 1981: 68).

The early administrators of these institutions were often the same reformers who had struggled so hard to create them. These women believed they had a moral duty to improve the lives of their female charges. The early group of advocates had a kind of religious fervor and felt kinship with their fallen sisters (Rafter, 1985: 66). As these women retired, they were replaced by "professional administrators," who were less zealous than their forerunners. Freedman writes that women entering prison reformatories as paid administrators during the 1880s and 1890s did not share the missionary spirit that had motivated the founders (Freedman, 1981: 109). These later women, who had experience in education and settlement houses, had different reasons for entering prison work. Fewer had a religious "mission"; and those who had training in social work, law, medicine, and the social sciences approached prisoners as subjects or clients (Freedman, 1981: 110). Rafter wrote that some were patronizing and showed condescension and contempt for their charges (1985: 66).

Staff who worked in early institutions had no easy task. As Rafter wrote:

> Meager salaries, long hours, and unpleasant working conditions undermined the morale of staff members. According to a report of the late 1920s, at Marysville matrons worked twelve-hour shifts with only two days off each month. Some lived in rooms designed for inmates, and both they and the superintendent received salaries that were "disgracefully low" (1985: 75).

Primary complaints centered on inadequate resources, overcrowding, and lack of programs (Rafter, 1985: 77). Female staff proved to be as prone to abusive treatment of prisoners as their male counterparts. A scandal at Bedford Hills in 1915 involved the use of physically abusive punishments. Eventually, some of these problems led to riots, such as those at Bedford Hills in the 1920s (Rafter, 1985: 77–79).

Those given reformatory terms were carefully chosen. The women who found themselves in reformatories were young, relatively unhardened, guilty of misdemeanors, or victims of difficult circumstances. Most were under the age of twenty-five, white, and native-born. Two-thirds were married at some time but were widowed, divorced, or separated. Most had no prior convictions and their crimes were minor: more than half had been incarcerated for drunkenness and prostitution (Freedman, 1981: 78–79). Rafter wrote that some of the women sent to Albion were there not for prostitution but because "exasperated mothers or embarrassed husbands" charged them with sexual misconduct (1985: 117). It is instructive to note that these "new" penal institutions were being used to control female behavior in much the same way as bridewells had been used in earlier times. In short, prisoners were usually young moral offenders with short sentences (Freedman, 1981: 82).

Women in reformatories were younger than those in custodial institutions. Rafter reported that half the women at custody institutions were between the ages of thirty-one and fifty, whereas reformatory (Albion) women were between the ages of fifteen and thirty (1985: 126). Reformatory women were also disproportionately white; blacks were almost entirely excluded. Albion, for instance, was 97 percent white. This exclusion of black women occurred despite the fact that blacks composed a disproportionate share of prison commitments. In New York, blacks comprised 12.5 percent of the commitments in 1831; this figure had risen to 40 percent by 1934 (Rafter, 1985: 132). Tennessee had even higher figures. Between 1860 and 1887, blacks comprised 70 percent of the women incarcerated; in 1900 they comprised 90 percent. The figure declined to 65 percent by 1926–1934 (Rafter, 1985: 132). Those blacks that were placed in reformatories were segregated into separate cottages (Rafter, 1985: 37).

The institutions offered domestic training and very little else. Academic classes were underfunded; industrial training was opposed by civilian industry; and only a small number of women could get jobs in skilled trades (Freedman, 1981: 90). Many women were trained in the "domestic sciences." In Massachusetts, an indenture law was passed in 1879, and 1,500 women went into service in family homes (Freedman, 1981: 92). Rafter wrote: "Albion provided trained, inexpensive household help. It was the institution's policy 'to place our girls in the home of a woman who will take a motherly interest in them'" (1985: 163). One-quarter of the prisoners were paroled directly to live-in domestic positions. In fact, parole revocation usually occurred because of sexual misconduct or "sauciness" to employers (Rafter, 1985: 125).

Some institutions, however, had an expanded view of domesticity. At Bedford Hills, the women did outdoor work, such as gardening, slaughtering pigs, and draining a swamp (Freedman, 1981: 134). Women there also "poured concrete sidewalks, laid floors for new buildings, painted cottages, graded the grounds, filled washouts, put up fences, planted trees and began a farm" (Strickland, 1976: 47). Clinton Farms, in New Jersey, also took a nontraditional view of women's work and included an early form of inmate self-government (Freedman, 1981: 137). Most institutions emphasized a feminine ideal, however, and women were rewarded for maintaining ladylike decorum and cleanliness with privileges such as prettier uniforms (Rafter, 1985: 39).

Women incarcerated in the early reformatories were not serious criminals and did not often pose a security risk for the staff, but those that did found that punishment in a women's reformatory was the same as in any other prison. "Dungeons," rooms with no ventilation or light, were available for those who attacked officers, destroyed property, or threatened safety (Freedman, 1981: 99). Some serious disturbances did occur in 1888 in Framingham, Massachusetts, and in 1899 in Hudson, New York (Freedman, 1981: 100). These disturbances may have been caused by inefficient security and overcrowding. A more prevalent problem, according to early discipline reports, might have been homosexuality between the races. Because of this "unnatural attraction," staff wanted to segregate blacks in Bedford Hills and other institutions (Freedman, 1981: 140).

Overall, the interaction between female staff and female prisoners was one of mutual dependency. Freedman wrote that the prisoners transferred their dependency needs to the female staff members. The staff became surrogate mothers to their female dependents. The staff, in turn, needed the prisoners because they were the only appropriate outlet for the female professionals' training and energy (Freedman, 1981: 105). Women who studied women prisoners were outcasts from the male professions of medicine and science (Freedman, 1981: 121). Some institutions, like Bedford Hills, became centers of research on female criminality. Interestingly, these women researchers pointed out factors in crime causation, such as poor family life and temptation, years ahead of their "discovery" by male criminologists; yet this earlier work was largely ignored.

Katharine B. Davis was one such early physician and superintendent who conducted research with female delinquents (Freedman, 1981: 116). In 1910, she obtained a grant for psychological testing of feebleminded mental defectives and established the Bureau of Social Hygiene at Bedford Hills. These women were isolated on the reformatory grounds and studied by female researchers (Rafter, 1985: 69). The thrust of this testing and research was eugenics. Women were thought to be the breeders of future classes of criminals; the logic of the research was to test for defectiveness and then prevent those found to be defective from having children. In one sense, the reformatory might be considered a method for restraining defective women from getting pregnant and producing children who would be criminal, defective, or both. Certainly concern about reproduction may have been the reason for the longer sentences given for relatively trivial crimes committed by women considered promiscuous (Rafter, 1985: 54). Albion inmates served an average term of 33.8 months compared to 28 months for those incarcerated in Ohio's custodial institution, despite the fact that Ohio's inmates were probably there for much more serious crimes whereas Albion's inmates were all misdemeanants (Rafter, 1985: 121). It is also possible that reformatories were considered such a good idea that many courts decided to keep women in them for longer terms. Some legislatures granted courts more discretion in sentencing women, and longer sentences were available for women (Freedman, 1981: 129). For instance, in 1869 Michigan had an indeterminate sentencing law for women only (Rafter, 1985: 25). These discriminatory sentencing laws will be discussed in more detail in a later chapter.

Rafter discussed the fate of those many women who did not spend their sentences in reformatories. In other regions of the country, such as the West and the South, only makeshift arrangements were available for women prisoners long into the 1900s. The prison farm camps popular in the South were thought to be extremely inappropriate places for women. Consequently, the female felon was dealt with by alternative methods, unless she was an extremely serious offender or black. If she met either of those criteria, she may have ended up on the prison farm and been expected to do less arduous physical work, such as gardening or housework in the home of the superintendent (Rafter, 1985: 88).

In the South, inmates were often "leased out" to private farmers for labor. Women were not wanted by private lessees because they were not considered economically productive. Consequently, the state kept them with the old and sick men (Rafter, 1985: 151). In 1910, all women prisoners in Texas were transferred to a central state farm called Goree. Here, black women worked in the field and white women worked at sewing and in the garden. This institution was in a dilapidated condition, and all sixty inmates—except for the few white women there—were housed in one building (Rafter, 1985: 89).

Table 3-1 State and federal correctional institutions for women, 1873–1975

State	Title at Opening	Date
Indiana	Woman's Prison	1873
Massachusetts	Reformatory Prison for Women	1877
New York	House of Refuge for Women, Hudson	1887
New York	House of Refuge for Women, Albion	1893
New York	Reformatory Prison for Women, Bedford Hills	1902
New Jersey	State Reformatory for Women	1913
Maine	Reformatory for Women	1916
Ohio	Reformatory for Women	1916
Kansas	Industrial Farm for Women	1917
Michigan	Training School for Women	1917
Connecticut	Farm for Women	1918
Iowa	Women's Reformatory	1918
Arkansas	Farm for Women	1920
California	Industrial Farm for Women	1920
Minnesota	Reformatory for Women	1920
Nebraska	State Reformatory for Women	1920
Pennsylvania	State Industrial Home for Women	1920
Wisconsin	Industrial Home for Women	1921
United States	Industrial Institution for Women (Alderson)	1927
Delaware	Correctional Institution for Women	1929
Connecticut	Correctional Instutution for Women	1930
Illinois	State Reformatory for Women	1930
Virginia	State Industrial Farm for Women	1932
North Carolina	Correctional Center for Women	1934

(continued)

State	Title at Opening	Date
California	Correctional Institution for Women	1936
Kentucky	Correctional Institution for Women	1938
South Carolina	Harbison Correctional Institution for Women	1938
Maryland	Correctional Institution for Women	1940
Alabama	Julia Tutwiler Prison for Women	1942
West Virginia	State Prison for Women	1948
Georgia	Rehabilitation Center for Women	1957
Missouri	State Correctional Center for Women	1960
Louisiana	Correctional Institution for Women	1961
Ohio	Women's Correctional Institution	1963
Nevada	Women's Correctional Center	1964
Oregon	Women's Correctional Center	1965
Tennessee	Prison for Women	1966
Colorado	Women's Correctional Institute	1968
Washington	Purdy Treatment Center for Women	1970
Oklahoma	Women's Treatment Facility	1973
South Carolina	Women's Correctional Center	1973

Source: Estelle Freedman, *Their Sister's Keepers* (Ann Arbor: University of Michigan Press, 1981), pp. 144–145.

Freedman concluded that early reformatories did accomplish good things: they prevented sexual abuse, allowed freedom from exploitation of labor, and provided services for women such as nurseries that were possible only in centralized prisons. However, problems did remain, and some were actually created by the reformatory. Women's sexual needs were still unmet, overcrowding and classification were still problems, and the reformatory ideal created a legacy of differential feminine care. This legacy lingers, exemplified in sexual stereotypes in work and vocational training programs and treatment of women prisoners as "children" (Freedman, 1981: 152).

Rafter concluded that the custodial institutions present a truer picture of women prisoners in the early years, since most women were sent to these institutions. Only a small portion of women ended up in the "nicer" reformatories; most served their sentences in grim custodial institutions or prison farms in the South. Only young, white misdemeanants escaped these conditions.

IIIII The 1930s

Reasons given for the demise of the reformatory ideal include the increasing disinterest with prostitution as a national issue and the gradual exit of the zealous reformers described previously. The

Depression also hastened the end of interest in reformatories (Rafter, 1985: xxiii). By the 1930s, the population of reformatories had changed in response to increasing numbers of women criminals. Felons were sent to women's reformatories because states started closing custodial units (Rafter, 1985: 81). For instance, in 1933 a portion of the custodial unit for women at Auburn Prison in New York was closed and the women were transferred to Bedford Hills (Strickland, 1976: 48). For all practical purposes, the transfer of these women ended the reformatory experiment at Bedford Hills; the emphasis after this time was on custodial issues.

Institutions were continuing to be built through the early and mid-1900s—indeed, into the 1970s!—primarily under a modified reformatory model. In the early 1900s, a Dutch lawyer came to this country to conduct a comprehensive survey of women's reformatories. She described the common characteristics of women's institutions she found at the time:

> All of them have been established as the result of an action of socially minded women in the community, in reaction to bad conditions existing where women were confined in the same penal institutions with men; they usually have a more vaguely defined population than the reformatories for men, nearly all of them comprising both misdemeanants and felons, and very few placing any age limits upon admission; almost all of them which were newly built (and not, for reasons of economy housed in a remodeled old institution) are on the cottage plan; nearly all are equipped with farms; everywhere women were placed at the head of the institution; all make sincere attempts to establish a truly reformatory regime, and they usually belong to the better and more progressive penal institutions; in several states, indeed, they are more advanced than the corresponding institutions for men (Lekkerkerker, 1931: 112).

Institutions for women built in the 1920s and 1930s were in rural areas and they were originally well kept and quite attractive. Lekkerkerker's portrayals at times read more like travel brochures than descriptions of penal institutions; for instance, when describing the prison farm for women in Connecticut, she wrote:

> The Farm certainly has charms: the buildings, scattered wide apart, form an attractive whole with the romantic lake, the wood and thicket, the rolling hills and green pasture, which offer the women abundant opportunity for healthy outdoor sports, such as hiking, swimming, fishing, sleighing and skating in winter, picking berries, chopping wood, etc. which, in fact, is often done by them (1931: 121).

Lekkerkerker describes the prisons that existed in the 1930s as varied in staff size. Bedford Hills had a ratio of one staff person to three inmates, whereas the Ohio reformatory had a ratio of one to fourteen. Staff were both custodial and educational; there were sewing instructors and farm supervisors as well as matrons (Lekkerkerker, 1931: 255). Lekkerkerker bemoaned the fact that the matron's low pay and absence of responsibility was insufficient to attract the quality of staff thought desirable for the position (1931: 265).

The life of a matron was a difficult one. In the 1930s she was expected to live at the institution and, in some institutions, to eat with the prisoners during all meals. She had only a day off each week with vacation days determined by how many years she had worked for the institution. Twelve-hour shifts were not uncommon (Lekkerkerker, 1931: 279–280).

Lekkerkerker described the daily routine in early institutions as follows:

> The inmates get up at six-thirty or seven o'clock in the morning, except those having kitchen or farm service who frequently have to rise earlier. Usually each inmate fixes her own room either before or immediately after breakfast. After this, the women go to their respective departments for work or instruction. For the rest of the day different systems prevail. In some institutions one half of the population goes to work in the morning and to classes in the afternoon, while the other half follows the reverse order; in other institutions classes are spread over the whole day and the work is made more or less subservient to the classwork; in others the women work all day while classes and further activities, if any, are held in the evenings. . . . Usually, the women cease working for about an hour at noon time for dinner, and finish their work or classes at about five o'clock in the afternoon. Recreation is provided in some institutions for half an hour after dinner, in others no free time is provided during the day except a little time before or after meals or between the periods to enable the girls to go from one building or department to another. . . . After supper, which is about five or half past five, there may be various activities, such as sports and gymnastics, cottage or community entertainments, singing or bible-classes, lectures, self-government meetings, etc., or the inmates may simply stay "at home" to mend their clothing, to read, do fancy-work, play games, or converse with each other. . . . At nine-thirty or ten o'clock the lights are usually turned off (Lekkerkerer, 1931: 410–411).

Lekkerkerker also found differences between institutions in the rules, regulations, visitation and mail privileges, and entertainment provided (1931: 413–415). Her descriptions of the discipline used in early prisons and reformatories indicate that the power of persuasion was used more than force. Sympathy and emotion usually were used to appeal to women inmates, rather than either rationality or force (1931: 424–425). However, harsher punishments did exist, including forfeiture of wages, distinctive dress, cutting the hair close to the scalp, and solitary confinement (1931: 427). One must remember that Lekkerkerker described only the northeastern prisons, providing no information about the early institutions in the South and West.

IIIII Conclusion

Prisons for women today have inherited the legacy of the reformatory ideal. Although two specific types of institutions for women emerged—the custody institution and the reformatory—the ideas surrounding them merged together, and the institutions that were built followed vague ideals that mixed both types. Women housed in reformatories were hardly criminal. They were more sinned against than sinning, since they often came from environments in which they were exploited or abused. The reformatory provided a home for them and placed them in domestic service upon release. Women felons more often were placed in custodial institutions that had less pleasant surroundings but were still feminized versions of the male penitentiaries. Lekkerkerker notes that European prisons for women were indistinguishable from those for men in routine and appearance; yet in this country, even the most custodial prison for women in the northeast often had separate rooms and a domestic routine. Women on southern prison farms were apparently treated most harshly of all. These women usually were incarcerated because of their race or the seriousness of their crime; other women were sentenced to alternative punishments.

We see that throughout the early 1900s, women's prisons tended to continue to follow the same vague ideals that defined women as different and institutions for women as a place to prepare them for womanhood. At least we assume they did; little was actually written detailing the methods or goals of these institutions. We see no attention directed to women's prisons from the time Lekkerkerker did her study in the early 1930s to the mid-1960s, when Giallombardo, Ward and Kassebaum, and Strickland looked again at the women's prison. Subsequent chapters will describe women prisoners of today and the institutions that house them. It becomes clear that the history of women's prisons has shaped contemporary prisons. Further, the conceptions that influenced early institutions—that women are different from men, that they need "feminizing" and domestic training, and that they are not so much criminal as sexually immoral—are still very prevalent today.

References

Dobash, R., R. Dobash, and S. Gutteridge. (1986) *The Imprisonment of Women*. New York: Basil Blackwell.

Feinman, C. (1984) "An Historical Overview of the Treatment of Incarcerated Women: Myths and Realities of Rehabilitation." *The Prison Journal* 63, 2: 12–26.

Fox, J. (1984) "Women's Prison Policy, Prisoner Activism, and the Impact of the Contemporary Feminist Movement: A Case Study." *The Prison Journal* 64, 1: 15–36.

Freedman, E. (1974) "Their Sister's Keepers: A Historical Perspective of Female Correctional Institutions in the U.S." *Feminist Studies* 2: 77–95.

Freedman, E. (1981) *Their Sister's Keepers: Women's Prison Reform in America, 1830–1930*. Ann Arbor: University of Michigan Press.

Lekkerkerker, E. C. (1931) *Reformatories for Women in the U.S.* Gronigen, Netherlands: J.B. Wolters.

Rafter, N. (1985) *Partial Justice: State Prisons and Their Inmates, 1800–1935*. Boston: Northeastern University Press.

Strickland, K. (1976) *Correctional Institutions for Women in the U.S.* Lexington, Mass.: Lexington Books.

4 ||||||||||||||||||||||||||||||||||||||||||||||||||||||||||||||
Women Prisoners

Glick and Neto's 1977 survey described women prisoners as young, black, and poor. Two-thirds were under thirty years of age; half were black. Only 20 percent were currently married. Most had children (73 percent). And most were poor: more than half had been on welfare at one time. Drugs and alcohol were a problem in the lives of 22 percent of these women.

The typical female prisoner has changed somewhat over the years. One study compared the incarcerated female between 1960 and 1970 and found that the average age had declined; no significant differences in offense type appeared but use of drugs had increased; the average sentence length had declined; and the number of previous incarcerations had decreased. The study also found a trend toward more divorced and single women in prison (Hannum and Warman, 1964).

Ryan (1984) described women inmates as more likely to be white and a little older than those in earlier years. Slightly more than half (55 percent) of the inmates in Ryan's survey were between the ages of twenty and thirty. About half were white and 38 percent were black. Most (58 percent) had fewer than 12 years of schooling. Property crimes accounted for 35.6 percent of the women's convictions, and the average sentence length was fairly short—44 percent were serving a sentence of two to five years (Ryan, 1984). In 1986, 70 percent of incarcerated women were mothers; 50 percent of them were between the ages of twenty-two and thirty; and 78 percent were from the lowest income groups (Bloom, 1988).

Other studies published in the early 1980s give us additional information on the female offender. Goetting and Howsen (1983) found that the proportion of women inmates increased from 3.5 to 4.4 percent of the total number incarcerated. In 1979 they used a random sample of 2,255 women inmates to compile the following profile. The women inmates sampled had a mean age of 29.66 (male mean age was 29.03); the women were 48.89 percent black, 47.36 percent white, and 2.75 percent other races (black male inmates made up a slightly lower percentage, 46.60 percent). About 36 percent of the women had never been married, 33.97 percent were separated or divorced, 21.15 percent were currently married, and 8.51 percent were widowed. The highest average grade in school completed was 10.59 (which compares roughly to the male average of 10.24). Fewer than half (43 percent) of the women held full-time jobs before incarceration, while another 8.59 percent held part-time jobs and 48.06 percent were unemployed. This compared to the average male unemployment figure of 28.69 percent. About 60 percent of women and 63 percent of men said no immediate family member had served time in prison. Women were more likely to have used heroin, amphetamines, methadone, or barbiturates on a regular basis, while men more commonly used marijuana, hashish, or LSD. No significant differences were found in the use of cocaine or PCP (Goetting and Howsen, 1983: 37).

A recent survey conducted under the auspices of the American Correctional Association is the most current source of women prisoner demographics (Crawford, 1988a). The survey was administered to a sample of 2,094 inmates. Results show that women continue to be disproportionately black (36 percent) and Hispanic (15 percent), although this percentage is less than what Goetting and Howsen found in 1983. Women continue to be in their late twenties and early thirties. They have changed hardly at all in their marital status. Again, similarly to what Goetting and Howsen found, women surveyed were never married (36.5 percent), divorced or separated (33.8 percent), and married (21.6 percent). Educational attainment was also similar to the women surveyed earlier. Most had completed some years of high school, although only 39 percent had graduated or attained an equivalence degree. Results show that more than one-third of the women who quit high school quit because they were pregnant. Eighty percent of the women had at least one child. Almost one-third of these women had their first child before they were seventeen years old (Crawford, 1988a).

The rate of imprisonment has increased for women offenders. In 1976, 11,000 women were incarcerated in state and federal prisons. In 1986, the number increased to more than 26,000; this is an increase of 138 percent, compared to an increase of imprisonment among men during the same time period of 94 percent. Chapman (1980) described the rate of imprisonment as peaking in 1931–1935, during the Depression, and in 1961–1963, when the country underwent an economic recession. There is no doubt, however, that women are increasingly sent to prison. Chapman pointed out that in 1970, 45 percent of convicted female murderers were sent to prison, whereas in 1975, 73 percent were sent; in 1970, only 25 percent of women convicted of robbery were sent to prison, whereas in 1975, 61 percent were sent; and only 15 percent of women convicted of writing worthless checks were sent to prison in 1970, but in 1975, 33 percent were incarcerated. She further described the woman prisoner as ordinarily a nonviolent economic criminal, with an extremely low economic status, usually responsible for small children, and exhibiting high levels of dependency and disorganization. Interestingly, Dobash, Dobash, and Gutteridge (1986), writing of women offenders in Great Britain, also emphasized the petty, economic nature of women's crime. They indicated that one reason for women's incarceration is that they cannot pay the fines assessed against them, unlike men who commit the same type of crime and receive no imprisonment (Dobash et al., 1986: 93).

The woman defendant today is probably more likely to find herself sentenced to prison than she was ten or twenty years ago. As discussed earlier, some evidence indicates that judges may have taken dependent children, marital status, and the like into account when sentencing women. These factors are likely no longer as important; women, whatever their crime and circumstances, are more likely to receive prison sentences. The increase in imprisonment of women has had drastic implications for prison populations and also probably for prison management, since women with children are more likely to be sentenced and sentenced to longer periods of time.

Chesney-Lind and Rodriquez (1983), reporting on a very small sample of Hawaiian women inmates, found they were basically similar to their counterparts on the mainland. They tended to be in their late twenties or early thirties, high school dropouts, unmarried but with children, and usually poor. More than half said they committed crime because of drugs. Most had suffered disrupted home lives and reported abuse. Three-fourths were involved in some way in prostitution. The women in co-correctional (which house both sexes) facilities described their practice of exchanging sexual favors for drugs inside the prison, continuing to subject themselves to the exploitive relationships they had with males on the outside. Despite their history with men, most still had fantasies of meeting the "right man" and having a perfect marriage and children.

IIIII Crimes

As has been mentioned, women in prison tend to be there for economic crimes. Further, women tend not to have the criminal backgrounds that imprisoned men have. In one study of the New York prison population, it was found that whereas only 11 percent of male prisoners had no prior records, 28 percent of women prisoners had no prior criminal history. Women are also less likely to become recidivists. It was found that 12 percent of the women offenders were returned to the Department of Correctional Services for the State of New York within five years, while 36 percent of the men released were returned within that time. About half the women (55 percent) committed the crimes with the lowest return rates (murder, manslaughter, drugs), whereas about half the men (53 percent) committed crimes with the highest return rate (robbery, burglary, youthful offender) (McDonald and Grossman, 1981). It must be noted, however, that a federal study found no differences in the recidivism rates of men and women as measured within risk categories (Hoffman, 1982).

DeCostanzo and Valente (1984), reporting on Georgia inmates, indicated that the number of women admitted to prison in the 1970s for violent crime decreased while the number admitted for property crime increased (1984: 122). Goetting and Howsen found in their sample that 48.68 percent of the women were serving time for violent offenses (men: 56.24 percent); 38.48 percent were committed for property offenses (men: 33.46 percent); 10.75 percent were in for drug-related offenses (men: 7.08 percent); and 2.07 percent had committed crimes against the public order (men: 2.84 percent) (1983: 34). Crawford reports that 37 percent of the women incarcerated were there for violent crimes—murder, rape, robbery, aggravated assault, arson, other assaults and weapons (1988b: 8). Women were more likely to be admitted to prison as adults rather than as youthful offenders and were less likely than males to have been admitted while on some form of conditional release or escape status. A little more than half (54.55 percent) of women prisoners reported having been on probation at least once, whereas 65.55 percent of the men had experienced at least one probation sentence. Only 22.25 percent of women served a probation sentence as juveniles, whereas 41.19 percent of men had juvenile probation records (Goetting and Howsen, 1983: 36).

There are increasing reports of the number of women in prison for killing their abusive husbands (Browne, 1987; Mann, 1988; Ewing, 1987). It seems that a percentage of the violent crime women are convicted and sentenced for may take place because of a history of abuse. Ewing, for instance, reports on samples where from 40 percent to 78 percent of women who killed their husbands or boyfriends had been abused (1987: 23). Nationally, an average of 11 percent of adult incarcerated women are in prison for domestic violence (Crawford, 1988b: 8).

The woman who has been battered and psychologically abused by her husband or boyfriend for a period of time may see no way out of her pain and danger other than to kill him. When she does, the same criminal justice agencies that were unwilling or unable to protect her are now ready to prosecute. Many of these women, historically and today, serve long prison sentences for their actions. Ewing reports that of the one hundred battered women he surveyed, twelve received life sentences and seventeen more received sentences in excess of ten years. Many others also received shorter prison terms (Ewing, 1987: 42). Although some celebrated cases have resulted in acquittals due to the defense based on the "battered woman syndrome," many others have resulted in years of imprisonment for women convicted of murder or manslaughter. Acceptance of the self-defense argument based on the battered woman syndrome has been mixed. Some courts are unwilling to allow jurors to hear expert witness testimony explaining the psychological state of the woman who suffers over a long period of time. Absent that evidence, jurors find it hard to understand why the woman doesn't just leave the abusive husband or seek outside help. In many cases, of course, there is substantial evidence that women have tried to leave, have sought help, and have suffered increased violence and threats because of their attempts.

Self-defense requires that the person alleging it be in imminent danger, believe his or her life is at stake, and use "equal force" to meet the aggressor (Ewing, 1987: 41–51). Many killings by battered women do not strictly meet these elements. Women may attack their abuser when he is incapacitated, either asleep or passed out from alcohol. Women may kill when there is no obvious external threat, for instance when the battering has stopped or during a verbal exchange rather than a beating. Women almost always use weapons to kill, either firearms or knives; if the male has no weapon, the prosecution can argue that she used unequal force. Each of these factors has been explained by the proponents of the battered woman syndrome defense. The woman kills while the husband is incapacitated because she would have no chance whatsoever to defend herself if he were awake. The danger is imminent in her mind regardless of the external circumstances because of a direct threat made by the husband ("I'm going to kill you tomorrow") or because something becomes the "last straw" for her and she realizes that either she or her husband is going to die. Browne, in her study of battered women who kill, found that there was "an absolute conviction that death was inevitable within a certain timeframe; usually this conviction was based on specific threats by the men" (Browne, 1987: 135). The equal force argument is ridiculous when one considers the weight and strength differential between men and women and the fact that most women would never be able to fight against most males without a weapon.

One case in Browne's study is that of a woman who struggled to protect herself and almost ended up in prison because of it. Sharon had separated from Roy because of his abuse, but he continued to follow her and threaten her and her infant son. He attacked and severely injured her at work; he continued to find her despite frequent moves; he threatened her on the phone. In the last incident he broke down the door of her apartment and yelled, "Get the gun, you bitch, 'cause I'm going to kill you and the bastard." Sharon, believing he meant the baby, got the handgun and warned him not to come any closer. He continued to approach and she shot him once; then, because he continued to advance on her, she shot him again. At this point he walked outside, told someone to call an ambulance, then sat down and died. Sharon also called an ambulance. The police arrived and, on their loudspeaker, told her to come out with her hands up. She was charged with first-degree murder and for thirteen months was pressured to plea bargain to a lesser charge. Although she finally escaped prosecution, she was forced into bankruptcy by the loss of her job and by legal expenses (Browne, 1987: 139). Her experience is shared by hundreds of women, many of whom do plead guilty and receive prison sentences.

Browne found that battered women who killed their abusers, as compared to battered women who did not kill, more often had husbands who used drugs and alcohol and were more frequently intoxicated. The men had also used more threats and had exhibited assaultive behavior more often; the men had been more likely to threaten not only the woman but her children or other family members as well; many of them had abused the children; and the abuse of their wives was more likely to include sexual abuse (Browne, 1987: 182).

Mann (1988) offered a cautionary note in her study, which found that not all women who kill their boyfriends or spouses may be excused by the battered woman syndrome. She analyzed 145 cases of homicide where the victim had been sexually intimate with the offender and found that the relationship was most often common law; the offender and victim were most often nonwhite; and alcohol or drugs were more likely to be a factor than in nondomestic killings.

Although 58.9 percent of the women claimed self-defense as a motivation for the killing, Mann observed that the circumstances of the killing did not seem to warrant such a justification in many cases. Also, 30 percent of the women had records of previous arrests for violent crimes, including assault, battery, and weapons charges (Mann, 1987: 45). Thirty-seven percent of the women charged with domestic killings received prison sentences, and the average sentence was ten years (1987: 47). Mann concludes that in many cases, because of premeditation, previous criminal histories, and use of alcohol or drugs by both victim and offender, the battered woman syndrome, may not be an accurate defense.

Several sources offer brief glimpses into the lives of women criminals (Mann, 1984; Carlen, 1985). These vignettes indicate that women in prison are there sometimes for extremely brutal crimes and sometimes for behavior that seems hardly criminal and often sad. Although full details are lacking, the case of Emma Ruth Cunningham hardly seems to illustrate a hardened criminal, even though she is on death row. Married at eighteen and convicted of murder at twenty-seven, she waited in the car, arguably in ignorance, while her husband beat the victim to death. She alleges she was coerced into signing a statement that implicated her in the planning of the crime by threats that her children would be taken away. She was tried and convicted of murder and armed robbery and received a death sentence (Mann, 1984). In contrast to Cunningham, with her relative lack of active criminality, is Pamela Perillo, twenty-four years old and on death row in Texas for a strangulation murder. The victim picked up Perillo and two companions while they were hitchhiking. After the victim gave them a place to stay for the night, Perillo and a male companion each pulled on one end of a rope tied around the struggling victim's neck until he died (Mann, 1984).

Women's stories of crime emphasize men and money. Many women participate with their husbands or boyfriends in various illegal activities up to and including murder; at times the husband or boyfriend is the target of homicide by the woman or the reason she kills a suspected rival. However, women are often active criminals by themselves or in conjunction with other women—especially in prostitution, shoplifting, and even some types of robbery.

A British study offers some insights into the criminal lives of a few British offenders (Carlen, 1985). One of the women described her methods in this way:

> After serving an 18 months' sentence for shopbreaking, I came out aged twenty. I then met some women I knew from the past who had a one-room set-up which was designed for robbing the "steamers," the name which we gave to men who used prostitutes. There was one bed in this room and what seemed like a makeshift

wardrobe behind slightly-open curtains. Just in front of the curtain-rail there was an armchair. The light was a dim red one. The men had a choice of putting their clothes on the floor, the bed or the armchair and they nearly always chose the chair. Whenever possible we had music on the radio, turned low. There were five of us using the room. Someone would be hidden behind the chair, ready to rob the men's clothes. We used hand signals to communicate while the man was on the bed having sex and we made sure to keep his face turned away. One hand signal would mean, "lots of money; keep talking; walk out of the block with him; make sure he doesn't pay much notice to where he is." Another meant, "Get rid of him quickly, nothing worth robbing." For a short while I was in my element because I was getting my own back on men. Then I experienced it as being bad for me and suddenly turned against it. Shortly after, I stopped prostituting altogether (Carlen, 1985: 74–75).

This woman later went back to shoplifting and became quite successful until she was caught again, convicted, and sentenced to a long prison term.

Women who commit crimes such as robbery at times resort to violence when the victim attempts to resist. Violence may be more common when the victim is male, since he may be tempted to offer resistance: "I put the knife up to his throat and took the money, but as I was coming out of the shop he started to fight me, and three old women coming past the shop went next door and rang the old bill" (called the police) (Carlen, 1988: 20).

An element of excitement is also mentioned by many women who try to explain why they could not stay out of trouble. For these women, trouble started early, often beginning as teenage pranks and dares that only later developed into serious crime. Carlen wrote that four major factors are correlated with women's criminality: poverty, being in foster or state care as a child or teenager, drugs, and the quest for excitement (1988: 12).

Prison, to some women, represents a rest from criminal activity; for some, it is a banishment and painful separation from family and children. For some—such as Jean Harris, the upper-class headmistress who killed her lover—the worst part of prison is the proximity to rejected and rejecting fellow prisoners and cruel staff members. Some women report that they learn new scams in prison; some gain insights into themselves; some learn to hate—themselves, the people who imprison them, or both.

lllll Children

One of the overwhelming differences between men and women incarcerated is the importance of children to the women. As mentioned previously, the majority of women prisoners have children, and they often were the sole breadwinners for their children before being incarcerated. Separation from children is often considered one of the worst aspects of prison for women. Imprisoning the woman breaks up the family much more than incarcerating the man of the family does. Imprisoned men may have wives who work or receive support and preserve the family so it is relatively intact upon his release. An imprisoned woman may not have had a stable family life to begin with, and even if she does have a husband, he is unlikely to keep custody of the children and often deserts her during her prison term.

Problems are even more severe for the woman who is pregnant and has her baby while in prison. Researchers document the fact that prenatal care is often sadly lacking in women's institutions, and women have difficulty meeting the nutritional requirements of pregnancy (Mann, 1984: 228). If a woman is addicted, forced withdrawal may injure the fetus or even cause a miscarriage. The institution's practice of waiting until the woman is in labor before transporting her to the hospital increases the risk of birth complications. The quick return to prison after birth—usually within a few days—and the separation from the baby in most cases is extremely traumatic and perhaps harmful to both mother and baby. These issues have been the source of court cases challenging prison practices and will be covered again in a later chapter dealing with legal issues involving women prisoners.

Many researchers have documented the pervasive presence of children in the women's prison. Either they are physically present or their presence is felt in the increased social and legal problems they create. Women prisoners also experience depression and guilt because of their children, which may have behavioral manifestations. One of the earliest studies on children of women in prison was conducted during the early 1960s in California. Questionnaires were distributed to women inmates, and 26 percent were identified as mothers. This percentage was very low, and it may not be representative of inmate mothers in general. This sample was used to uncover what happened to children after their mother was incarcerated. Findings indicated that 50 percent were placed with relatives, 24 percent went to the father, and 26 percent were placed in foster homes. More white children were placed in foster homes than black children, who were more likely to be placed with family. The study also showed minimal contact between the agencies responsible for the children and the incarcerated mother, and it advocated better communication (Zalba, 1964).

A comprehensive study conducted with samples from Kentucky and Washington found that the majority of the 190 women surveyed were mothers (70.4 percent), and they each had an average of 2.2 children (Baunach, 1979: 19). Now this figure is 80 percent (Crawford, 1988a: 9). In Baunach's sample, 82 percent of the children were living with relatives of the mother; 36 percent with the mother's parents; 25 percent with other relatives; and 20 percent with the father of the child. Other reports reinforce these findings. Bloom (1988) reports that only 10 percent of the fathers in his study had custody of children.

Baunach also found that blacks were more likely to have relatives caring for the children and whites were more likely to be found in foster care or other care by nonrelatives (1979: 29). Only half of the women still had legal custody of their children (1979: 33). About three-fourths of the children had been living with the mother before her incarceration, and 62 percent had never been separated from the mother before her incarceration. During incarceration, fewer than half visited the mother regularly; the reason most frequently given was the inconvenience and difficulty of getting to the prison (Baunach, 1979: 32).

One fairly recent study by Koban (1983) compared a sample of Kentucky women prisoners to male prisoners and their children. Findings included the fact that women were more likely to have children than men (76 percent, as compared to 56 percent) and were more likely to have lived with them prior to prison. Men's children were more likely to be living with their mother, while women's children were more likely to be living with other family members—one-third lived with the father, one-third with a grandparent, and one-third with friends, relatives, or foster placements (Koban, 1983: 174). Women whose children were in foster placements experienced fear and frustration because of the arrangements due to limited contact and ignorance of what was happening in the children's lives. Only 31 percent of the men but 58 percent of the women still retained legal custody (Koban, 1983: 175). While 72 percent of the women expected to be consulted over decision making related to the child, only 52 percent of the men expressed this view (Koban, 1983: 177). These findings indicate the different responses separation entails for incarcerated men and women who have children.

Crawford's 1988 study shows that family members continue to take care of the children of incarcerated women (68.3 percent). Only 10.6 percent of the women reported that a spouse or boyfriend was taking care of their children. Seventy-two percent of the women retained legal custody, and most also expected to live with their children upon release (Crawford, 1988a: 10).

The effects of separation on the child can be severe. Although some studies show slight effects, all indicate that the child does experience trauma. Baunach's study, for instance, found that 38 percent of the mothers reported no problems and another 13 percent said they were unaware of any problems. The rest said children experienced physical, emotional, or psychological, and academic problems, including hypertension, aggressive behavior, withdrawal, and trouble in school (Baunach, 1979: 31). McGowan and Blumenthal (1978) reported that children, especially infants and children of preschool age, responded with constant crying, little response to stimulation, little effort to crawl, and incidents of self-punishment. School-age children showed difficulty with social relationships.

Stanton reported that the separation itself may not be connected with psychological problems and juvenile delinquency as much as the disruption in the child's life (1980: 7–9). She looked at the effects of separation on children and found that a high percentage showed short-term behaviorial symptoms, such as expressions of sadness, withdrawal, and a drop in school performance. Antisocial behavior continued in a small number of children; children also experienced feelings of shame and demoralization (Stanton, 1980: 10). She found that more than half of the jailed sample's children displayed poor classroom behavior and created disciplinary problems at school, compared to 22 percent of a probation sample's children. There was a significant difference in academic standing as well. Jailed mothers' children were more likely to be below average academically: 70 percent were below average, compared to only 17 percent of the probationer's children. Only 4 percent of the jailed sample's children were in the top third of their class, compared to 33 percent of the probationer's children (Stanton, 1980: 92). Other factors may be influencing these statistics, but it seems likely that incarceration, especially of the mother, affects the children in a negative manner.

One problem the incarcerated woman faces is explaining to the child why she is in prison. Baunach reported that 68 percent of the children in her sample knew their mother was in prison, but the rest were told she was in a hospital, or did not know where she was (1979: 34). Only about half of the women had told their children they were going to prison or why. Sometimes the barrier to children visiting their mother is that the mother either does not want to tell her children she is in prison or does not want the child to visit her while she is in prison.

The majority of women in prison expect to live with their children after imprisonment. In Baunach's study, 89 percent of the women reported that they expected to regain custody and live with their children; only 20 percent, however, indicated they didn't expect to have difficulties in reestablishing a relationship (1979: 44). Many women feared that their children would reject them or not respect them. Others feared the economic problems they would face with housing and support (Baunach, 1979: 45).

Another complicating factor of release is that the woman may have lost custody of the child during or because of her imprisonment. Although only a few states have laws specifying that imprisonment alone is enough to negate parental rights, others do use imprisonment as one factor to deprive the woman of her legal custody. Obviously, if the mother is in prison she will not be able to appear at a hearing concerning the child's welfare and defend herself. Legal help is often nonexistent and consequently no one is there to represent the woman's interests. It is possible in some states for the woman to lose all rights and to lose the child completely to adoption proceedings, despite her objections. Often the woman's pre-prison behavior may have included behaviors that would give rise to a motion by the state to take the children, such as drunkenness, abandonment, or abuse. One study found that although the mother often lived with children prior to her incarceration, she also believed that the primary responsibility for child care often belonged to relatives, especially her own mother (Henriques, 1982). Although it does seem to be true that some women in prison often abdicated their responsibility to other family members before being incarcerated, this failure only reinforced their views that they were "bad" mothers who let their children suffer. Such a view often influences feelings of depression and powerlessness in prison, and contributes to fantasies about what life will be like outside after release.

Programs for Children

All concerned recognize the importance of improving or encouraging the relationship between the mother and the child. Visiting is usually difficult because of the distance between the prison and where the children are living. Uncooperative or economically distressed caregivers, who don't want or can't afford to bring children to visit, complicate the problem. The prison itself is an uncomfortable, intimidating place for children. Some prisons have programs that attempt to alleviate these problems, but not all of them. One study in 1980 found that of three federal and thirty-seven state prisons and twenty-two jails surveyed, only 60 percent had play areas for children, and only 37 percent had special visiting hours for those who couldn't make the regular time periods (Neto and Ranier, 1983: 125). Some states have special visiting programs. In addition to those discussed next, some prisons have conjugal or family visiting where children of certain ages are allowed to stay with the women in a special setting for a weekend or a period of days (Neto and Ranier, 1983).

Other innovative programs have been implemented to improve the relationship between mother and child. For instance, a Sesame Street program for the children of women incarcerated at Bedford Hills provides the children a more comfortable, nonthreatening place to visit than prison visiting rooms typically provide. One corner of the visiting room is sectioned off, and Sesame Street characters are painted on the wall. Children's furniture and toys further enhance the goals of the program. Inmates serve as day-care aides to watch the children when the inmate mother visits with adult family members privately (Haley, 1977).

Bedford Hills also has one of the few prison nurseries in the country: on the top floor of the prison hospital is a nursery and mother's rooms. Here the woman can stay for up to a year after her baby is born when she gives birth during her sentence. Only a few states—Florida, New York, Minnesota, and California—have laws that allow women to keep their babies in prison. Even in these states, prison authorities have discretion to refuse the request if there are security or health concerns, and it is rare indeed for a woman to be able to keep her child for any length of time.

In Florida, despite an old statute that allowed infants to be kept by inmates, prison policy prevented women from keeping infants with them in the institution until 1979 when Terry Jean Moore, sentenced to prison for twelve and a half years for a "'$5 robbery and a jailhouse mattress 'frustration fire'" became pregnant by a male correctional officer. She demanded to keep the child with her until she was paroled five months later, and evidently in response to this case, the Florida legislature enacted a new statute that gave courts discretion to allow women to keep their infants or to require that infants be placed elsewhere. The inmate mother had to petition the court and make a case that keeping the child with her was in the best interest of the child. In 1981 a bill was passed that closed even this possibility (Mann, 1984: 231).

In these prison nurseries, one has the strange experience of seeing babies behind bars. Uniformed officers, both male and female, often play with or feed the babies, and when they are taken outside for an afternoon of fresh air, inmates in the general population stop by to play with and admire the infants until they are sent on their way by patrolling officers.

In California, a halfway house was created for women inmates with children. If the women met the requirements—no history of violence, child abuse, or neglect; primary caregiver; and good prison record—she could be paroled early to the halfway house setting where she could live with her children under six years of age and receive employment training and rehabilitative services (Bloom, 1988). Unfortunately, the requirements were very strict, and the halfway house has been underutilized.

In Kentucky, the MOLD (Mothers Offspring Life Development) program provided weekend visits and a parenting program. Women could have their children—girls up to fifteen years of age and boys up to twelve years—visit them in prison for an entire weekend and have open privileges across the prison grounds. Activities were also scheduled. Problems with this program included difficulties in transportation, lack of consistency in scheduling, and no continuity between parenting classses and weekends. When the women inmates were transferred to a new institution, the program was reduced to only daylong visits rather than weekend ones. In 1983, an overnight component was added, but the visit took place in isolation from the rest of the prison (Baunach, 1979: 84). A MOLD program is still in operation in Nebraska that allows weekend visits for the children (Neto and Ranier, 1983).

Purdy Treatment Center in Washington state has a foster day-care program that increases the potential for continuous communication between mother and child during the term of incarceration. One of the difficulties of foster placement is that the child is often far away from the prison, and the foster family is not inclined or encouraged to help the child and mother communicate. In the Purdy program, foster parents are found close to the prison, and the foster mother agrees to keep the child in touch with the imprisoned mother through frequent visits and letter writing (Baunach, 1979: 101). Another program at Purdy is an apartment complex outside the prison walls for work-release and minimum-security women. Here, the women can have their children stay with them for overnight visits (Baunach, 1979: 86). One more program at Purdy is day-care and nursery school. Women prisoners learn about rearing children and nutrition, and they work with children of incarcerated mothers and even community children in a day-care center (Baunach, 1979: 87).

In one prison, a converted motel, forty women were surveyed on their feelings regarding their children. Here, the children could visit up to three days and stay in the mother's room. More than half of these women had lived with their children before incarceration. A majority (65 percent) kept in touch with their children through these visits, telephone calls, and letters. Two-thirds of the women were satisfied with the placement of their children. Interestingly, although the mothers felt that the visits did a lot to dispel children's fears about their mother's whereabouts and whether she was being mistreated, some felt that the visits were counterproductive, because the place was "too comfortable" and the mother didn't want the child to think prison was a fun place (Datesman and Cales, 1983: 151).

Upon release, women experience serious problems in regaining custody, finding housing, and securing employment sufficient to support themselves and their children. As noted earlier, mothers may have to fight the state to regain custody. Children are often in foster homes and relatively settled. State workers will resist a separation until the mother shows that she has a job and a home to care for the children. Ironically, if she has a job to afford a home, she is not in the best position to show that the children will be cared for adequately. Halfway houses typically are not designed for women and their children; thus, women who need to spend some time in a transitional facility must delay a reunion with their children. Often, this is the hardest time for the women because children do not understand why their mother can't live with them when she is out of prison. If the woman attempts to live independently, housing poses a problem. In many cities inexpensive housing close to employment does not exist. Women are forced to live in poverty-stricken areas and in apartment complexes that are havens for drug dealers and pimps. These locations only tempt the woman to crime again, if only to get enough money to get her children to a safer neighborhood. The programs described in this section illustrate some attempts of prison administrators to alleviate the problems caused by separation. The increasing rate of imprisonment of women will necessitate continued expansion of such programs and others, including furlough programs, expanded visiting, and early release.

IIIII Sex Differences

One of the more interesting subjects of study is the analysis of sex differences between incarcerated men and women. Many of the findings discussed here lead to hypotheses regarding behavioral differences between men and women, particularly in prison. Unfortunately several problems prevent such studies from being more than merely suggestive. The major problem is the difficulty of getting comparable samples. The small number of imprisoned women leads to studies that compare a small number of women with a large number of men, or compare women to a sample in one male facility that is not representative of the total imprisoned population. Ages may not be comparable, nor offense histories. If one is comparing men and women in a co-ed prison, the comparability of the sample is the issue. If one is comparing men and women in single-sex institutions, comparability of the institution is a problem. Any measurements of prison behavior are suspect because of different measuring tendencies; for instance, findings that compare male and female inmates' infractions are suspect because there may be a greater, or lesser, tendency to report infractions in a prison for women.

Another problem in the studies that purport to show sex differences is the contamination of popular stereotypes. One article in particular shows how sex roles popular in culture may bias an observer's perceptions. For example, in describing women in a training school: "It is common knowledge, for instance, that women become upset if another female wears the same style dress" (Catalino, 1972: 122). When discussing two females aiding a runaway boy: "It seems doubtful the girls would have done the same thing for another girl, whereas boys have performed similar 'services' for other boys" (Catalino, 1972: 125). Finally, in describing reaction to a sick girl: "Despite the facade of genuine empathy with the sick girl, an appearance of superficiality was evident. Male relationships appear to be based on firmer fidelities. . . ." (Catalino, 1972: 126). These examples of subjective interpretations are rare in the descriptions of women inmates today but were very common not too long ago; they are examples of the difficulty of separating popular stereotypes from "general knowledge."

Pollock (1986) examined correctional officers' perceptions of sex differences and found that both male and female officers perceived inmates as reflecting sex differences commonly ascribed to males and females in society. For instance, they described female inmates as emotional and manipulative and males as cool and aloof. They also reported that women were more difficult to supervise, primarily because they were less respectful of officers' authority and more argumentative. Although one must be careful in accepting perceptions at face value, the consistency in responses of people who work with males and females in custody and their descriptions of differences lend some support to the idea that women may exhibit different behaviors from men in the prison environment. The source of these differences may be sex differences, socialization, or different treatment by officers; probably it is a mixture of all three.

Emotionality

One of the differences noted between male and female inmates by those who work with them is the greater emotionality of women. This difference is no doubt partly cultural and partly stereotypical. Basically, the emotionality of women as described by officers can be broken into three constructs: expressiveness, attachment, and mood swings (Pollock, 1984). Expressiveness relates to the tendency to spontaneously and openly display emotions. Whether it is sadness, anger, happiness, love, or any other emotion, women inmates are observed to be more open in their display.

> Men hold emotion in. It comes out aggressively or they're aloof. Women are tearful and crying.

> First time I ever had an inmate cry on my shoulders I was here two days. I never thought that would happen in a jail.

> Women can hug and show expression to each other but the public doesn't accept men hugging and showing affection to men (Pollock, 1981).

Another related component of emotionality is attachment. Attachment is a tendency to become involved with other people. Women inmates are observed to care more for one another, even though some researchers report that this caring seems superficial or transitory. Attachments may be stronger love attachments or the tendency of women inmates to be concerned with one another's problems.

> One of the females in the group may be having an emotional problem, may be having a physical problem, a family problem that's got her all upset and all her friends would congregate around her to give her sympathy and console her, to give her direction, to give her moral support, whatever. . . .

> Men will take their problems to their cell, close the door and read a book, whatever, but a woman will take theirs out and share it, display it, let everybody see what was bothering them (Pollock, 1981).

The final component of emotionality is the greater variability in moods observable among many women inmates. Although this variability may simply be another measurement of openness, many officers and treatment professionals do report that women inmates tend to undergo extreme mood swings with drastic behavioral consequences. Further, these mood swings may or may not be related to external events. Finally, the mood swings may be relatively rapid, so that a woman can show various moods even during one particular day.

> Men seem to be more stable than women. One woman can be at a high one day and the next day she can be very low and the men generally you get one man and he's generally that way most of the time unless something comes up, you know, to push him over the edge, but generally they're the same way the whole time you know them. The women go up and down (Pollock, 1984: 87).

Rule Breaking, Violence, and Suicide

Many of the studies available on women in prison document differences in their behavior, self-concepts, or tendencies toward violence. Women in prison may exhibit more spontaneous, emotionally based behavior. Women in prison tend to be more open, emotional, and spontaneous in their affection and aggression. Men, on the other hand, tend to be more covert and less open in their relationships as well as in their business dealings—gambling, drugs, or black market—in prison (Pollock, 1984).

One well documented difference between men and women is the greater rates at which women break rules. Lindquist, for instance, found that women committed on average 4.38 offenses in prison, compared to males' 2.61. Usually women received less serious punishments for their infractions (1980: 307). About 33 percent of the men's violations involved fighting or assaults, while 23.8 percent of the women's violations were for fighting or assaults (Lindquist,

1980: 310). Another study by Selksky (1980) found that the ratio for Bedford Hills in New York was one assault per 24.8 inmates, whereas at Great Meadow, a prison comparable in size but housing males, the ratio was one assault per 27.7 inmates. Studies in other institutions have made similar findings. McKerracher, Street, and Segal (1966) found that women in a forensic unit of a British mental hospital also exhibited more aggressive acting-out behavior than did male patients. They found that women committed more aggressive acts toward others, property, and themselves. They were also more likely to commit noisy disturbances and exhibit psychiatric symptoms.

Obviously it is dangerous to assume comparability among institutions in the rules and patterns of recording rule breaking. Staff in women's prisons may tolerate much less in the way of acting-out behavior before they issue disciplinary tickets. There may also be more rules in women's institutions. It is also possible that much of male's rule breaking is covert and not subject to discovery. Assaults, drug dealing, and the black market are hidden; rarely do officers have evidence to discipline such behaviors.

Officers offer a possible explanation for the greater number of recorded assaults by women inmates.

> Women tend to showboat, men don't. Like even here if a girl was going to fight, quite often she'd wait until she got in the messhall so that all the girls were around, not just three or four girls on her unit. Where men will, at least from what little I've observed here and what I know the male officers have said, they'll tend to get you later, on the side of the building and that way nobody gets hurt—I mean not have to go to lock. We've had a couple instances here where a guy has shown up with a black eye and we ask and they give you some bull story about tripping down the stairs and yet after it all comes out eventually you hear that somebody met him out behind the gym or something and cleaned his clock (Pollock, 1981).

> With females you get yelling spats that some people think are regular barroom brawls—you know, a little yelling back and forth that gets out frustration as far as I'm concerned (Pollock, 1981).

One study that did not find greater rule breaking by women found that nearly 41 percent of women had been guilty of breaking prison rules during incarceration, but 47.74 percent of men had; men also obtained more serious punishments, such as solitary confinement, loss of good time, or transfer (Goetting and Howsen, 1983: 37). This finding seems to be replicated in British institutions as well, where professionals report more incidences of self-mutilation, more aggressive rule breaking, and more psychiatric disturbances among women prisoners than male prisoners. Of course, these perceptions also may be influenced by an expectation that women will react more emotionally and cause more trouble than male inmates; the reporting may reflect the expectation (Heidensohn, 1985: 74).

The woman who is most often disciplined seems to fit the profile of those offenders most prone to prisonization (adaptation and socialization to the prison subculture) and the inmate subculture. Faily and Roundtree (1979) found that the women most likely to commit violations were black, in their late twenties, incarcerated for manslaughter or narcotics, from urban areas, single, with no children. They had sentences of six to ten years and often were sentenced without parole (Faily and Roundtree, 1979: 82–83; Roundtree, Mohan, and Mahaffey, 1980). Some of these characteristics (black, urban, and convicted for a violent crime) are shared by male prison assaulters.

One older theory for women's apparently greater rule breaking harks back to some of the early theories of crime. Ellis and Austin (1971) attempted to show a relationship between menstruation and rule breaking in a women's prison. They found that the frequency of aggressive behavior increased during the premenstrual and menstrual period. Almost half (41 percent) of the acts took place during eight days of the 28-day cycle. Their data sources were self-reports and officers' observations. Although this study is somewhat interesting, the methodology may be flawed in that they depended on self-reports and officer observations that might have been biased by expectations. Also, it must be noted that the causes of violence are complicated. One study that looked at a range of factors found that the factors most highly correlated with violence included maternal loss before age ten, severe parental punishment, neurological disorders in relatives, the "discontrol syndrome" (a pattern or lifestyle of impulsiveness), and easy access to weapons. These findings emphasize the multidisciplinary nature of violence (Climent et al., 1977: 987).

Although women may be responsible for more minor rule breaking, they are much less likely to engage in large-scale riots. In Crawford's recent study, 82.6 percent of the facilities reported that they had experienced no major disturbances, fires, riots, or demonstrations for the previous five years (1988b: 16). Only a few examples of collective disturbances have been documented at women's prisons. For instance, a 1971 riot occurred at Tennessee's State Prison for Women. In the four hours it lasted, thirty of the nearly hundred women incarcerated there overcame the guards who were bringing them back from an evening meal. One officer ran, leaving the other to face the inmates. She was taken hostage, and the women demanded certain changes, most having to do with unreasonable rules and "racist" staff who treated the women "like animals." The women involved were transferred to a maximum-security section of the Central State Hospital a few days after the incident. In 1971, women in Alderson, a federal facility, rioted in support of the male prisoners who were rioting at Attica. The women's riot lasted four days and required extreme force to quell (Mann, 1984: 210). A 1973 riot in Georgia forced the warden to use a ten-man riot team, which took control over the rioting women (Baunach, 1973: 8). Various incidents have occurred at Bedford Hills over the years. In one fairly serious incident in the early 1980s, the women in segregation overpowered the guards, took them hostage, and armed themselves with boiling water and other makeshift weapons. In other incidents, the male correctional officers from a nearby male prison had to be called in to take control. Despite these few examples, very few prison administrators take these disruptions seriously. The fear of a take-over in a women's prison is not a major issue. Consequently, some say that the women's complaints are not taken as seriously as those of male inmates.

A related problem of rule breaking and aggression in prison is self-aggression—either suicide or self-mutilation. Women may be more prone to such expressions of despair. Women may attempt suicide or mutilate themselves because of emotional problems that existed prior to imprisonment, but there is no doubt that the deprivations of the prison also spur some women to such desperate acts. Women may experience the deprivation of family roles more severely. They may find that the institutionalized lifestyle of the prison provides little comfort or succor. One study in England showed an average of 1.5 incidents of self-injury each week in Holloway prison (Cookson, 1977). The women involved tended to be younger with more previous incarcerations or psychiatric institutionalizations, and most had committed self-injury at least once before. They had higher hostility scores, indicating the close relationship between inwardly and outwardly directed aggression. Also, self-injury tended to occur in copycat epidemics at times (Cookson, 1977: 347).

Fox (1975) also studied self-mutilation among imprisoned women. His study at Bedford Hills indicated that women were more likely than men to attempt suicide or injure themselves; in other words, women tended to turn their aggression inward, whereas men turned their aggression outward. An officer described this tendency in the following way:

> I have seen it on a number of occasions. She won't harm anybody else but she will start to destruct her own body. I've seen them have cuts from here up to their shoulders. They've had stitches in; brand new stitches were put in and they got back here from the hospital and they would sit here and pull the stitches back out again. If you look at their arms, the men don't do it as much as the women, but if you look at the females' arms, they'll sit and they'll just cut and cut and cut. They don't want to hurt anybody else and the only person that they think of hurting is themselves (Pollock, 1981).

The women inmates also identify different reasons for "cutting up" than male inmates do. Women primarily feel the loss of relationships and support in prison; men suffer from other deprivations. Women are less able to retreat into a "manly stance" and consequently feel the loss of interpersonal support more than men. Women also are prone to release their emotion in a catharsis: 64 percent of the females sampled had this self-release theme in their responses, whereas only 13 percent of the males sampled exhibited this theme (Fox, 1975: 194). This theme involves the need to express pent-up emotions, with a resulting feeling of relief when the person "explodes."

IIIII Self-Esteem and Other Characteristics

This section will summarize a wide range of other studies that have examined various characteristics of women in prison. Some studies compare men and women; others look only at samples of imprisoned women. Some studies attempt to validate commonly held perceptions, such as the belief that women inmates have lower self-esteem than nonincarcerated women. Others use personality tests to discover profiles of women prisoners. Some find that women in prison are statistically different from women outside on one or several indices; others find that women in prison represent their sex fairly accurately.

Self-Esteem

One long-standing belief is that women in prison have very poor concepts of self. Tittle (1973) reported that women experienced lowered self-esteem during a prison term, although their self-esteem increased as they neared release. Hannum, Borgen, and Anderson (1978), using a sample of fifty-seven women inmates, found that self-concept improved after a time in prison. No correlation was found between age and self-concept, but those with higher educational levels had lower self-concepts (Hannum et al., 1978: 276). Widom (1979) reported no difference in a prison group and a control group of women on measures of self-concept, masculinity, or personal autonomy. The only difference between the groups was that the nonoffender group scored higher on the femininity scale—"feminine" being defined as affectionate, loyal, sympathetic, sensitive to needs of others, understanding, and compassionate (Widom, 1979: 371).

Officers and treatment professionals report that women inmates express low self-esteem in their interactions. As one professional observed:

Women tended not to feel successful with anything. They didn't feel successful as wives—they didn't feel successful as lovers—they didn't feel successful as mothers—they didn't feel successful as daughters, whereas men felt a lot more success relatively speaking I found than women did. Men could say I was a good carpenter or I did this well or I screwed more women than anybody else on the block or again anything from sex to sports to whatever although the men didn't have much going for them either. . . . Women were always zero in their own eyes. In fact, they even showed this by self mutilation (Pollock, 1981).

A recent study by Culbertson and Fortune (1986) reviewed the earlier research and concluded that much of the methodology was flawed; for instance, some studies used stereotyped descriptions of the women's role. Culbertson and Fortune used the Tennessee Self Concept scale with a sample of 182 women in the Dwight Correctional Facility. The women were classified into role types: butch, femme, or dependent; and the cool, the life, or the square. The authors found that low self-concept varied with education and social role. Those who had higher educational levels had a higher self-concept. Those who played a self-perceived "butch" role had a higher self-concept. Those who had low "femme" scores had a lower self-concept (Culbertson and Fortune, 1986: 44-48). These findings indicate that self-esteem is related to self-identity; and any strong identity, whatever it might be, may improve self-concept.

Family Background

Some researchers have found that women in prison may come from more disordered backgrounds than men in prison do. Velimesis (1981) reviewed the literature and found that previous studies suggested women inmates come from families marked by alcoholism, drug addiction, mental illness, erratic use of authority, and desertion. Other studies showed that in samples of incarcerated women, a majority had been abused as children (Chesney-Lind, 1983). Another study showed that the majority of women involved in prostitution had been sexually abused as children, often by family members (James, 1976). In Chesney-Lind's study, half the women sampled had been raped as children, and 63 percent had been sexually abused (1984: 54). Another study showed that of one sample of men and women inmates, women were more likely to come from broken homes and had greater difficulties in their interpersonal relationships with family and peers. In addition, 24 percent of the female sample, compared to 12 percent of the male sample, had been treated for mental problems (Panton, 1974: 333).

Crawford's recent study further supports the view that incarcerated women have had difficult backgrounds. Almost half had other family members incarcerated (48.4 percent). Almost half had run away from home while growing up (46.5 percent). Thirty percent said they took drugs to make themselves feel better, and almost 28 percent had attempted suicide. Consistent with the other studies, the women reported victimization by relatives and the men in their lives. Over half (53 percent) reported being physically abused, either as a child (35 percent) or by a husband or boyfriend (49 percent). They had also experienced sexual abuse (35.6 percent). More than 60 percent of these women had been sexually abused before the age of fifteen (Crawford, 1988a: 12–21).

By all accounts, the lives of many women prisoners before prison often involved economic distress, victimization, and self-abuse through the use of drugs and alcohol. Often, they have had a series of negative relationships with men, being either exploited or physically abused. Children come early, and the women typically have little in the way of skills or resources to take care of their children. The women's families often have similar instabilities and economic problems and are not able to care for the women's children either, although typically that is where children are placed, sometimes even before incarceration.

Values

A few studies have examined the different values of men and women in prison. Kay (1969) found that in a sample of 258 women and 335 men in prison, women showed significantly more negative attitudes toward law and legal institutions than did men, as measured on a survey instrument. There was no significant difference between the two groups on a "moral value scale." In another study examining values, Cochrane (1971) found that women in prison have a more "masculine" value system than a female control group did. The female prisoners valued such things as an exciting life, freedom, independence, and intellectualism. The female prisoners rated freedom more highly even than male prisoners did. Although it is obviously sexist to label these values as "masculine," it is interesting to note the differences in the priorities of men and women. It may be that this study reflects the prevalent view that women do "harder time" than males do, since women's responses indicate that freedom is very important to them.

IIIII Activities while in Prison

More incarcerated women than men spent the better part of their day in some form of work assignment, classes, or training; women spent significantly fewer hours walking, exercising, and playing sports (Goetting and Howsen, 1983: 39). Women also reported more frequent outside communication with family members than men did. Of females, 46.07 percent received at least monthly visits from family, whereas only 41.12 percent of males received monthly visits; 73.08 percent of women had telephone contact monthly, whereas only 54.31 percent of men had monthly contact (Goetting and Howsen, 1983: 41). Visitation is crucial to the woman's ability to maintain family connections and a stable state of mind. As already noted, however, because women's prisons tend to be in locations far removed from cities where the women come from, visitation may be infrequent for some. These issues will be covered in chapter 5.

Women spend the day in vocational programs, educational programs, or job assignments. Their leisure time is often spent watching television or playing card games and board games. The events that brighten the day are few. Women look forward to the commissary where they can buy candy, soda, and luxury items (sometimes these are not so much luxuries as necessities—for instance, a gentler shampoo than prison issue). Some women spend as much time as they can in their cells, removed from other prisoners by their own choice. Other women are involved in the social organization of the prison and gather around them a group of "family" who provide needed items and social support. These interactions will be covered in a later chapter.

IIIII Conclusion

The women in prison are not necessarily representative of the women who commit crime. They are more likely to be members of a minority group and poor, and more likely to have had problems with drugs or alcohol. They also are more likely to have been single, not taking care of their children at the time of sentencing, or both. They have often committed violent crimes, or been parties to violent crimes. Very often, however, their victims have been family members and, for some, husbands who have abused them. Women have also committed crimes independently or in conjunction with other women. Their orientation toward crime is more professional, and they use prison to pick up more scams and techniques of crime commission. For most, prison is difficult. Separation from children and family is painful. The loss of autonomy and the incessant boredom also cause women to hate the time they must spend there. Some women find support and friendship in relationships with other prisoners. Others scorn and are distressed by their forced proximity to their fellow prisoners. For these women, isolation and prison "niches" are important to maintain sanity.

References

Baunach, P. (1979) "Mothering Behind Prison Walls." Paper presented at American Society of Criminology Conference, Philadelphia.

Baunach, P. (1985) *Mothers in Prison*. New Brunswick, N.J.: Transaction Books.

Baunach, P., and T. Murton. (1973) "Women in Prison, an Awakening Minority." *Crime and Corrections* 1: 4–12.

Bloom, B. (1988) "Women Behind Bars: A Forgotten Population." Paper presented at the 1988 Academy of Criminal Justice Sciences conference, San Francisco.

Browne, A. (1987) *When Battered Women Kill*. New York: Free Press.

Carlen, P., et al. (1985) *Criminal Women*. Cambridge, England: Polity Press.

Carlen, P. (1988) *Women, Crime and Poverty*. Philadelphia: Open University Press.

Catalino, A. (1972) "Boys and Girls in a Co-educational Training School Are Different, Aren't They?" *Canadian Journal of Criminology and Corrections* 14: 120–131.

Chapman, J. (1980) *Economic Realities and Female Crime*. Lexington, Mass.: Lexington Books.

Chesney-Lind, M., and N. Rodriquez. (1983) "Women Under Lock and Key: A View from the Inside," *The Prison Journal* 63, 2: 47–65.

Climent, C. E., A. Rollins, and C. J. Batinelli. (1977) "Epidemiological Studies of Female Prisoners." *Journal of Nervous and Mental Disease* 164, 1: 25–29.

Cochrane, R. (1971) "The Structure of Value Systems in Male and Female Prisoners." *British Journal of Criminology* 11: 73–79.

Cookson, H. M. (1977) "Survey of Self-Injury in a Closed Prison for Women." *British Journal of Criminology* 17, 4: 332–347.

Crawford, J. (1988a) "Tabulation of a Nationwide Survey of Female Offenders." College Park, Md.: American Correctional Association.

Crawford, J. (1988b) "Tabulation of a Nationwide Survey of State Correctional Facilities for Adult and Juvenile Female Offenders." College Park, Md.: American Correctional Association.

Culbertson, R., and E. Fortune. (1986) "Incarcerated Women: Self Concept and Argot Roles." *Journal of Offender Counseling, Services and Rehabilitation* 10, 3: 25–49.

Datesman, S. K., and G. Cales. (1983) "I'm Still the Same Mommy: Maintaining the Mother/Child Relationship in Prison." *The Prison Journal* 63, 2: 142–154.

DeCostanzo, E., and J. Valente. (1984) "Designing a Corrections Continuum for Female Offenders: One State's Experience." *The Prison Journal* 64, 1: 120–128.

Dobash, R., R. Dobash, and S. Gutteridge. (1986) *The Imprisonment of Women*. New York: Basil Blackwell.

Ellis, D. P., and P. Austin. (1971) "Menstruation and Aggressive Behavior in a Correctional Center for Women." *Journal of Criminal Law, Criminology and Police Science* 62, 3: 388–395.

Ewing, C. (1987) *Battered Women Who Kill*. Lexington, Mass.: Lexington Books.

Eysenck, S. B. G., and J. J. Eysenck. (1973) "The Personality of Female Prisoners." *British Journal of Psychiatry* 122: 693–698.

Faily, A., and G. A. Roundtree. (1979) "Study of Aggressions and Rule Violations in a Female Prison Population." *Journal of Offender Counseling, Services and Rehabilitation* 4, 1: 81–87.

Faily, A., G. A. Roundtree, and R. K. Miller. (1980) "Study of the Maintenance of Discipline with Regard to Rule Infractions at the Louisiana Correctional Institute for Women." *Corrective and Social Psychiatry and Journal of Behavior Technology Methods and Therapy* 26, 4: 151–155.

Fox, J. (1975) "Women in Crisis." In H. Toch, *Men in Crisis*, pp. 181–205. Chicago: Aldine-Atherton.

Glick, R., and V. Neto. (1977) *National Study of Women's Correctional Programs*. Washington, D.C.: U.S. Government Printing Office.

Goetting, A., and R. Howsen. (1983) "Women in Prison: A Profile." *The Prison Journal* 63, 2: 27–46.

Haley, K. (1977) "Mothers Behind Bars: A Look at the Parental Rights of Incarcerated Women." *New England Journal of Prison Law* 4, 1: 141–155.

Hannum, T. E., F. H. Borgen, and R. M. Anderson. (1978) "Self-Concept Changes Associated with Incarceration in Female Prisoners." *Criminal Justice and Behavior* 5, 3: 271–279.

Hannum, T. E., and R. E. Warman. (1964) "The MMPI Characteristics of Incarcerated Females." *Journal of Research in Crime and Delinquency* 1: 119–125.

Heidensohn, F. (1985) *Women and Crime*. London: MacMillan.

Henriques, Z. W. (1982) *Imprisoned Mothers and Their Children: A Descriptive and Analytical Study*. Lanham, Md.: University Press of America.

Hoffman, P. B. (1982) "Females, Recidivism and Salient Factor Score: A Research Note." *Criminal Justice and Behavior* 9, 1: 121–125.

James, Jennifer. (1976) "Motivations for Entrance into Prostitution." In L. Crites, ed., *The Female Offender*, pp. 23–36. (Lexington, Mass.: Lexington Books.

Joesting, J., N. Jones, and R. Joesting. (1975) "Male and Female Prison Inmates' Differences on MMPI Scales and Revised Beta IQ." *Psychological Reports* 37, 2: 471–474.

Kay, B. (1969) "Value Orientations as Reflected in Expressed Attitudes Are Associated with Ascribed Social Sex Roles." *Canadian Journal of Corrections* 11, 3: 193–197.

Koban, L. A. (1983) "Parents in Prison: A Comparative Analysis of the Effects of Incarceration on the Families of Men and Women." *Research in Law, Deviance and Social Control* 5: 171–183.

Lindquist, C. (1980) "Prison Discipline and the Female Offender." *Journal of Offender Counseling, Services and Rehabilitation* 4, 4: 305–319.

Mann, C. (1984) *Female Crime and Delinquency.* Birmingham: University of Alabama Press.

Mann, C. (1988) "Getting Even? Women Who Kill in Domestic Encounters." *Justice Quarterly* 5, 1: 33–53.

McDonald, D., and J. Grossman. (1981) "Analysis of Low Return Among Female Offenders." Department of Correctional Services, Albany, New York.

McGowan, B., and K. Blumenthal. (1978) *Why Punish the Children? A Study of Children of Women Prisoners.* Hackensack, N.J.: National Council on Crime and Delinquency.

McKerracher, D. W., D. R. K. Street, and L. S. Segal. (1966) "A Comparison of the Behavior Problems Presented by Male and Female Subnormal Offenders." *British Journal of Psychiatry* 112: 891–899.

Neto, V., and L. Ranier. (1983) "Mother and Wife Locked Up: A Day with the Family." *The Prison Journal* 63, 2: 124–141.

Panton, J. (1974) "Personality Differences Between Male and Female Prison Inmates Measured by the MMPI." *Criminal Justice and Behavior* 1, 4: 332–339.

Pollock, J. (1981) From interviews conducted with correctional officers.

Pollock, J. (1984) "Women Will Be Women: Correctional Officers' Perceptions of the Emotionality of Women Inmates." *The Prison Journal* 64, 1: 84–91.

Pollock, J. (1986) *Sex and Supervision: Guarding Male and Female Inmates.* New York: Greenwood Press.

Roundtree, G., B. Mohan, and L. Mahaffey. (1980) "Determinants of Female Aggression: A Study of a Prison Population." *International Journal of Offender Therapy and Comparative Criminology* 24, 3: 260–269.

Ryan, T. E. (1984) *Adult Female Offenders and Institutional Programs: A State of the Art Analysis.* Washington, D.C.: National Institute of Corrections.

Selksky, D. (1980) "Assaults on Correctional Employees." Department of Correctional Services, Albany, N.Y.

Shaffer, E., C. Pettigrew, C. Gary, D. Blouin, and D. Edwards. (1983) "Multivariate Classification of Female Offender MMPI Profiles." *Journal of Crime and Justice* 6: 57–65.

Stanton, A. (1980) *When Mothers Go To Jail* Lexington, Mass.: Lexington Books.

Tittle, C. (1973) "Institutional Living and Self Esteem." *Social Problems* 20, 4: 65–77.

Velimesis, M. L. (1981) "Sex Roles and Mental Health of Women in Prison." *Professional Psychology* 12, 1: 128–135.

Warman, R. E., and T. E. Hannum. (1965) "MMPI Pattern Changes in Female Prisoners." *Journal of Research in Crime and Delinquency* 2: 72–76.

Widom, C. (1979) "Female Offenders: Three Assumptions About Self-Esteem, Sex-Role Identity and Feminism." *Criminal Justice and Behavior* 6, 4: 365–382.

Zalba, A. (1964) *Women Prisoners and Their Families.* Los Angeles: Delmar Press.

5 ||||||||||||||||||||||||||||||||||||||||||||||||||||||||||
Women's Prisons Today

In 1930, many states still did not have separate women's prisons. Either women were housed in county jails or in separate wings of male institutions, or they were transferred to other states. Between 1930 and 1966, several states built small institutions to house women offenders. These institutions typically used the cottage model or a modified cottage model. In 1966, after conducting a nationwide survey, Strickland described women's institutions as typically small and patterned after the cottage model. In thirty reporting institutions, two-thirds had populations less than 200 (1966: 237). Most of the prisons had less than 150 staff; fourteen employed fewer than 50 staff members (1966: 240). Many of the prisons were located in the northeast and north central region of the country (1966: 237). Inmates' age distribution went from sixteen to sixty-five (Strickland, 1966: 238). Living units were typically cottages; thirteen of twenty-eight reporting institutions were on the cottage model exclusively or in combination with other living-unit types. The majority of institutions used simple classification techniques to assign inmates.

Strickland also described the women's institutions in terms of their orientation or management philosophy. Of those she surveyed, 17.85 percent were termed "custodial," 32.15 percent were termed "custody-oriented," 17.85 percent were "mixed," 14.3 percent were considered "treatment-oriented," and 17.85 percent were deemed "treatment institutions" (Strickland, 1966: 206). This distribution is interesting, since the general belief is that women's institutions are more treatment-oriented than institutions for men. Women's institutions are described as "softer" or "nicer" and as having fewer formal and custodial aspects. According to Strickland, however, a larger number of institutions for women fell closer to the custody than to the treatment end of the continuum. The variables she used for her determination included the ratio of treatment staff to inmates and meeting frequency. This observation was supported by later studies, such as those done by Burkhardt (1973) and Taylor (1982), which also described the women's institution as having many rules and strict policies governing every aspect of the inmate's life.

Schweber (1984) reported that in 1971 there were two federal institutions for women, and only thirty-four states had completely separate institutions for women. All other states housed women in prisons for men or in county jails, or else they contracted with other states to take the few women criminals they deemed in need of institutionalization. In 1985, only two reporting states still did not have institutions for females. New Hampshire left female inmates in county jails or sent them to Massachusetts or federal facilities, and West Virginia sent its female prisoners to Alderson, a federal prison for women (Ryan, 1984: 13).

Most women's prisons in the country are designated medium-security prisons. One of the biggest differences between facilities for men and women is the absence of custody-graded institutions. Typically only one or two facilities are available for women in the state. Consequently, the single facility must house the whole range of security-graded inmates. Men, on the other hand, are sent to a prison that matches the risk they present. Minimum-security prisons exist for those male prisoners who pose little risk, medium- and maximum-security institutions are for those who pose a more serious risk. There are even "maxi-maxi" prisons in some states for exceptionally violent or escape-prone inmates. Women, because all of them are in the same facility, are not classified, or if they are, the classification grade has little meaning. In reality, most women, regardless of the risk they present, are subject to medium- and maximum-security measures because of the few who need them. Classification systems that result in risk-factor scores are developed with males and may not be useful for a female inmate population. Crawford found that only 22 percent of female facilities used a classification system designed especially for women (1988b: 15).

Many women are housed in co-correctional facilities. Generally, when women offenders are housed in an institution also housing males, a male superintendent is in charge. Even in some cases where the women's institution is physically and administratively separate from institutions for men, the superintendent or warden is male unless, as in California, a state statute makes it mandatory that an institution for women be managed by a woman. In fact, only slightly more than one-half of the administrators at women's prisons are female (Crawford, 1988b: 12). Males are also increasingly employed as correctional officers in women's prisons. Crawford reports that only 65.3 percent of the correctional officers at women's prisons are female (1988b: 13). Women have fought for and won the right to work in male prisons; however, the consequence has been that correctional departments are now placing greater numbers of males as officers in prisons for women. Perhaps due to this increase, there have been reports of sexual harassment and sexual aggression against female inmates by male officers. This problem seems to be more prevalent in county jails, where some female prisoners have been raped and impregnated by male deputies. Mann discusses this problem and offers the following quote from another researcher:

> In my interviews with more than 50 women serving time in southern jails or work-release programs, inmate after inmate repeated virtually the same stories of what happened to them, or to the woman in the next cell: the oral sex through bars; the constant intrusion of male trustees who slither in and out of the women's cells as unrestricted as the rats and roaches; the threats of "you do, or else . . ." (Sims, reported in Mann, 1984: 245).

Unfortunately, no studies have documented how much of a problem sexual abuse is in prisons. It must be noted also that women may exchange sexual attentions for favors from male officers, thus becoming somewhat willing participants in the exchange. However, because of the powerlessness of the woman inmate, and the fact that she may feel she has nothing but her sex to bargain with in order to gain needed or desired freedoms or privileges, one can hardly characterize the woman as able to give full and free consent even if she agrees to the interaction.

Women's institutions typically do look different from institutions for males. Often, there are rooms for inmates rather than open cells or dormitories. Typically, women are allowed to have curtains and bedspreads. Decorated with pictures and handiwork, their rooms take on a personal appearance. Women are more likely to be allowed to wear their own clothing, at least in the living units. They may have more access to personal items from the commissary, such as cosmetics and shampoo. Some may have cooking facilities on the floors or washers and dryers. The uniforms, if provided, may be available in more variety than men's institutions—for example, in different colors or combinations.

Despite these characteristics, it is unlikely that one could mistake a women's institution for anything but a prison. Officers are in uniform, just as in a prison for men. Rules and regulations govern everything from showers to letters. Women are frequently prohibited from visiting in one another's rooms or exchanging clothing. Although the atmosphere may seem almost jovial at times in the living units, it is also sometimes punctuated with physical altercations between angry inmates or the cries and screams of women who "go off," reacting to imprisonment with violent self-destructiveness or madness.

Upon entry, a woman is fingerprinted and photographed, stripped, searched, and deloused. Reception may include a medical exam, a psychiatric exam, and educational testing. Prison orientation indoctrinates her to the extensive rules and regulations of the prison and what is expected of her. She may share a cell or be lucky enough to be in an institution where overcrowding has not forced administrators to place bunks in cells designed for one.

Her day starts at 6:00 A.M., or earlier if she is on kitchen duty, and typically ends at 10:00 P.M. with lights out. After breakfast the women are sent to their various assignments: school, training or work. Relatively few women stay in the living units during the morning or afternoon hours unless they are on "daylock," in which a woman is locked in her cell all day as punishment, or they have a medical excuse for staying in. The women come back at 11:30 or 12:00 for count and lunch and then are sent to their afternoon assignments. Dinner is relatively early, sometimes as early as 4:30, in order for kitchen staff to have the meal cooked, served, and cleaned up by a reasonable hour. Count is taken periodically during the day, usually before breakfast, before lunch, and after dinner. If there is a discrepancy in the figures, women are kept in their cells until the numbers can be reconciled. They may wait for hours if the error cannot be found. The noon count is most problematic, and an error or a missing inmate may mean afternoon classes are postponed or canceled, visitors are kept waiting, and women who need to go to the medical unit must wait. Yard time is typically in the evening after count. Women may and sometimes are forced to spend the evening hours walking and playing cards in the recreation area. Many prefer to stay indoors and watch television in the living-unit lounge. Typically the inmate must spend the evening in one location or another; there is no possibility of movement once the doors are locked.

Food in prison is uniformly criticized as bland, starchy, and unappetizing. Some women, if they have the means, ignore the mess hall meals altogether and use food bought in the commissary. Jean Harris describes how she practically lived on raisin bran, shunning the food and company of the mess hall. In Bedford Hills, where Harris is serving time, women have access to stoves in the living units. Groups of women share supplies and cook dinners in these small kitchens. This luxury is not available in most prisons, however, and is a remnant of the cottage days of Bedford when women were expected to need the domesticity of home.

Burkhardt (1973) provided a journalistic account of women's prisons in the early 1970s, which emphasized the psychological effects of imprisonment and the infantilization of adult female prisoners by the correctional staff. She visited twenty-one jails and prisons for women and conducted formal and informal interviews with more than 400 women. She painted a bleak picture of institutional life: staff patronized and taunted the women offenders, and the inmates spent prison time in useless pursuits, often turning to one another in homosexual relationships that served as a cushion against the anomic life of the prison. She pointed out that many of the programs offered to help women prepare for release, such as cosmetology, were outdated and sex stereotyped.

In 1977 Glick and Neto published a comprehensive examination of programs and services in women's prisons and also provided a demographic profile of the incarcerated female offender. They included sixteen state prisons, forty-six county jails, and thirty-six community-based programs in a total of fourteen states in their survey. In all, 1,607 women were surveyed. In 1978, Chapman (1980) surveyed a number of different women's prisons and community programs, and she too presented summary data on their policies and available programs. The National Institute of Corrections published a "state of the art" analysis of programs in adult female institutions in 1984 (Ryan, 1984). The most current information on programs is provided by Crawford's recent survey of seventy-one facilities for women and girls (1988b). With these sources, one can get some sense of what is going on in women's prisons today. Three major areas will be explored in this chapter. First, we will look at what programs are available for women inmates; second, we will explore rules and discipline procedures; and third, we will look briefly at co-correctional programs for women and men.

lllll Programs

Programs for women fall into five major categories. The first would be those activities necessary for the maintenance of the institution—activities such as clerical work in administration, food service for inmates and staff, and general cleaning and maintenance work around the grounds. The second category is education. As is true of men in prison, the majority of women prisoners need remedial education, although a few could take advantage of college programs if any were offered. The third category of programs is vocational training; ordinarily in prisons for women, these programs fall into sex-typed categories, such as cosmetology and office skills. The fourth category of programs is designed to rehabilitate the prisoner through personal growth or individual change—for example, group therapy, transactional analysis, or Alcoholics Anonymous. The fifth category is medical care. Arguably not a program at all but a needed service, medical care is included as a program because it is usually placed under the treatment branch of institutional management.

Most women in prison do something during the day. Fox (1984) reported that in 1972, 20 percent of the women in Bedford Hills held full-time work or program assignments and another 40 percent held part-time assignments. Moyer (1984) described prison vocational programs as primarily falling into stereotyped areas, such as cosmetology, food service, laundry, nurses' aide training, housekeeping, sewing, garment manufacturing, clerical work, and IBM keypunch. Whether the woman is interested in education, vocational education, or personal growth, the problem seems to be that most institutions do not have the resources or interest to offer a broad range of programs. Although education and some vocational programs seem to be fairly prevalent, more specialized or nontraditional programs are rare. Another problem is the number of women who can take advantage of these programs. Some programs have the capacity to serve only small numbers of imprisoned women, and consequently there are long waiting lists to enter.

Maintenance jobs and prison industry use women inmates to perform needed services and jobs in the prison community. Almost all (95 percent) of the facilities require women to perform some maintenance or institutional work assignments (Crawford, 1988b: 23). Ordinarily the pay is almost nonexistent: the U.S. average is $1.66 per hour (Crawford, 1988b: 23). Prison industry may provide some skills and work experience for the woman inmate. Industry was present in 53 percent of Ryan's responding institutions (1984: xi).

Work assignments are typically menial and often are performed over and over again for the mere purpose of keeping the women busy. For instance, floors may be scrubbed every day or sometimes twice a day. The laundry employs many women and is considered by most to be the worst of assignments because of the heat, the physical toil of the work, and the potential for danger from the chemicals and boiling water available for aggressors. In some states, the women's institution houses the laundry for the whole system, and large truckloads of institutional laundry come and go every day filled with prison uniforms, sheets, and towels. Women inmates are also employed to do clerical tasks in the administration building; at times, if they prove capable, they may be given quite a lot of responsibility. Much of any prison's daily maintenance, in fact, is performed by the inmates who live there. This is true for men's as well as women's prisons. There has been a tendency in women's institutions to employ more outsiders to perform typically "masculine" tasks, such as lawn care, electrical and plumbing work, and construction or renovation tasks. Some prison administrators, however, have started to use female inmates for these tasks, supervised by a civilian foreman. Some women, like some men, attempt to refuse to work for the prison, maintaining the view that the prison sentence itself is their punishment and refusing to help the state in their own imprisonment. These women are quickly labeled as troublemakers; either they are forced to work or face being sent to segregation, or if left without a work assignment, they often receive disproportionate punishment for even slight infractions of prison rules.

Chapman (1980) discusses the great need for education. She found that 60 percent of the women inmates were high-school dropouts. Similarly, Crawford found that only 33 percent of inmates in her sample had completed high school (1988b: 26). In 1975, 83 percent of women's prisons offered educational and reading programs (Chapman, 1980: 103). A national survey in 1984 showed that 83 percent of the respondents, covering forty-five states, had GED programs, and 83 percent had adult basic education programs. College programs were present in 72 percent of the institutions (Ryan, 1984: x). In a 1985 survey, all but one of the institutions offered educational programs (Weishet, 1985).

Adult basic education (ABE) was present in most of the institutions surveyed in national studies. This type of education comprises basic literacy and living skills. Ryan reports that the hours women spent in ABE courses ranged from two to thirty-five hours per week. The average was fifteen and the mode was twenty (Ryan, 1984: 15). In Crawford's sample, 35 percent of the institutions required women to participate in ABE programs (1988b: 26). GED programs are designed to give the women the equivalent of a high-school diploma. Ryan reports that most institutions have GED programs, but 27 percent of them had fewer than 10 women enrolled. New York, on the other hand, reported 175 women enrolled in its GED preparatory course. The average enrollment across the country was 26 (Ryan, 1984: 15). The mean number of hours spent in these programs was fifteen hours per week; the mode was twenty and thirty hours. Crawford reports that 17.5 percent of the facilities in her survey required GED participation for those women who needed it (1988b: 26). Three states had programs that led to high-school diplomas instead of GED certificates—Texas, Maine, and Washington (Ryan,

1984: 15). Fewer institutions have college programs. Ryan reported that only 72 percent of the responding facilities had college programs for women inmates. Enrollments ranged from 0 in Maine to 198 in Texas (1984: 18). Most of these programs were offered at the institution, but a few were community programs.

Crawford reports that about half of the facilities reporting paid women for classroom attendance (1988b: 26). Payment is important, because when women were forced to choose between an institutional job that paid at least some amount of money and education that did not, they often would have to choose the assignment that resulted in money. This money is especially important for those women who have no family or whose families are too poor to provide packages from home or money to put into their institutional accounts. The candy, shampoo, and foodstuffs obtained in the commissary often provide the only treats in the woman's day. Some are necessary—for instance, products for women whose skin is too sensitive for institutional soap or products designed for black women's hair and skin not available in institutional supplies.

Vocational programs in women's institutions have been the target of criticism for years. Ordinarily, women's institutions do not have the same number or kind of vocational programs as are offered at institutions for men. For years, the only vocational programs available were those that prepared women for domestic service, clerical work, or cosmetology. Although nothing is wrong with such programs, and they continue to exist at a number of institutions, many women have no interest in these fields or will need more lucrative employment upon release to support themselves and their children adequately. Also, in some states that train women in cosmetology, state licensing is required to work in the field and is denied to ex-inmates.

Both the number and variety of vocational programs have increased. Ryan reported that 83 percent of facilities responding to his survey had at least one vocational education program. The number of programs varied, ranging from one to thirteen (Ryan, 1984: xi, 17). Texas, California, Georgia, Nevada, Oklahoma, and Pennsylvania offered the most programs (twelve to thirteen each) (Ryan, 1984: 17). Crawford reports that 90.2 percent of the facilities responding to her survey had some type of vocational program. Further, she reports that 57.5 percent of these facilities pay the women for their vocational training assignment (Crawford, 1988b: 25).

Interestingly, some states have vocational program offerings but report no enrollment. Ryan presents information that Oklahoma reported thirteen program offerings and no enrollment. Arizona reported four program offerings and no enrollment. Oregon reported nine program offerings with only one female offender enrolled (Ryan, 1984: 17). More research needs to be done to uncover why such programs are not being utilized. It may be that the qualifications for program entry are too difficult or have disadvantages attached to them that outweigh the advantages. For instance, many vocational programs, especially in the clerical area, require at least a ninth- or tenth-grade reading level. Many inmates may not meet this entry qualification. Faced with problems associated with overcrowding, prisons often do not have the staff to continue the few vocational programs they have.

The courses with the largest enrollments are those in the business education and clerical field, cosmetology, nurse's aide training, and home economics, cooking, or food service (Ryan, 1984: 17). Although cosmetology and clerical skills are popular programs in women's institutions, auto repair and carpentry have been added to the vocational offerings at some institutions. Chapman (1980) reported that of the prisons surveyed in her study, the offerings included upholstery, drapery making, ADP keypunch, welding, marine electrical, auto mechanics, clerical, college, cosmetology, and cleaning services. The smallest enrollments seem to be found in nontraditional programs. Women in prison may be more committed to the traditional feminine role-type than their middle-class sisters when it comes to choosing vocational programs. Institutions that have instituted nontraditional programs have found they need to do public relations work and "consciousness-raising" to get women inmates interested.

Part of the reason for the increase in the number and variety of vocational programs has been litigation that challenged the lack of programs under an equal opportunity argument. Cases such as *Glover versus Johnson*, 478 F. Supp. 1075 (E.D. Mich. 1979), which will be discussed more fully in a later chapter, helped encourage prison administrations to institute new programs for women. Although such challenges typically object to the number of programs available, criticism is also directed at the nature of such programs. Ryan (1984) reported that in 1983, twenty-seven states were involved in litigation concerning adult female offenders. The allegations included (in order of frequency) inadequate medical services, inadequate facilities, inadequate educational programs, inadequate vocational training, invasion of privacy, inadequate prison industry, inadequate mental health services, inadequate provisions for child care, discrimination, inadequate and inequitable program level system, inadequate law library, and segregation practices (Ryan, 1984: 23).

Weishet (1985) reported an association between the size of the institution and the number of programs it offered. Weishet's study also found an increase in the number of nontraditional programs. In 1973, none of the prisons surveyed had nontraditional programs; in 1979, four had started such programs; and in 1985, fifteen had nontraditional programs. Taylor studied the programs available to the women incarcerated in California Institution for Women-Frontera in California. She compared the programs available there to those for men incarcerated at Chino and found that women had access to thirteen vocational programs; however, five of those programs had slots for only five women, because they were located at Chino and the women had to be bused back and forth. She notes that although men have access to only thirteen programs at Chino, they may transfer to other institutions in the state and thereby gain access to twenty-eight programs state-wide (Taylor, 1982: 102).

Table 5-1 Available programs

Program	Number of Institutions Offering	
	n = 36	n = 58
Sewing	30 (83%)	31 (53%)
Food services	28 (78%)	15 (36%)
Secretarial	31 (86%)	26 (45%)
Education	35 (97%)	51 (83%)
College	28 (78%)	40 (72%)
Basic skills	32 (88%)	48 (83%)
Domestic	20 (56%)	n/a
Cosmetology	16 (44%)	15 (36%)*
Auto repair	8 (22%)	11 (27%)*
Welding	9 (25%)	11 (27%)*
Carpentry	15 (42%)	10 (24%)
Computer	21 (58%)	8 (20%)
Electrical	15 (42%)	9 (22%)
Plumbing	12 (33%)	2 (5%)

*Data was reported by state: n = 41

Sources: Weishet, 1985; Ryan, 1984.

One nontraditional program for women is Wider Opportunities for Women (WOW). A private program operating primarily in northeastern prisons, (Washington, D.C., and New York), it combines nontraditional jobs with self-assertion training to help women learn to be independent (Kestenbaum, 1977). This program and others like it promote nontraditional careers in such areas as carpentry, welding, electrical work, and so on. The primary reason these occupations are touted is that they are far more lucrative than traditional women's work. WOW places women in construction jobs and helps with day-care and housing.

Other innovative programs include an Arizona program implemented in conjunction with Best Western Corporation. In this program, women inmates book reservations for Best Western motels across the country and are paid $3.65 an hour. Illinois offers an apprenticeship program in which women inmates can get training and apprentice certification in baking, building maintenance, food services, cosmetology, environmental control, sewing machine repair, and water and waste treatment (Ryan, 1984: 22). On the whole, one can say that vocational programs for women prisoners are improving, but programs are still far too few, and too many programs do not prepare a woman to support herself upon release.

Treatment-oriented programs help women prisoners to experience personal growth or to acquire other introspective or social skills. Weishet (1985), in his survey of women's prisons, found that almost all prisons offer some sort of treatment programs. All surveyed offered alcohol programs, drug programs, and mental health programs. Thirty-three of thirty-six surveyed offered parenting classes. Twenty-five of the thirty-six offered personal etiquette classes, with no explanation as to what was taught in such a class, and thirty-four of the thirty-six offered health programs.

Treatment programs may range from group therapy to art therapy. Results of evaluations show that most programs have limited influence on the women participating (Ross and Fabiano, 1986). Individual psychotherapy may be more available in women's prisons than prisons for men, but women prisoners are no less suspicious of prison staff psychiatrists. Group psychotherapy may take many forms, and results with regard to its effectiveness are mixed. Studies show that the type of therapist, the type of offender, and the type of therapy are all important variables in the success of group therapy. Therapeutic communities emphasize inmate participation, open communication, and shared decision making. Some programs in women's prisons may be therapeutic communities in name only, practicing none of the elements crucial to the theory behind the therapy. Behavior modification may be less effective with female offenders than with male offenders. In one study reported on by Ross and Fabiano, female delinquents who were participating in a behavior modification program increased their rate of self-mutilation, vandalism, escape attempts, and assault (1986: 18). In general, behavior modification programs may be more successful in community rather than institutional settings, because the offender must be more committed to the program in the community. All of the various programs described here may be found in women's institutions as well as institutions for males; little research is available to determine which programs work best with women.

Programs that help women learn better parenting skills or increase and better utilize the women's visitation time with children are in the greatest demand by women inmates. In one report, women wanted more family programs and services, increased visitation, and increased support in legal and post-release areas (Chapman, 1980: 121). Weishet reported that twenty-five of thirty-six reporting institutions allowed weekend visits with children, and twenty of these prisons provided transportation for children of inmates

(Weishet, 1985). Taylor's comparison of Frontera, for women, with Chino, for men, in California showed that women had more access to family visiting programs than did male inmates. There were not only more family visiting units (apartments or trailers), but women had to wait for a shorter period of time before becoming eligible (Taylor, 1982: 164). Women's relationships with their children are very important to an understanding of women's prisons; this topic was covered in a separate chapter, which described the specific programs that attempt to increase mother–child ties.

Visiting is a necessary and important tool to continue family ties and aid in reintegration. Unfortunately, many women's prisons are far removed from the urban areas where most prisoners come from and where their families live. Visiting poses problems for the families of women prisoners even more than for the families of male prisoners. Because there are fewer women's prisons in any particular state, the woman prisoner is likely further removed from her family than the male prisoner is. This problem is especially acute in the federal system, which has only a few institutions for women in the whole country. Despite traveling difficulties, prisons often allow for no flexibility in visiting times; visiting may be restricted to specific hours during the day and may be limited to a couple of days a month. This discourages families from traveling sometimes hundreds of miles to see the incarcerated woman.

DeCostanzo and Valente (1984) described how the Georgia prison system attempted to fashion a comprehensive program for the needs of the female offender. They explained that the typical offender is thirty years old, has few years of education and undeveloped work skills, and is the single head of a household with one or more children. She tends to be incarcerated for property crimes (DeCostanzo and Valente, 1984: 122). The proposed Georgia program has 15 components: restitution, street probation, specialized case load, probation to client's residence (curfew), out-client/diversion center, out-client to "storefront," specialized living arrangement, central diversion center, satellite women's center, co-residential diversion center, institution, community residential correctional center, specialized living arrangement on inmate status, transitional center, and supervised earned release. However, three years after this comprehensive program was suggested, most of the components had not become reality. Georgia may be more advanced in its planning than in its implementation, since this state, along with North Carolina, still sends women inmates to the Governor's mansion as housemaids (Mann, 1984: 217). This "vocational training" is in keeping with the traditional stereotypical programs for women inmates, which prepared them for nothing but a domestic role.

Although one must be cautious of case studies and not extrapolate individual administrative differences to institutions across the country, Taylor's comparison of Chino and Frontera is interesting. She summarized the differences between the institutions, and some of her relevant observations include the following. Women's education was more humiliating because adult education materials were not used. Fewer external school learning centers were available for women. A higher percentage of women were enrolled in vocational programs, but they had fewer to choose from. No apprenticeship programs were available to women inmates. Women had less opportunity to be paid for prison work. Only one industry, sewing, was available for women, whereas men had six. Women were, in general, further from their homes. Women had fewer visitors than men. Rules for visiting were stricter for women inmates, except in a comparison of maximum-security inmates in each institution. Men had easier access to telephones. There were more volunteer programs at the men's institutions. Men had more limitations on their personal property. Seemingly irrational differences existed in the rules regarding what could be sent in inmate packages. Known homosexuals were segregated at the institution for males and allowed in the general population at Frontera. Finally, at Chino all males were given a battery of psychological tests, but this was done only for selected women at Frontera (Taylor, 1982: 238–242). These findings lend support to observers who contend that women are treated differently and often receive fewer services than male inmates.

Health care for women has been the focus of some litigation. Typically, women are in greater need of medical services. This seems to be so for reasons having to do with the needs of women versus men in general as well as the special needs of women offenders. Women are more likely than men to seek health care in the society at large; they are no different in prison. Women's requests for medical care far exceed those of men. Women have more medical problems related to their reproductive systems than do men. Women in prison also have a barrage of problems related to the poor health care they received while on the street. They may be pregnant upon entering prison, which would increase their need for medical services. They might also be suffering from sexually transmitted diseases; they might be alcoholic, with all the medical problems associated with that addiction; or they might be addicted to other drugs.

Women have reported that they received no care during pregnancy, and that they were misdiagnosed or did not receive medical care for diagnosed illnesses. They report that pills have been withheld during punishment, but also that drugs, especially tranquilizers, are used excessively in women's prisons (Mann, 1984: 212). Women's prisons, unlike men's, typically do not have the numbers to justify an extensive hospital on the prison grounds. Consequently, although a doctor is on call and there is a scheduled examination period, emergency cases and women with serious medical problems are taken to hospitals outside the prison. The time involved in arranging and transporting may pose a potential danger to the inmate-patient.

Todaro versus Ward, 431 F. Supp. 1129 (S.D.N.Y. 1977), aff'd, 565 F.2d 48 (2d Cir. 1977), was a case challenging health care delivery at Bedford Hills in New York. The prisoners' complaint, which included the charge that no physician was on permanent duty at the institution, was upheld by the court. The complaint also included the fact that women had to be bused out of the institution to a local hospital for many types of medical problems, which resulted in delays and possible further risk. However, even when inmates win a court case, compliance tends to be slow and not completely ideal. Courts typically allow prison administrators a great deal of flexibility in the time and manner in which they comply with court mandates. If no monitor is appointed to oversee compliance, another court case is necessary to bring violations to the court's attention.

Ryan reports that forty-two of the forty-five responding institutions in his survey provided medical care through intake screening and health appraisal, yearly checkups, gynecological and obstetrical service, and twenty-four-hour emergency service (1984: xi, 19). Only forty-one of the states provided annual checkups for women inmates. Ryan reports that medical service for women offenders has roughly doubled in the period between the Glick and Neto study in 1977 and his own study in 1983 (1984: 20).

Psychiatric and psychological counseling is often inadequate in women's prisons. Women are much more likely than men to take advantage of such services, but they may not be adequate to meet the demand. For instance, women prisoners, like male prisoners, complain that psychiatrists and psychologists often have restricted office hours and that for many of them, English is a second language, so that they are hard to understand. Typically, the inmate does not feel comfortable or able to identify with mental health professionals. A large part of treatment has been reported to be the administering of psychotropic drugs (Velimesis, 1981: 130). Psychologists may be used to classify inmates rather than to provide psychotherapy. In this branch of medical services, court cases and complaints have led to an increase in the available services. Ryan reported that psychological and psychiatric services doubled between 1977 and 1983 (1984: 28). Several observers have noted the greater tendency to characterize women's problems as psychiatric. This expectation may be projected to women, leading to their belief that they have "problems." It is important to keep this in mind when discussing the need for mental health services, in order to avoid the stereotype that women need these services more than male inmates.

Recreation is also an important component of any institution's offerings, and in this regard women's institutions again tend to offer less than comparable institutions for men. As one writer noted, the most common recreational facilities available for women were television and board games (Mann, 1984: 215). There is a belief that males are in greater need of recreational outlets, and consequently in a male prison one may find basketball courts, weight-lifting equipment, and a range of supplies for handicrafts. Women tend to be less enthusiastic about physical sports such as softball when they are offered; consequently, authorities justify the lack of such programs by the apparent disinterest on the part of women inmates. It is not clear, however, that women would not be interested in other types of physical activity, such as swimming, aerobics, or gymnastics, if these were offered to them.

IIIII Rules and Punishment

The impression one receives on entering a women's institution is that it might be a pleasant, albeit restricted, place to spend some time. Grounds are typically attractive, and rooms may be decorated in homey ways. Upon further examination, however, one discovers that the institutions typically operate by means of dozens of serious and trivial rules governing behavior. Women may not be allowed freedom of movement except in groups and with passes. They may have their letters from or to home read and censored. They may be forced to go eat in the cafeteria whether they want to or not. Officers constantly check passes and interrogate women accused of being out of place. Several observers agree that the rules in women's prisons may be stricter and cover more petty details than those in prisons for males (Mann, 1984: 209). One explanation for this disparity may be that women's institutions do not have the same physical security present in male facilities; thus, in the absence of guns, towers, and stone walls, prison security is based on minute rules of behavior that govern the movement and interactions of the female prisoners.

The most obvious fact of life in women's prisons is that women are dependent on the officers for practically every daily necessity. Women may have to ask for personal items such as tampons or napkins from the officer in the living unit, and the number issued per day may be regulated. While commissaries provide the "luxuries" of life, they are relatively expensive, and the inmate must either have some sort of prison work or financial source on the outside to pay for things like candy and cigarettes. Further, she is limited in the number of items she may buy and the amount of money she can spend each month. Women in segregation must ask for everything, including toilet paper and razor blades. They are dependent on the officers to bring them everything, including food. If the officer is busy or irritated, the food cart may sit undistributed until the food is cold. To ask another adult for permission to do such mundane things as use the kitchen facilities or go to the bathroom is demeaning and humiliating. Women inmates may adapt by adopting an abrasive and hostile attitude toward the experience; thus a request is phrased as a demand, often capped with an obscenity for good measure. This tactic only results in making the situation worse, however, since the officer may then ignore the woman, demand that she rephrase the request, or write her up for insolence.

Strickland's study of women's institutions observed that a basic list of rules for women's prisoners included strictures regarding personal cleanliness, what type of clothing could be worn, and what items were considered contraband, which included "immoral" magazines and dice; and prohibitions against exchanging presents, bartering, offensive language, gambling, and disorderly conduct, including sexual conduct (Strickland, 1966: 114). Women inmates seem to be more strictly controlled than male inmates are, at least in personal areas such as dress and living-unit activities. Female staff tend to take a maternal approach to their charges and demand that the women brush their hair or take better care of their appearance—concerns that are likely rarely expressed in an institution for men.

Punishments Strickland described included confinement; loss of movie, recreation, or store privileges; loss of visitation privileges; loss of good time; or loss of smoking and letter-writing privileges (Strickland, 1976: 239). These punishments are roughly the same today. Several reports indicate that there are a greater number of infractions in women's facilities than in those for men. Infractions most often have to do with some variation of insubordination toward staff. It is not clear, but this greater number might be attributed to the greater tendency of women officers to write up relatively minor incidents, such as insolence; it is also possible that women inmates have a greater tendency to speak their mind to officers rather than to remain quiet.

Fewer women receive serious punishments, such as loss of good time and segregation; this difference is related to the lack of serious infractions in women's facilities, such as drug violations or weapons. Women tend to be involved frequently in minor personal altercations, contraband other than drugs, and insubordination. For these infractions, daylock or some type of privilege deprivation is common. However, some women may be subject to such serious punishment as segregation, the most punitive legal means of causing pain to individuals. As Burkhardt described them, the segregation units fully illustrate the extent of the women's powerlessness in the face of state control:

These cells are drearily the same in every jail I've visited—window-less and bare. Some have one thin, dirty and bloodstained mattress on the floor. Some have no mattress. Some jails provide blankets for the women confined, some do not. In some quarters, women locked in solitary are allowed to wear prison shift—in others they are allowed to wear only their underwear or are stripped naked. Toilets are most often flushed from the outside, and women complain that on occasion sadistic matrons play games with flushing the toilets—either flushing them repeatedly until they overflow or not flushing them at all for a day or more at a time (Burkhardt, 1973: 148).

lllll Co-Correctional Facilities

In 1971, Ft. Worth, a co-correctional facility for federal inmates, was opened. Thus we had come full circle from the date in 1873, almost a hundred years earlier, when the female reformers were finally successful in establishing a separate female facility. Schweber reported that approximately 61 percent of adult women were housed in co-correctional facilities in 1984 (Schweber, 1984: 5). Crawford reported that 27 percent of the facilities for women in her survey were co-correctional (1988b: 10). Although the co-correctional institutions of today bear no resemblance to those of the past, there are still disadvantages as well as advantages to housing male and female inmates together.

The observable effects on inmates of a sexually integrated prison, which in many ways is a microcosm of society, appear to provide a more humane environment, albeit one in which women often assume a subservient position. Inmates and staff at coed facilities frequently comment that women humanize the prison atmosphere; that all inmates care more about their appearance, and sloppiness or bad language is unusual; that coed women are "softer," more ladylike, and they assume traditional helping/dependency roles; and that homosexuality and violence among men is drastically reduced (Schweber, 1984: 6).

As Schweber points out, however, there are real trade-offs between single-sex institutions and co-correctional facilities. While women and men may enjoy the more normal environment of both sexes housed together with some interaction, more often than not the situation creates more control and security precautions for at least one of the sexes. It also appears that women less often take advantage of program opportunities in a co-correctional prison. They also may be less likely to take leadership roles or to express themselves in a positive, assertive manner. Staff also may be more restricted in a co-correctional facility, and female staff may have fewer opportunities for advancement.

In 1984, Ryan reported that six states had co-correctional facilities (Ryan, 1984: x). He also reported that of the forty-eight facilities that reported vocational education, 31 percent of them had co-correctional vocational programs. These programs may bus the inmates to a nearby prison or have the program in the women's facility (Ryan, 1984: 17). Some studies have been done on the differences in activities between the two groups of inmates. Wilson discovered that more women than men appeared to be involved in academic pursuits (66.7 percent, compared to 57.7 percent). More men than women, however, set a goal of a college degree (21.2 percent, compared to 1.3 percent). Men and women were about equal in their requests for vocational education (73.1 percent to 74.4 percent). However, as might be expected, there were sex differences in program requests. Both sexes preferred programs traditionally associated with their own sex (Wilson, 1980).

Just because a facility is co-correctional does not necessarily mean that male and female inmates are able to interact. Crawford indicates that some co-correctional facilities do not allow recreation, leisure activities, eating, or working together (1988b: 10). Often this means that women are the ones who suffer from increased restrictions on their movement.

An exhaustive look at co-correctional facilities is beyond the scope of this text; however, the interested reader may find several good sources that document the success of co-correctional facilities and their stated goals.

IIIII Women's Prisons in England and Scotland

British women are held in six "closed" and three "open" facilities, two Youth Custody Centers and three Remand Centers. The combined daily population in 1987 was roughly 1,600 (O'Dwyer et al., 1987: 177). We have a few enlightening descriptions of how women prisoners fare in Great Britain. These studies point up international differences in the treatment of prisoners. Mawby (1982) explains that British prisons may hold more petty and first-time offenders than prisons for women in the States. He describes the difference between open prisons and closed prisons, the latter being more similar to American prisons.

Carlen (1983) studied Cornton Vale, a women's prison in Scotland. She pointed out that it is very rare indeed for women to be incarcerated; if they are, their sentences are likely to be fairly short, 115 days on average (1983: 13). Carlen describes Cornton Vale as a well kept place composed of cottages, lined with "trim paths" and flower gardens. The rooms are brightly furnished and "light and airy in summer" (1983: 14). She further explained, however, that within the walls, females are disciplined by being socially isolated from one another. This practice creates a situation where women are dependent on their keepers for everything, including affection. Training tends to be solely in the "domestic arts," reinforcing the idea that the women imprisoned have violated social rather than legal norms—and indeed very few are in for more than petty crimes. One-third are committed for property crimes without violence, and one-third are there for public-order crimes (breach of the peace). Half of these involve the failure to pay a fine (Carlen, 1983: 115). Carlen proposed that the women who end up in prison are there because of their failure as mothers, rather than for criminality per se. If a woman shows herself to be the caregiver to children, she will escape imprisonment, almost regardless of what offense she has committed. On the other hand, a woman who has no children, or who has not taken care of her children, is considered no great loss to society, and thus finds herself in prison (Carlen, 1983: 68).

The "family life" artificially created at Cornton Vale is said to be a substitute and training for the family life these women have been deprived of or have deprived their children of and need to learn. Carlen explained that since some of the women ran away from home or husband in order to escape this type of family life, it is ironic indeed that they are forced to submit to it in prison. She further proposed that it is hypocritical to promote a family atmosphere when women are punished for truly helping one another or for getting involved with one another's problems. In fact, the division of the blocks into small family units is primarily useful as a discipline device, since it further increases women's isolation and dependency (Carlen, 1983: 73).

At Cornton Vale, the women lead a much more structured and strict life than at any American prison. All letters are censored, there are no phone calls, and visiting is rare. The women get little time to socialize with one another, and all conversations are monitored. Carlen, like many American researchers, described how the institution for women encourages them to be childlike, and in response many of the women act in immature ways. Suggested explanations for the apparent immaturity of female inmates include the following: women themselves are essentially childlike (some officers believed this); the hierarchical organization created the childishness; or disciplinary and security measures were "actually designed" to induce feelings of infantile dependency in the prisoners (Carlen, 1983: 109).

Dobash, Dobash, and Gutteridge (1986) also described Cornton Vale and other British prisons. They provided a historical account as well as current descriptions of women's prisons that indicate that British women are treated similarly to American women, although probably the routine and procedures are harsher in British prisons. During the rehabilitative era in the late 1960s and 1970s, women's prisons in England were reformed, and a medical approach to corrections was adopted. It was much more common to explain female criminality through resort to medical and psychiatric termi- nology than male criminality; and the "treatment model" was used more often in female institutions than in male prisons (Dobash et al., 1986: 126). Adherence to a treatment ethic was probably more superficial than real, however, since the authors suggest that the social work staff pressured women to be pleasant and ladylike rather than engaging in any real attempt to deal with personal problems (Dobash et al., 1986: 144). Useful vocational programs are less apparent than domestic and maintenance work.

> Failure to consider the needs of women prisoners for work and training is evident in the official government papers which dis- cussed the setting up of Cornton Vale and the rebuilding of Holloway. While a great deal was said about therapy and treatment, very little attention was paid to work and training. Where these are mentioned, they are considered primarily for their supposed ther- apeutic value (Dobash et al., 1986: 163).

The authors go on to describe the women as having fewer outlets for physical recreation or social programs. Women tended to be involved in individual pursuits such as sewing or handicrafts and, to a lesser extent, education. It certainly seems to be the case that British and American female inmates share similar experiences both before and in prison.

IIIII Conclusion and Summary

This chapter attempts to illustrate in general terms what prisons for women are like today. Obviously, one cannot be completely accurate when describing prisons across the country. Generalities reduce accuracy. While some prisons are cottages, others are of the ware- house variety. Some may have more liberal policies and procedures than what has been described. Some may not allow the amenities that make women's prison life more comfortable physically, if not psychologically. Even in the area of programs offered to women inmates, dramatic differences appear. Whereas some prisons offer none, others offer more than a dozen. Some have continued to stick with the traditional sex-typed programs, while others are remark- ably innovative.

Despite these problems with generalization, some general prin- ciples can be gleaned from this broad look at institutions across the country. First, it seems obvious that more programs are needed, with a better rationale for program distribution. It is not clear that programs are now offered according to women's needs or desires. Rather, it seems that program development has been hodgepodge and ad hoc, perhaps related to staff interests or chance happenings. After surveying the "state of the art" in women's programming, Ryan offers the following suggestions for improvements in women's prisons. First, he suggests that prisons develop policies to facilitate communication and the growth of interagency agreements and cooperation among correctional agencies. Second, he urges that managers and supervisors in correctional systems with adult female offenders expand their networking activities. Third, he suggests the creation of regional and national forums for the exchange of ideas and models and the identification of resources. Fourth, he urges special issue-training programs for managers and supervisors of female offenders to address identified needs and problem areas and to develop skills, techniques, and tools for addressing these needs and problem areas (Ryan, 1984: 29).

Although litigation, increased attention, and more professional training of officers may have lessened the paternalism described in women's prisons of the 1960s and 1970s, an atmosphere and treatment of women inmates by staff different from that commonly described in institutions for men still prevails. Arguably less harsh physical surroundings and treatment are used to control women inmates, but the psychological control seems much more pervasive—resulting in an institution that looks nice but within which the incarcerated women feel that staff attempt to control every aspect of their lives. They are confused because on the one hand they receive signals that indicate they should be grateful for the opportunities and pleasant aspects of the institution ("They have nothing to complain about"), yet on the other hand they are also constantly besieged by signals that tell them they are children or incompetent adults who need to be told what to do. This situation results in an institution remarkably similar to a high school with rowdy students. Staff spend a great deal of time concerned with such behavior as walking and talking loudly and rough horseplay, because there are no serious infractions like drug dealing or homicide to worry about.

It is a strange place, this institution housing women and controlled by other women. It is a place where women inmates may pleasantly and animatedly discuss hairstyles with women officers then a short while later swear bitterly at the same officer for refusing to allow them extra time outside their cells. It is a place where women forty years old are called "girls" and mothers are treated like children. It is a place where a new officer can be the target of a vicious game played by inmates, who subject her to taunts about her ignorance, her body, and her personal life as she attempts to understand her duties and deal with the new job. If she is reduced to tears, the inmates may never forget her weakness and will constantly intimidate her until she requests a position with less contact or quit. The women's prison is not as violent as the prison for men, but it still possesses an undercurrent of fear. There are the "stud broads" who control others by sheer force of personality and occasional violence. There are instances of officers, with full riot gear, subduing female inmates who might be breaking up a cell or attacking other inmates or officers, either because of intentional hostility or undirected anger borne of frustration and hopelessness. The women's prison is a place that can only truly be experienced from the inside.

References

Burkhardt, K. (1973) *Women in Prison*. Garden City, N.J.: Doubleday.

Carlen, P. (1983) *Women's Imprisonment: A Study in Social Control*. London: Routledge & Kegan Paul.

Carlen, P., ed. (1985) *Criminal Women*. Cambridge, England: Polity Press.

Chapman, J. (1980) *Economic Realities and Female Crime*. Lexington, Mass.: Lexington Books.

Crawford, J. (1988a) "Tabulation of a Nationwide Survey of Female Offenders." College Park, Md.: American Correctional Association.

Crawford, J. (1988b) "Tabulation of a Nationwide Survey of State Correctional Facilities for Adult and Juvenile Female Offenders." College Park, Md.: American Correctional Association.

DeCostanzo, E., and J. Valente. (1984) "Designing a Corrections Continuum for Female Offenders: One State's Experience." *The Prison Journal* 64, 1: 120–128.

Dobash, R., R. Dobash, and S. Gutteridge. (1986) *The Imprisonment of Women*. New York: Basil Blackwell.

Fox, J. (1984) "Women's Prison Policy, Prisoner Activism, and the Impact of the Contemporary Feminist Movement: A Case Study." *The Prison Journal* 64, 1: 15–36.

Glick R., and V. Neto. (1977) *National Study of Women's Correctional Programs*. Washington, D.C.: U.S. Government Printing Office.

Kestenbaum, S. E. (1977) "Women's Liberation for Female Offenders." *Social Casework* 58, 2: 77–83.

Mann, C. (1984) *Female Crime and Delinquency*. Birmingham: University of Alabama Press.

Mawby, R. (1982) "Women in Prison: A British Study." *Crime and Delinquency* 28, 1: 24–39.

Moyer, I. (1984) "Deceptions and Realities of Life in Women's Prisons." *The Prison Journal* 64, 1: 45–56.

O'Dwyer, J., et al. (1987) "Women's Imprisonment in England, Wales and Scotland: Recurring Issues." In P. Carlen and A. Worral, *Gender, Crime and Justice*, pp. 176–190. Philadelphia: Open University Press.

Ross, R., and A. Fabiano. (1986) *Female Offenders: Correctional Afterthoughts*. Jefferson, N.C.: McFarland and Co.

Rubick, R. B. (1975) "The Sexually Integrated Prison: A Legal and Policy Evaluation." *American Journal of Criminal Law* 3, 3: 301–330.

Ryan, T. E. (1984) *Adult Female Offenders and Institutional Programs: A State of the Art Analysis.* Washington, D.C.: National Institute of Corrections.

Schweber, C. (1984) "Beauty Marks and Blemishes: The Coed Prison as a Microcosm of Integrated Society." *The Prison Journal* 64, 1: 3–15.

Strickland, K. (1976) *Correctional Institutions for Women in the U.S.* Lexington, Mass.: Lexington Books.

Taylor, B. (1982) *Sexual Inequities Behind Bars.* Ph.D. diss., Claremont Graduate School, Claremont, CA.

Velimesis, M. I. (1981) "Sex Roles and Mental Health of Women in Prison." *Professional Psychology* 12, 1: 128–135.

Weishet, R. (1985) "Trends in Programs for Female Offenders: The Use of Private Agencies as Service Providers." *International Journal of Offender Therapy and Comparative Criminology* 29, 1: 35–42.

Wilson, N. K. (1980) "Styles of Doing Time in a Coed Prison." In U. Smykla, *Co-Corrections*, pp. 160–165. New York: Human Services Press.

6 ||||||||||||||||||||||||||||||||||||||||||||||||||||||||
Staff

The uniqueness of women's prisons may be due in part to the correctional officers found there, the majority of whom are also women. Although many similarities appear among the staff of any "total institution," a place described by Goffman (1961) as one where the boundaries of work, play, and sleep are eliminated, certain unique characteristics arise when the staff is largely female. At the women's institution, as at any total institution, a chasm stretches between the staff and residents who live within the walls. The relationship between these two groups is part of the nature of the total institution. As Goffman wrote:

> Each group tends to conceive of members of the other in terms of narrow hostile stereotypes, staff often seeing inmates as bitter, secretive, and untrustworthy, while inmates often see staff as condescending, high-handed and mean. Staff tends to feel superior

and righteous; inmates tend, in some ways at least, to feel inferior, weak, blameworthy and guilty. Social mobility between the two strata is grossly restricted; social distance is typically great and often prescribed; even talk across the boundaries may be conducted in a special tone of voice. The restrictions on contact presumably help to maintain the antagonistic stereotypes. In any case, two different social and cultural worlds develop, tending to jog along beside each other, with points of official contact but little mutual penetration (Goffman, quoted in Glaser, 1964: 114).

Indeed, that is an apt description of any prison. Officers stereotype inmates as worthless and evil; inmates stereotype officers as lazy and ignorant. The lack of meaningful communication between the two groups makes the job harder for the officer and life more difficult for the inmate. The social distance between the groups makes casual mistreatment possible: officers may use their power to withhold necessities or humiliate inmates forced to ask for needed items. Note how Jean Harris, a firsthand observer, describes the predicament of being under the power of a correctional officer (c.o.).

One must have experienced prison as an inmate to know into what kind of hands this power of destruction has been placed. The young c.o. who is presently pregnant with her third illegitimate baby . . . the woman who goaded me daily to get me to hit her so she could scream "assault" and have me put in solitary, the male c.o.'s who impregnate inmates, the female c.o. who gets so stoned on duty I have seen her struggle to unlock a door while pushing the key in to the door two feet above where the lock was. Anyone of these and many more like them could walk into my cell as I sit here and tear up the pictures of my sons and the manuscript I am writing and anything else that strikes their fancy (Harris, 1988: 238).

The relationship between male inmates and officers has been documented by Sykes (1956), Crouch (1980), and Johnson and Price (1981), among others. However, the women's prison is different from the male prison in many ways. Much of what is written concerning male officers and their relationships with male inmates does not apply to institutions housing and staffed by women. For example, the social boundaries are not as severe in women's prisons; a social distance still exists, characterized by a lack of informal communication, but it is not as great as that found in prisons for men.

As previously noted, separate institutions for women offenders originally were created to enable female role models to influence their charges without the brutalizing and corrupting presence of men. This original premise led to the development of female staff, who were socialized to approach their role differently from male officers in parallel positions. Moreover, most of the women in early institutions did not come from a military background, as did many of the male officers, but rather from social work and teaching backgrounds. They had no experience in custody control and approached their charges as they would a dependent client, child, or student. Consequently, the early histories reported staff and women inmates working together hand in hand to build new buildings or plant in the fields. Many of those attracted to corrections work were educated in women's colleges or possessed an almost religious fervor to change the lives of women offenders for the better.

As is true of all innovations in corrections, gradually the great experiment in women's reformatories slipped off track. The educated and zealous women reformers who had started the movement lost interest or became exhausted from their efforts, and they were replaced by those who saw corrections as a job rather than a vocation. Partly because qualified women were so rare and partly because administrators never really believed women could handle the responsibility of management, males stepped in to take control of the early institutions, and women were relegated to lower positions of authority. Over time, the women's institution in any particular state correctional system became last on the priority list for funds and other considerations. Women correctional officers did not follow the same pay grade as males, nor was a position in a female facility considered comparable to a similar position in a male facility. Women who worked in corrections as correctional officers did so for very pragmatic reasons rather than the idealistic motivations of their forerunners. The female correctional officer, up until recently, was very different from the male correctional officer—in how she was treated, in her reasons for entering corrections, and to a very large degree in her opportunities for career advancement.

In the past, women workers were believed to have different habits, motivations, skills, and worth than men. Despite recent advances, women are still clustered in "female occupations," such as nursing, social work, and education—fields that emphasize nurturant skills and traditional, "feminine" attributes. Most women work in nonmanual white-collar occupations, as do most men, but men are also distributed across other categories. A much larger percentage of women than men are in clerical and manual blue-collar positions (Baker, 1987: 172). Fields with large numbers of women are observed to be more centralized, with less autonomy for the individual worker. This tendency supposedly resulted from the psychological characteristics of women workers, including a greater deference to authority, greater need for approval and association, guilt about expressing aggressiveness, and less opposition to centralization because of less commitment to the job and less concern with decision making (Marrett, 1972). More recent research disputes these assumptions. Much of the current literature either finds no differences or explains the differences as resulting from differential job demands or other factors (Nieva and Gutek, 1981: 85; Baker, 1987: 183). Further, women were believed to have personal characteristics—compliance, submissiveness, emotionality—that made them unsuitable for leadership or supervisory positions (Nieva and Gutek, 1981). These supposedly feminine traits also made women unsuitable for work with offenders, except for juveniles and adult women.

Whether women in leadership roles perform differently from males is not clear. Results of research are mixed. Some studies report that women emphasize "human" factors, while men emphasize "task" factors. Other research, however, can find no differences between the two groups. Older studies indicate that the nurturant role of women may be carried with them into the workplace. For instance, female supervisors have been perceived as performing more supportive functions than males in a similar position (Lipman-Blumen and Tickmayer, 1975). Even when women and men have the same occupation, it has been observed that the women may bring more nurturing qualities to the job. For instance, female teachers may carry on more personal relationships with their students, female social workers and counselors may emphasize the importance of the relationship over achievement goals, and female managers may use a more personal style of supervision. However, studies that rate women's and men's leadership find negligible differences on certain objective measures (Nieva and Gutek, 1981: 86). One might conclude that women may emphasize a less task-directed and more personal style of supervision when they have the flexibility to do so, but when the environment demands a certain style of supervision—for instance, the military, where some studies finding no differences were performed—women follow the standard style.

Perceptions concerning the behaviors women and men may employ in their supervisory functions are also different. Whereas women are rated more negatively for direct approaches and authoritarian, unemotional styles of supervision, they are rated less negatively than men for using an emotional style of supervision (Nieva and Gutek, 1981: 87–88). These findings indicate that, despite work pattern changes and the employment of the majority of women outside the home in modern society, sex roles are hard to change. Women are still restricted by and large to certain occupations and may bring different characteristics to an occupation or adapt themselves to it. Women who enter corrections not only inherit the legacy of early reformatory ideals but also are influenced by their socialization and predilections for how they see and respond to others. Research in corrections has found that the female correctional officer performs her role differently from male c.o.'s in some ways. The prison for women is different as a result.

IIIII Matrons

As already noted, most early women's prisons were built so that women staff could guide and advise women inmates in a setting away from the influence of men. This separation from men was felt to be important because women offenders were perceived to have only experienced negative male–female relationships and either had been exploited by men or had manipulated men to their own advantage. Before the emergence of this concept of the fallen or misguided woman, women offenders were thought of as worse than male offenders and irredeemable. They were guarded by men in separate wings or buildings in male facilities and subjected to various forms of mistreatment and sexual exploitation. Parisi (1984) notes, for instance, that women were isolated in a separate wing in Auburn Prison in 1825, but no matrons were hired until 1832. Even then, the managers and administrators were men until the women were moved to Bedford Hills and other separate facilities for women in New York.

The rise of the reformatory movement opened new avenues of employment for educated women and provided them with opportunities to use their newfound skills and experience independent careers. Some of the early administrators were influenced by religious motives as well as altruistic ones. Few of the early administrators were feminists per se; that is, they did not necessarily support equal rights for women but rather believed women had a special and exalted place in society, as the bearers of children and keepers of the home. Because of the importance of the woman's role, it was necessary to guide the women offenders back to an ideal of womanhood (Rafter, 1985).

Lekkerkerker (1931) found that almost all who came in contact with women offenders in women's prisons were female, even the physicians. The sole exceptions were sometimes dentists and the farmers who supervised the fields. Some states had laws specifying that the officers be women, and several states had laws requiring that a woman be hired as the superintendent (Lekkerkerker, 1931: 272). These early women administrators initiated many reforms in institutional corrections that are still with us today. The presence of libraries, music programs, recreation, and formal education and other reforms were initially embraced by female administrators in reformatories for women. Because of the lower security risk presented by women offenders, women's prisons were the locale for many forms of innovative programming. For instance, some early institutions had very little in the way of security. Women were not placed behind bars and stone walls, since they were not considered dangerous. Some programs placed women in the community as house servants, in a kind of early work-release program. Women administrators often had the luxury of starting from scratch, since women's prisons were being built with no models to pattern themselves after, thus allowing the administrator to create her own conception of an ideal prison.

The line staff in these early reformatories may have had some education, but many took their positions for purely pragmatic reasons. The reformatories offered bed and board as well as a small salary, an attractive aspect of the job for those who had to support themselves. The women sacrificed a great deal of freedom and privacy for this privilege, however, and were watched almost as closely as the inmates in their private lives and personal habits.

Lekkerkerker (1931) described the life of the matron in early institutions. They were usually paid no more than a domestic except in a few institutions and the federal system, although the salaries of those who worked in institutions for white women were much higher than those who worked in institutions housing black women (1931: 278). The shifts were long and there were few days off. For instance, Lekkerkerker reports that in Iowa, women staff had one half-day off every third Sunday and one to three weeks' vacation a year, depending on length of service. In Ohio, matrons worked twelve-hour shifts and received two days off each month. Massachusetts, perhaps the most lenient state, allowed a day and a half off each week and three weeks' vacation (Lekkerkerker, 1931: 279). Officers were prohibited from cooking for themselves and had to take their meals in a common dining room; they were not allowed visitors and had nowhere to go during free time because of the isolated location of the institution. Cottage matrons lived with the inmates. Even when officers did not live in the inmate quarters, staff housing was not much better than that provided for inmates, and in some cases it was the same as inmate housing.

Despite these drawbacks, institutional corrections was one of the few fields in which educated women could work. Lekkerkerker described the importance of good matrons as essential for the institution:

> There is a real place in the reformatory for "matrons" in the good sense of the word, women of great refinement and intelligent social workers, who know not only to create a fine home atmosphere, but who above all have the confidence of their charges and know how to help them in re-adjusting their personalities. Viewed in this light, the work of the cottage matrons should be considered a "key-position" only to be trusted to the best. Unfortunately, rather the opposite meaning seems to prevail in many institutions, if one considers the low salaries of the matrons and the position these officers occupy (1931: 265).

The type of person who could handle this important function was very special.

Generally, reformatory officers should be physically and mentally
healthy, well-balanced, even-tempered, socially mature women,
with steady moral standards and a cheerful disposition. . . . The
officers should undoubtedly be women who know life and the world
at large, and who have what may be called a convincing personality;
the woman who feels her own life as a failure or who is emotionally
repressed usually has small success with delinquent women who
instinctively sense her weaknesses and have only contempt for her.
It is especially important that the officers have a wholesome and
objective understanding of and attitude towards sex, for they will
often have to deal with sexual problems, and it is almost entirely
through the attitudes and reactions of the officers that the inmates
have to gain a correct interpretation of sexual questions which
many of them so badly need (Lekkerkerker, 1931: 273).

In the 1930s Lekkerkerker observed that the matron, who was
responsible for all aspects of the inmate's supervision, was being
replaced by specialists in education and counseling. This change
was accompanied by instructions to the matron staff prohibiting
them from becoming involved in the personal lives of the inmates
(Lekkerkerker, 1931: 262). Obviously, the increasing professionalization of counseling staff during this period changed the role of the
female matron. The author bemoaned the specialization and the way
it deprived the matron of the more important features of her role;
she was relegated to mere supervision by this time and was not
expected to know or influence the women offenders she supervised.
The other problem with decreasing the responsibilities of the matron
was that educated and ambitious women no longer were interested
in the position. As other avenues of employment opened up for
women, especially in education and social work, it was no doubt
more difficult to attract them to corrections. Consequently, the
matron role grew to be less important as a role model for female
inmates and instead became more custodial. Women were attracted
to the matron job for increasingly financial and pragmatic reasons.

The history of women's reformatories implies that the early
institutions were havens of enlightenment and good staff care. This
depiction is probably not accurate. For every educated and enlightened administrator or matron, many more saw their function in a
harsher light. Although brutality has never been as prevalent in
institutions for women, certain practices, such as cold baths and
isolation, were just as painful as practices found in prisons for men.
A few staff in any custodial institution succumb to the temptation
to abuse their position. Women, unfortunately, are no better than
men in this regard; women staff are just as capable of using their
positions to unnecessarily taunt and humiliate the inmates under
their control. Outright abuses, however, are rarely documented. The
more insidious tendency of the female staff in women's prisons is to
maternalize their relationship with inmates, treating them in a

manner that does not recognize their adulthood. This tendency holds as true today as it did in the first reformatory for women in 1873.

lllll Female Correctional Officers Today

Women who work in corrections today are very different from their forerunners in the reformatory era or even in the early 1900s. Women today often seek correctional positions for the same reasons, however; that is, they are attracted by the security and by the salary, which is hard to match in any other unskilled position. Some women hope for a career in corrections, and these women seek more education and pursue advancement through diverse work assignments and affiliation with professional organizations. Many women, however, like many men, view the work as "just a job" and one with substantial drawbacks, especially for women with children.

A 1979 survey reported that only 29.3 percent of correctional workers were female; moreover, these women were overrepresented in clerical and support functions, and only 41 percent of them had contact with prisoners. Many of these women worked in institutions for females and juveniles. Women, on average, were younger and had less experience than male correctional officers, and their salary levels were lower. Parisi (1984) reported that in 1966, only ten female institutions were headed by females, although the number of female administrators has increased since then. Strickland reported in 1976 that of the thirty facilities for women in existence, only three were headed by men (1976: 139). Crawford's more recent survey, however, reports that only 56 percent of the facilities for women are headed by women (1988: 12). Females in corrections seem to be less likely than men to list corrections as a career goal; they more often chose it because of financial reasons or because the job was close to home. They seem to have lower career aspirations than men, lower job satisfaction, and less positive attitudes toward employee relations (Chapman, 1983).

Because corrections is somewhat like a paramilitary organization, women staff members may feel uncomfortable operating within it. The nature of a bureaucracy leaves little room for flexibility and personality; thus, women may have a hard time adjusting to the constraints of such an occupation, whereas men may have experienced more similar situations before. Women in corrections usually have children to support—in fact that is often why they work as correctional officers in the first place, since it provides a steady source of income to someone likely to be unskilled and without a college degree. Correctional work, however, is peculiarly unsuited to the working mother. The shifts are long, and overtime, even involuntary overtime, is not uncommon. There is often no chance to leave work during an emergency, and sometimes it is very difficult for family or child-care workers to reach the officer-mother at work.

Institutions are often far away from urban centers, and women either live in the small towns where the institutions are located or commute long distances. Often women come from the rural area that surrounds the prison, in which case they have very little in common with the primarily urban inmate population. Women correctional officers may come from a corrections family; that is, they may have fathers, brothers, or husbands who also work in corrections—especially in areas where there is more than one prison, so that the woman works in the institution for females while her male relatives work in the institution for men. Although working in corrections as a family allows the family to share problems and discuss their work, facilities for men and women often differ in regard to rule enforcement and other practices. As women enter facilities for men, family members may face different issues, with a sister, mother, or daughter in the same facility.

When the woman has no family involved in corrections, she is often forced to explain and defend her reasons for entering such a profession. Lurid movies that portray women's institutions as hotbeds of lesbian activity and guard brutality feed the fuel of friends' and relatives' imaginations and provide further misperceptions about the nature of the work. When black women from urban areas enter correctional work, they face unique problems. Often they come from the same neighborhoods as the women they supervise; they may even know people in common with the prisoners. The women correctional officers are viewed as "cops," and many inmates are openly hostile to what they see as betrayal on the part of the officers.

Although most states have academies now that train correctional officers before placing them into facilities, little training is provided to prepare the female officer for the facility for women. The academies are largely geared for male officers who will be transferred to prisons for men. Consequently, all the rules, procedures, and problems discussed relate to facilities for males. If women's institutions are mentioned, it is often in a comparative manner, indicating the "peculiarities" of women's prisons. Typically, state correctional systems have moved from an approach that isolates and differentiates the women's institution to an approach that alleges that all inmates and all prisons are the same in terms of rules, supplies, assignments, and other factors. This latter approach is no more helpful than the benign neglect that previously characterized the central office's attention to facilities for women; women's prisons obviously have unique needs, different from men's institutions.

One of the more interesting developments for female correctional officers has been their entry into prisons for men. An early study found that few correctional institutions did not have female staff—in fact an average of 8.4 percent of the staff in surveyed facilities were women—but they typically had restricted assignments, such as in the administration building or in the visiting room where they were employed to search female visitors (Parisi, 1984: 95). In *Dothard versus Rawlinson,* 433 U.S. 321 (1977), a woman presented the first challenge to the state's right to bar her from working in a facility for males. In this case, the U.S. Supreme Court overturned the use of height and weight restrictions unless the state could show how they were related to the job; but it did uphold the state's argument that, because of the violence and conditions of the Alabama state prison, it would be dangerous to allow women to work there. However, *Dothard* was a narrow ruling, applying only to Alabama's prison, and many states interpreted the dictum in the case as supportive of women's right to work in men's prisons (Jacobs, 1979). Title VII of the Civil Rights Act forbids sex discrimination at all levels of employment except when sex is a bona fide occupational qualification. Since states have been unable to show that height and weight restrictions or sex itself influences what is necessary to be an effective correctional officer, the number of women in male prisons has increased substantially.

This hesitancy in allowing females to work in male facilities is the same as the resistance met by women who entered the police force as patrol officers in the early 1970s. Basically, what have been considered "feminine" traits in our society are inconsistent with the tasks of correctional and law enforcement personnel. Women's control has tended to be emotional and affectional in this society, not derived from the use of fear or intimidation. Since it is difficult to imagine any emotional ties between inmates and staff, the general consensus was that females would be unable to control male inmates; also their peculiarly "feminine" traits, such as seductiveness, fearfulness, and weakness, would make them a danger to themselves and to colleagues. "Male" traits such as emotional detachment, assertiveness, and aggressiveness are considered more suited to the prison environment (Coles, 1980). It was felt that women not only would be poor officers, but their presence also would entice male inmates to sexual assault or acts of homosexuality. Just as women police officers did and continue to do, women in corrections have had to struggle against strong resistance. Yet most evaluations to date show that, except in a few areas, they do their job as well as men and receive support from male colleagues for doing so.

Other similarities between police officers and correctional officers exist. In both fields, women have been present for a long time, but only recently have their positions been equal to those of men. In law enforcement, women had been placed in juvenile departments and as matrons in local jails since the late 1800s. Women in corrections, of course, have been relegated to institutions for women and juveniles. In both areas, the placement of women was due to the perceived role of women in society and the unique contributions women could make in working with those special groups of offenders. However, when women became tired of being limited to narrow career ladders and restricted assignments and recognized that these restrictions also meant lower salaries, they sought court help in breaking employment barriers based on sex.

Evaluations of women in both fields have been uniformly positive. Studies that evaluated women police officers found some differences in the way women patrolled. They were said to patrol "less aggressively," meaning they made fewer arrests and had fewer altercations with citizens. They also had more "good arrests" and fewer complaints. Some weak areas included shooting firearms and driving skills, but in most areas of evaluation, such as number of sick days, calls for help, use of backups, or departmental ratings, the men and women were rated as substantially the same (Block and Anderson, 1974; Martin, 1980).

Evaluations of women correctional officers in prisons for men or in co-correctional institutions indicate that women may not get assigned to certain posts where administrators feel security might be risked. However, they are perceived as competent in giving first aid, cooling down angry inmates, and dealing with verbally abusive inmates. They are perceived as less competent in handling physical altercations. Most correctional officers surveyed got along equally well with both sexes, but males were less likely to rate female officers as excellent or good. This study found that inmates reacted to the presence of females by improving their appearance and language and behaving more politely toward the female officers. Three out of four male officers and 80 percent of the inmates gave female officers favorable ratings (Kissel and Seidel, 1980).

Martin (1980) found that one of the problems of women police officers, and by analogy women correctional officers, was that they lacked the anticipatory socialization men brought to the work. They had less experience with aggression in organized sports and less experience with teamwork or authority; they had to learn these patterns of behavior. They needed to develop an authoritative tone and learn new facial expressions that indicated authority rather than subservience. They had to restrain themselves from smiling as much as is natural for a woman socialized in this society. They needed to learn to use more direct language to convey instructions, rather than requesting or suggesting what they wanted. All of these "deficiencies" were due to the socialized role of women in this society, and the "masculine" characteristics of the law enforcement and corrections job.

It is debatable whether in any given situation, the "masculine" approach is more effective than the "feminine" approach; in many instances, one could imagine that a smile might elicit greater cooperation than a direct order would. Yet this is the pattern of behavior that has developed in corrections and law enforcement, and women must either adapt themselves to the expected pattern or change the expectations. It may be that women officers adapt in the prisons for men and change the pattern in the prisons for women, since the supervision patterns between the two types of institutions are quite different. Adherence to the authoritarian role is only a matter of degree, however; often women as well as men play down the heavy role and use other means to control, even in prisons for men.

Women in law enforcement and in corrections encountered a great deal of resistance on the part of their male colleagues. Although education and age had some influence on the receptivity of males to the entry of females, ordinarily a great deal of sexual harassment and scapegoating went on. While women police officers reported being made the target of sexual jokes and innuendos, and being prevented—sometimes physically—from engaging in physical altercations with suspects, women correctional officers reported much the same experiences when they entered the prisons for men. Women correctional officers still report male officers propositioning them in front of male inmates or having supervisors threaten them with poor assignments or termination to gain their sexual acquiescence. Hopefully, as the women's presence becomes less unusual in the prisons for men, these abuses will cease. Female correctional officers in institutions for women have not had these problems to the degree that those who work in prisons for men have, although their supervisors may still be male.

Women who adapt to correctional work and law enforcement by adopting male behavior patterns in voice and manner experience a fair degree of stress in other parts of their lives. Women report that it is hard to be authoritarian at work and go home to be "mommy." Relationships with male colleagues are often difficult in that a balance always has to be struck between being friendly and being thought of as sexually available—being "one of the boys" or designated as the fraternity whore. Arguably, there is less role dysjunction for female c.o.'s who work in institutions for women. The feminization of the institution guarantees that women officers need not adapt themselves to a role that emphasizes "machismo" as does the police officer role and the role of staff in prisons for men.

Obviously, along with female staff in male facilities will come male staff in facilities for women. This is not a new concept, of course; in fact the presence of co-corrections and opposite-sex officers has come full circle from the very beginnings of institutions for women. The impact of employing larger numbers of male correctional officers in female facilities has not been investigated to any great degree. It is argued that the risk of sexual abuse may be higher with men guarding women than vice versa, and some charges have been made that male c.o.'s use their position to view women inmates in the shower and while they are performing personal functions, as well as outright sexually harassing and propositioning them. It is clear that correctional officer unions will probably fight for equal assignments, rather than specialized assignment policies for women in male facilities. Thus, males in female facilities are sure to come, despite possible law suits. With more transfers back and forth between facilities for males and females, there is pressure to make prisons for women more "normal"—meaning more like prisons for men. Different security measures and more formalized interaction between inmates and c.o.'s may develop as a result.

On the other hand, one of the advantages of the transfer of both men and women officers among various prisons, including those for women, is the different perspective the transfer can give both sides on what methods are necessary to run a prison. Security issues are less likely to be emphasized in women's prisons; yet women's prisons experience fewer escapes and serious assaults than male facilities do. Often, an approach of negotiation is used rather than immediate resort to force. In the other direction, c.o.'s from prisons for men may also have contributions to make. Institutions for males must operate efficiently; their very size demands streamlined operations without complicated procedures. Women's institutions, because of their small size, have enjoyed the luxury of often being run in a manner more personal than efficient. Although there are procedures and rules, the top administrators are relatively accessible, and there is less of a hierarchy.

Female officers often prefer to work with male inmates, but male officers do not ordinarily prefer female inmates. Men find it difficult to interact with female inmates, they are troubled by the possibility of rape charges, and they find it difficult to disassociate their culturally induced attitudes toward women from their security role.

> I know how to handle [men]. . . . Now with females, all my life I've been brought up to protect them and respect them, so when you have to use force, it's difficult (Pollock, 1981).

The few men that do prefer to work with female inmates feel that way because of the greater degree of safety, the possibility of "reaching" the inmate because she is more expressive, and the more "lighthearted" nature of the institution (Pollock, 1986).

Female correctional officers who have supervised both sexes often prefer to work with male inmates because they are "more respectful" and don't demand the time and energy of the c.o. in the same way that women inmates are perceived as doing. Female c.o.'s complain that women inmates argue and refuse orders and that they are verbally abusive and expressive about frustration and anger. In other words, they're described as acting like children. On the other hand, female inmates complain that women officers treat them like children by calling them "girls" and scolding or patronizing them concerning dress, behavior, language, cleanliness, and other trivial issues in a heavy-handed, "maternal" way. Women officers who do prefer to work with women say they enjoy discussing things of mutual interest, and some who see their role as having more counseling elements prefer women inmates because they are perceived to be more open than male inmates.

Research illustrates the unique subculture of the correctional officer. As with police officers, the working hours, stigmatization, and frequent isolation of the job create a certain solidarity among officers. This solidarity is marked by reticence with outsiders and protection of members. Correctional officers who break rules are sometimes protected by their fellow officers in the same way that police officers are protected by the "blue shield of secrecy." In recent years, again similarly to police officers, this solidarity has been broken down by the integration of minority and female officers who neither come from the same backgrounds nor are as receptive to the same values as officers in years past. The homogeneity of the workplace gives way to heterogeneity, and officer solidarity is broken down and replaced by more formal and bureaucratic methods of dealing with daily events. In the correctional officer force, minorities and women have broken the ranks of the white, rural guard subculture, and the result has been similar to what has occurred in police forces. Also, civil suits and possible individual liability or perjury charges have resulted in more c.o.'s coming forward with evidence of correctional officer misdeeds. It is safe to say that the correctional officer subculture is a much different one from that of earlier years. There is greater professionalization, greater bureaucratization, and less solidarity. In the women's prison, the officer subculture never reached the degree of intensity observed in prisons for males. The reasons for this are unclear. It may be that there was less homogeneity in the female officer population, or that the less severe nature of the institution did not create a need for a strong subculture. It is also possible that there is a subculture so different from the male subculture as to be unrecognizable.

One can use the deprivation and importation theories to explain officer subcultures as well as inmate subcultures. Deprivation theory would suggest that because women staff members are not faced with the same degree of danger and isolation, they have less need to create an insulating subculture to protect them from these stressors. Thus, the subculture of women officers is more permeable; less stereotyping and physical brutality occurs because the same degree of anxiety and stress is not present to engender it. The importation theory would indicate that because women staff members, like women prisoners, are very concerned with children and family, they are able to find common ground as a basis for communicating. Obviously women officers and inmates are interested in other things besides children, but this bond seems to be very pervasive and bridges the gap between the two groups in some ways. However, it would be unrealistic to view the women's prison as a place where officers and inmates happily share baby stories all day long. The backgrounds of officers and inmates are usually very different. Officers are often judgmental about the inmate's lifestyle, especially as it has affected her children, and these issues may serve to separate rather than draw the two groups together.

Today, with all officers attending a central training academy, transfers between the facilities, and union activity, there is less of an institution-based subculture and more of a state identity among c.o.'s. Officers may share similar interests, regardless of what institution they are housed at, if they aspire to managerial positions and attend national conferences or are involved in higher education. Women officers who have worked in facilities for men before being transferred to a prison for women may have more in common with the male officers there who have worked in the same male facility than women officers who have not.

Women officers in prisons for women may still find some discrimination in the system. It is unlikely that the woman officer would be able to be promoted to another facility from a women's prison, since the general view is that an individual should have a wide range of experience in all types of settings—meaning the various custody grades of institutions for men. Obviously, men are not held back from promotion simply because they have not experienced the women's institution.

lllll Interactions with Inmates

When women guard other women, the social distance is noticeably less than that observed in prisons for men. Most observations of women working in prisons for men have emphasized the differences women bring to the officer role. The manner of supervision seems to be different, along with the relationship with the inmate. Crouch and Marquart (1980) have characterized the male officer as cynical and authoritarian. Often the male officer feels obliged to give orders using demanding tones and obscenities. The relationship between male officers and male inmates may, at times, reach a level of acceptance and respect, especially in isolated settings such as work assignments or in special niches, but these relationships are tenuous at best, and they are often fragmented and shattered when reality brings home the gulf between the two groups of men and polarizes each group, as when a lock-down or beating takes place. It must be noted that some writers describe much closer ties between men, even reaching the point where names such as "kid" and "dad" describe parental relationships between officers and inmates; but these accounts are rare (Webb and Morris, 1980).

Women officers are much more likely to use emotional tools to supervise their inmates and are even more likely to do so when working with juveniles or even adult females. The control from an emotional attachment is often more powerful than the fear that may be employed in facilities for men, but it comes at a cost. As Toigo explains, sometimes the staff person is also caught in the pull of emotional ties.

> The mutual relationship between such staff and girls may constitute a major "hold" the cottage parent has over a girl, say for disciplinary purposes. At the same time, it may impose limits on the parent's autonomy of action. Either from fear of possible responses of girls with whom a "warm" relationship has been developed or from the potential anxieties of losing such a relationship, a cottage parent may well hold in check disciplinary actions which would otherwise be employed (1962: 27).

Although this description is of a juvenile facility, the same observation may be made in a facility for adult women.

Even fairly recent accounts reinforce the concept that women staff members are meant to be role models and help the women inmates develop a more appropriate feminine identity. Eyman (1971), for instance, wrote that the purpose of female staff is to satisfy the emotional needs of the female inmates, so that inmates would not need to turn to pseudofamilies to meet their needs. Males as administrators could serve as father figures who could not be manipulated, thus helping the women to develop more positive relationships with the opposite sex, according to this author (Eyman, 1971: 139).

This perception of the female inmate as needing more emotional support and guidance in establishing her femininity is widespread in the literature concerning not only female juveniles but also adult women offenders. This view of female inmates creates an environment where women offenders are treated very often as children; they are called "girls" or "ladies," and the tone is often that used to discipline teenagers, or somewhat dense and naughty adults. Older women officers, perhaps as a result of their experience in a more paternalistic time period, are especially likely to use this approach with inmates, regardless of the age or experience of the inmate. Fox (1984) explains that often the supervision style whereby women officers treat the inmates as errant children is cause for frustration on the part of the female inmates.

> For a 33 year old woman to have another woman tell her that she is misbehaving, it's funny to me, it's funny! I have a child who is 15 years old and I wouldn't tell him that he is misbehaving. He'd look at me like I was crazy. To be 33 and have somebody tell you

that you're acting like a little child, and that means that you're going to be punished. It's funny (1984: 23).

Younger officers may not be able to carry off the maternal role and instead resort to either jocular friendships or a bureaucratic role, where the officer expects the inmate to do what she asks because "she says so." The bottom line of supervision in any prison is that much of the officer's power is illusory. Although the threat of officially sanctioned violence is ever present, on a day-to-day basis the officer must depend on the force of his or her personality to motivate the inmates to perform required behaviors. The officer must make inmates perform tasks they would probably prefer not to do. The c.o. is responsible to see that inmates leave the housing unit and arrive where they are supposed to be, keep the buildings and grounds clean, do not break rules (or at least not blatantly), and do not hurt themselves or others. How a c.o. manages this supervision is influenced by his or her own personality. Their day may be made either relatively pleasant or extremely difficult by the inmates they supervise. Women may take more liberties with officers, assuming they will not be subject to retaliatory force. In the following anecdote, Jean Harris describes why many officers do not enjoy working with female inmates.

> There is a woman currently on my corridor in lock for a month. There are three young, white males on duty from 7:00 a.m. to 3:00 p.m. She calls for their services by yelling, "One a you dumb motherfuckin' honkie assholes—" One always comes running to provide what she demands. "I'm the king," she yells. "We doin' it my way" (Harris, 1988: 126).

Even though there is less violence and danger in the institution for women, a few women offenders in any prison are known as violent troublemakers. Most women offenders pose a danger only when they are angry at another inmate. Then, in their emotional outburst, they may unintentionally injure an officer attempting to break up the fight. Women correctional officers in facilities for women may be less forceful in handling violent incidents, partly because of anticipatory socialization, partly because of lack of training, and partly because of the infrequency with which they are called upon to perform physically. Women c.o.'s may experience a degree of fear when dealing with these violent women, and they often cover their fear by overreacting to threats or advances or calling in male officers to handle the threatening women offenders. Many prisons now have a cadre of trained male and female officers to intervene in disturbances. These "goon squads" are feared and hated by female as well as male inmates. The display of reactionary force is all the more dramatic in its impersonality. Indeed, the special uniforms and appearance of the team are akin to an invading army. Some observe that this "innovation" may be necessary in an institution for males but is perhaps unnecessary and ill-adapted to institutions for women.

Many situations that would call for force in a male facility are handled by negotiation and persuasion in the facility for women. Female officers are much more likely to argue with women offenders or explain rules to them; they are much more likely to coax a recalcitrant inmate from a cell than to call for backup and the use of force. They are more likely perhaps to ignore some misbehaviors, even while emphasizing others. As one officer explains:

> In a male institution the rules are much more stringent and they are handled differently. They don't usually deviate, you know, like it is black and white where in the female [prison], usually goes by a set of circumstances, in some cases where it is not a serious offense, they'll take factors into consideration (Pollock, 1981).

It may be that the differences between male and female inmates force officers to behave differently.

> The female inmates come over and they always want a little bit more than what's there, you know, if you say you can't have this or this, they'll argue about it. They take up more time because you listen to them, you don't have to, you could say "you can't have it and that's all there is to it" and throw them out the door, but it is very hard to do because you know you prevent a lot of problems if you take the time to talk to them, even if it's just to explain, you know, the rule is changed and they usually then accept it, but they have to argue it all the time (Pollock, 1981).

Or it may be that because officers are more willing to explain rules or argue in an institution for women, that women have the opportunity to be more argumentative.

The personal style of supervision that seems to characterize the women's institution means that the female c.o. may interact with inmates with more sensitivity and attachment. For instance, one observer notes the differences between men and women: "On the women's division, there was not the denial of feelings and callousness observed on the men's division of the same institution" (Ackerman, 1972: 365). The reduced social distance may allow for productive bonds to form between women officers and inmates. On the other hand, some observers believe that the interactions between inmates and officers are superficial at best. Inmates do not share with officers real problems and may use a friendly relationship to manipulate the officer. Of course, this superficiality would be true of men's prisons as well.

On a final cross-cultural note, Dobash, Dobash, and Gutteridge (1986) describe female correctional officers in Scotland as being not too different from female c.o.'s in this country. They were attracted to the job as an alternative to what they considered boring clerical jobs. Some came to corrections from military experience; some entered corrections as a practical solution to a problem—they needed a place to live and one was provided. The authors report that female officers in Scotland received the same training as the male officers received (Dobash et al., 1986: 189). Similar to the officers in this country, Scottish female officers were closer to female inmates than male officers were to male inmates. This did not mean, however, that there was an excessive degree of trust between the two groups.

> Relationships with officers were described as a "game" where you communicated with them just enough to avoid being put on report for ignoring them. At the same time, unpredictability and lack of confidentiality meant that there was little trust and a large element of fear in staff/adult relationships. A commonly expressed feeling was that officers did not regard them as individuals, but treated them as one of a (sometimes subhuman) herd (Dobash et al., 1986: 189).

Genders and Player reported parallel findings in other British institutions. According to these authors, women inmates talked to staff about problems only when staff were able to provide concrete help—for instance, allow a phone call. Otherwise, the conversations were more superficial or the inmate deliberately "gamed" the officer by telling her what she thought the officer wanted to hear (Dobash et al., 1987: 172).

IIIII Conclusion

Any prison is made up not only of inmates but also of officers. The nature of the institution for females is influenced in large part by the women correctional staff employed there. Their different style of supervision and different interactional patterns with the inmates make the women's prison in some ways a better place and in other ways a more confining place to be. Although female correctional officers engage in more personal relationships with inmates and express sensitivity to women's problems and concerns, officers are prone to maternalize their role, which puts the woman offender into an infantile position. The women's prison does not have the same gulf in communication that separates officers and inmates in the prison for men, but the women's prison does suffer from too familiar relationships at times between inmates and officers. Inmates may overstep the boundaries of their role and treat the officer as less than an authority figure. Jean Harris provides a critical summing up of the officer and inmate in a women's prison.

> In this prison, c.o.'s harass the inmates, and the inmates harass the c.o.'s. I've seen a c.o. work laboriously for two hours writing charge sheets for women who didn't jump fast enough for him.

Having finished the job he chose, unwisely, to go to the bathroom. As soon as he closed the bathroom door a woman tiptoed to the bubble, grabbed the charge sheets, tore them and flushed them down the nearest toilet. The confused c.o. spent the next two hours looking for them. It's boarding school stuff played with Keystone Kops (Harris, 1988: 233).

Finally, one must remember that even in women's institutions, which are relatively small as prisons go, there are literally hundreds upon hundreds of correctional officers, all of whom touch the inmates' lives in some way. Some are professional; some are not. Some are cruel; some are kind. Some should not be there; some should be promoted. A few generalizations may be made, but in the end, each officer is an individual—as is each inmate.

References

Ackerman, P. (1972) "A Staff Group in a Women's Prison." *International Journal of Group Psychotherapy* 23: 364–373.

Baker, M., ed. (1987) *Sex Differences in Human Performance*. New York: Wiley.

Bayes, M., and P. Newton. (1978) "Women in Authority: A Sociopsychological Analysis." *Journal of Applied Behavioral Science* 14, 1: 7–28.

Becker, A. (1975) "Women in Corrections: A Process of Change." *Resolution* 1, 4: 19–21.

Block, P., and D. Anderson. (1974) *Policewomen on Patrol*. Washington, D.C.: Police Foundation.

Chapman, J. (1983) *Women Employed in Corrections*. Washington, D.C.: National Institute of Justice.

Charles, M. (1981) "The Performance and Socialization of Female Recruits in the Michigan State Police Training Academy." *Journal of Police Science and Administration* 9, 2: 209–223.

Coles, F. (1980) "Women in Corrections: Issues and Concerns." In A. Cohn and B. Ward, *Improving Management in Criminal Justice*, pp. 105–115. Newbury Park, Calif.: Sage Publications.

Crawford, J. (1988) "Tabulation of a Nationwide Survey of State Correctional Facilities for Adult and Juvenile Female Offenders." College Park, Md.: American Correctional Association.

Crouch, B. (1980) *The Keepers: Prison Guards and Contemporary Corrections*. Springfield, Ill.: Charles C Thomas.

Crouch, B., and J. Marquart. (1980) "On Becoming a Prison Guard." In B. Crouch, ed. *The Keepers: Prison Guards and Contemporary Corrections*. pp. 65–111. Springfield, Ill.: Charles C Thomas.

Dobash, R., R. Dobash, and S. Gutteridge. (1986) *The Imprisonment of Women*. New York: Basil Blackwell.

Epstein, C. (1976) "Sex Role Stereotyping, Occupations and Social Exchange." *Women's Studies* 3: 185–194.

Eyman, J. (1971) *Prisons for Women: A Practical Guide to Administration Problems.* Springfield, Ill.: Charles C Thomas.

Feinman, C. (1980) *Women in the Criminal Justice System.* New York: Praeger Publishers.

Freedman, E. (1974) "Their Sister's Keepers: A Historical Perspective of Female Correctional Institutions in the U.S." *Feminist Studies* 2: 77–95.

Fox, J. (1984) "Women's Prison Policy, Prisoner Activism, and the Impact of the Contemporary Feminist Movement: A Case Study." *The Prison Journal* 64, 1: 15–36.

Genders, E., and S. Player. (1987) "Women in Prison: The Treatment, the Control and the Experience." In P. Carlen and A. Worrall, *Gender, Crime and Justice*, pp. 161–176. Philadelphia: Open University Press.

Glaser, D. (1964) *The Effectiveness of a Prison and Parole System.* Indianapolis: Bobbs-Merrill.

Goffman, E. (1961) *Asylums.* Garden City, N.J.: Doubleday.

Harris, J. (1988) *They Always Call Us Ladies.* New York: Scribner's.

Jacobs, J. (1979) "The Sexual Segregation of the Prison's Guard Force: A Few Comments on *Dothard v. Rawlinson*." *University of Toledo Law Review* 10: 389–418.

Johnson, R., and S. Price. (1981) "The Complete Correctional Officer." *Criminal Justice and Behavior* 8, 3: 343–373.

Kassebaum, G., D. Ward, D. Wilner, and W. Kennedy. (1962) "Job Related Differences in Staff Attitudes Toward Treatment in a Women's Prison." *Pacific Sociological Review* 5: 83–88.

Katrin, S. (1974) "The Effects on Women Inmates of Facilitation Training Provided Correctional Officers." *Criminal Justice and Behavior* 1, 1: 5–12.

Kissel, P., and J. Seidel. (1980) *The Management and Impact of Female Corrections Officers at Jail Facilities Housing Male Inmates.* Boulder, Colo.: National Institute of Corrections.

Klofas, J., and H. Toch. (1982) "The Guard Subculture Myth." *Journal of Research in Crime and Delinquency* 19, 2: 258.

Kraft, L. J. (1978) "Integrating the Keepers: A Comparison of Black and White Prison Guards in Illinois." *Social Problems* 25: 304–318.

Lekkerkerker, E. (1931) *Reformatories for Women in the U.S.* Gronigen, Netherlands: J.B. Wolters.

Lipman-Blumen, J., and A. Tickmayer. (1975) "Sex Roles in Transition: A Ten Year Perspective." *Annual Review of Sociology* 1: 297–337.

Marrett, G. (1972) "Centralization in Female Organizations: Reassessing the Evidence." *Social Problems* 19: 221–226.

Martin, S. (1980) *Breaking and Entering: Policewomen on Patrol.* Washington, D.C.: Police Foundation.

Matusewitch, E. (1980) "Equal Opportunity for Female Correctional Officers: A Brief Overview." *Corrections Today* 42, 4: 36–37.

Nieva, V., and B. Gutek. (1981) *Women and Work: A Psychological Perspective.* New York: Praeger.

Parisi, N. (1984) "The Female Correctional Officer: Her Progress Toward and Prospects for Equality." *The Prison Journal* 64, 1: 92–109.

Pollock, J. (1981) From interviews conducted with correctional officers.

Pollock, J. (1986) *Sex and Supervision.* New York: Greenwood Press.

Rafter, N. (1985) *Partial Justice: State Prisons and Their Inmates, 1800–1935.* Boston: Northeastern University Press.

Ross, R. (1981) *Prison Guard/Correctional Officer.* Toronto: Butterworths.

Strickland, K. (1976) *Correctional Institutions for Women in the U.S.* Lexington, Mass.: Lexington Press.

Sykes, G. (1956) *Society of Captives.* Princeton, N.J.: Princeton University Press.

Toigo, R. (1962) "Illegitimate and Legitimate Cultures in a Training School for Girls." *Rip Van Winkle Clinic Proceedings* 13: 3–29.

Webb, G. L., and D. G. Morris. (1980) "Prison Guard Conceptions." In B. Crouch, ed., *The Keepers: Prison Guards and Contemporary Corrections,* p. 160. Springfield, Ill.: Charles C Thomas.

Wolf, W., and N. Fligstein. (1979) "Sex and Authority in the Workplace: The Causes of Sexual Inequality." *American Sociological Review* 44: 235–252.

Zupan, L. (1985) "Gender Related Differences in C.O.'s and Attitudes." Paper presented at the Academcy of Criminal Justice Sciences Conference, Las Vegas, Nev.

7 ▓▓▓▓▓▓▓▓▓▓▓▓▓▓▓▓▓▓▓▓▓▓▓▓▓▓▓▓▓▓▓▓▓▓
Prison Subcultural Adaptations

It has already been noted that prisons for women are not as harsh as the penitentiaries that house men. The architecture is softer, the atmosphere less oppressive. Yet women still acutely feel the deprivations imprisonment entails, especially the loss of freedom and the lack of emotional support. They feel isolated and surrounded by uncaring or hostile others, and the loss of their children is cause for acute worry and depression.

Researchers have engaged in a somewhat Kafkaesque inquiry into who feels the pains of imprisonment more deeply, men or women prisoners. For instance, Ward and Kassebaum wrote: "The impact of imprisonment is, we believe, more severe for females than for males because it is more unusual. Female inmates generally have not come up through the 'sandlots of crime,' in that they are not as likely as men to have had experience in training schools or refor-matories" (1964: 161). In their study of 832 women inmates, inter-viewing 45 of them, they observed that women indicated that, although prison was not physically difficult, it was emotionally stressful, both because of a fear of the unknown and because of severed ties with children. Women expressed frustration at not being able to depend on staff for help and emotional support. This frustration marks a theme pervasive throughout the literature; women evidently expect and demand more from the correctional staff, whether or not they receive it. They do not adopt the social distance and isolation that characterize the relations between male inmates and officers but rather look to staff, as well as one another, to provide support and nurturance (Ward and Kassebaum, 1964: 162).

Prison life leads to subcultural adaptations: *prisonization* is the term used to describe the degree to which an individual inmate has adopted the prisoner subculture and its value system. The prisoner subculture is a subterranean culture that exists within but is distinct from the formal culture of the prison and society. It is the sub rosa culture of norms, values, and social roles. This system of power and interchange occurs among prisoners more or less outside the control or even knowledge of prison officials. The formal prison culture, on the other hand, is what is seen; it is the product of all the actors in the prison environment, including prison administra-tors, staff, and the prisoners themselves. Elements of the subculture in prisons for men that have been studied include leadership (Schrag, 1954; Berk, 1966; Sykes, 1956) and social roles (Sykes, 1956; Hayner, 1961; Schrag, 1961). These elements have also been studied by at least a few researchers studying institutions for women. However, although gangs, violence, drugs, victimization, and other aspects of the subculture have been studied in male prisons, homosexuality has been virtually the only research topic to interest researchers in institutions for females. Part of the reason for this may be that homosexuality in women's institutions mani-fests itself in such a different way from what one finds in the prisons for men; part of the reason may be the importance placed on relationships in the women's subculture. But one can't help noting the almost prurient curiosity of so many researchers in the female's sexual identity and activity. This interest seems suspiciously similar to earlier days when female offenders, but not necessarily males, were questioned about their sexual history.

Obviously, to speak of one prisoner subculture is a misnomer. Every institution has a separate prisoner subculture. Each subcul-ture is molded and constrained by several variables, such as the demographic characteristics of the prisoners, the level of custody, population size, physical layout, regional location, characteristics of the city from which the prisoners are drawn, average length of sentence, and a whole range of other elements. The prison subculture ordinarily refers to an "inmate code," argot roles, and the social organization of the prisoners.

IIIII The "Inmate Code"

The "inmate code," a Magna Carta of prison life, was originally described in the 1940s and 1950s. Interestingly, very little current research has been done to redefine the code; instead, researchers are still measuring adherence to the code as if it had remained unchanged over the years. The major values the code has been described as endorsing are: "Don't interfere with inmate interests"; "Never rat on a con"; "Don't be nosy"; "Don't have a loose lip"; "Keep off a man's back"; "Don't put a guy on the spot"; "Be loyal to your class"; "Be cool"; "Do your own time"; "Don't exploit inmates"; and so on (Sykes, 1956).

The "do your own time" dictum seems to be more often followed by males in prison than by females. More women are involved in dyads or kinship systems. These relationships are tinged with emotional involvement and concern. Women prisoners seem not to share the subcultural proscriptions about getting involved in another woman's problems. The negative aspect of this element is that women will spread rumors and gossip about one another's activities as a form of social control or merely as a social pastime. Women's sexual involvements become community property; the latest break-ups provide more immediate entertainment than television. Emotional involvement often is unreliable; friends will fight; dyads will split and re-form, with other members. Sometimes a woman's problem will be taken up by a number of her fellow inmates; sometimes women will exhibit unconcern, depending on what else is happening at the time. Other women may pick up another woman's confrontation with staff or emotional crisis as their own; and depression or suicidal tendencies often have a contagious effect.

Women also do not have proscriptions regarding interaction with c.o.'s. In a men's prison, inmates tend to avoid officers so as not to be labeled a "snitch." Thus, correctional officers and inmates share very little and, except in special settings, tend to limit interaction to formal exchanges regarding duties or needs. Women seem not to have the subcultural proscription against interactions with c.o.'s, and there is more casual and social interaction as a result. Of course, some inmates share the view more dominant in the men's prisons, but they have little power to control other inmates' behavior.

Arguably, with changes brought about by the drug culture, a different racial mix, changes in the composition of offenders, and legal changes in the operation of the prison, the old system of values described by Sykes and others is probably quite different today. Because of differences in the composition of the inmate body (including offender criminal background), gender differences, and different institutional features, it should not be surprising that women prisoners have different values and a different inmate code. Unfortunately, researchers always use the male inmate code to measure prisonization.

IIIII Argot Roles

The social roles present in male institutions have been the topic of many articles and debates among researchers. Sykes' classic work specified rats, centermen, gorillas, merchants, wolves, ball busters, real men, toughs, and hipsters (1956). Hayner and Ash described real men, racketeers, smoothies, politicians, and dings (1939: 40). Schrag's typology, which is perhaps the best known, included square johns, right guys, con politicians, and outlaws (1961: 12). These roles describe the behavior patterns, motivation and place of the individual in the prison culture. Not all inmates can be categorized into a social role, of course, but some are easily recognizable. The real man was the type who populated the "Big House" of earlier days. He was an honest thief and subscribed wholeheartedly to a criminal subculture. Neither the administration nor brutal guards could break him; he would maintain control through any and all attempts to belittle or humiliate him. The "square john" was the innocent among wolves. He held middle-class values and identified more closely with the guards than fellow inmates. Consequently, he was never trusted and often victimized. The "con politician," because of verbal skills and intelligence, was the articulate manipulator, serving as liaison for the inmate body with the administration but ever watchful for opportunities to advance his own interests. The "outlaw" was the inmate others feared because he would use violence and force to take what he wanted, living outside the bounds of normal prison society. Finally, the "ding" was also feared, but because his violence was irrational and unpredictable. He was the inmate whose tenuous hold on sanity was destroyed by the hard edges of prison life, and he was shunned by those who did not trust his unpredictable fear and paranoia.

Apparently the social roles of the prisons for men and women are different. Although some roles have been observed in both prisons—namely, squares, snitches, and homies—others are different. Some are probably more similar than different. For instance, Simmons described a type of female inmate who worked well with the administration and probably was a type of politician (1975: 103).

She also mentioned women who used violence to get their way, and they may have represented a type of outlaw (Simmons, 1975: 108).

Interestingly, sometimes the same social role is explained in different terms. Giallombardo discusses the "homey" relationship found in the women's prison as one created to prevent gossipy women from spreading stories about one another on the outside. The woman befriends those who come from her neighborhood to guard against such "feminine" tendencies. Strangely, she does not recognize that homies exist in male prisons as well, nor would she probably attribute the presence of male homies to such sex stereotypes as gossip (Giallombardo, 1966b: 279). Giallombardo's social roles included snitchers (common to male prisons), inmate cops, squares (parallelled by square johns), jive bitches, rap buddies or homies (common to male prisons), boosters, pinners, and the cluster of roles associated with homosexuality (1966a: 105–123).

The "real man" is a term applied to old-style cons who possess characteristics such as generosity, integrity, and stoicism in the face of provocation from guards. Giallombardo wrote that there were no corresponding "real women," because the positive qualities associated with the role do not exist in the female prisoner, who was instead "spiteful, deceitful and untrustworthy" (1966a: 130). Heffernan, however, described the "real woman," who seems to come fairly close to the concept of the "real man," as one who is responsible, loyal, and willing to stand up for what she thinks (1972: 158). Heffernan's "square," "cool," and "the life" correspond almost identically to Irwin and Cressey's "square," "thief," and "con" subcultural roles. These two systems also exemplify the trend to identify several subcultures within a prison, which has helped explain differential adherence to the inmate code. According to Heffernan, the different normative orientations are more potent predictors of prison adaptation than length of prison sentence or other variables. They also have relevance, in the female institution, to participation in homosexuality; those who are in "the life" subculture are involved most heavily in prison homosexuality.

These three subcultures were indicative of differential attitudes and adaptations to prison. Findings indicated that those women in "the life" were more comfortable in the prison environment. Only 22 percent of those women rejected prison, compared to 60 percent of those described as belonging to the "cool" and 75 percent of those termed "square" (Heffernan, 1972: 67). Those in "the life" participated more often in the homosexual subculture and had more inmate friends. They totally immersed themselves in the prison life. This group also had the fewest contacts with the outside.

The cool type was described as the professional criminal. These women seek to do their time with as little trouble as possible. They participated the least in prison programs and limited contacts with other prisoners. They adhered most strongly of all the groups to the inmate code. Although these results seem valid, some problems exist with Heffernan's work, including an arbitrariness in the way individuals were assigned to subcultures. Part of the definition of the subculture uses the variables employed for assignment to it, and the subcultures are not discrete. Heffernan also used many staff perceptions in assigning individuals to the subcultures and in determining the degree of homosexuality.

Mahan discussed several types of women inmates in her descriptions of prison life. They include the junior c.o.'s, who are similar to Giallombardo's inmate cops; "inmates" who are opportunistic and want to do easy time, similar to Heffernan's cool type; and convicts, who were the long termers and probably similar to "the life" type of Heffernan's research (Mahan, 1984: 361). There are some differences, however, in that Mahan found that the convicts uphold some tenets of the inmate code, such as "Don't rat," and "Don't ask for protective custody," and "Take care of your people"—values that Heffernan and Irwin and Cressey identified with the thief or cool roles.

A large part of the inmate code is concerned with the proscription against ratting, or in any way conveying information about inmate activities to prison officials. The importance of the rat in the prisoner subculture is made clear by the number of argot terms related to the person who talks. The common perception is that this concern is present in both female and male prisons, but the rule against ratting is much more heavily enforced in male prisons.

Giallombardo believed that women showed greater propensity for snitching than men. Widespread ratting is common in male prisons, however, and the norm is not enforced as often or as severely as the early literature on the inmate code suggested. It is true that rats exist in both prisons, and there is no shortage of male or female prisoners who are willing to talk for personal reasons or for profit. The sanctions employed against rats, however, do seem to differ. In both prisons, social isolation is used against individuals, but gossip is used in women's prisons, and sometimes mild violence, in the form of threats or pushing and shoving sessions. Serious violence, however, is rare in women's prisons, although it does happen.

Several reasons can be suggested for these differences. The stakes involved are probably not as high in female prisons. Specifically, drug traffic probably does not approach the same level in women's prisons as it does in male prisons, and sanctions against inmates for illicit behaviors are probably much more extreme in men's prisons, including keeplock and physical assaults. Even though enough evidence shows significantly different sanctions against ratting in women's prison, it is still unclear how much difference appears in the reasons for and frequency of ratting or in the percentage of the prison population that takes part in ratting.

No systematic study has yet uncovered what kinds of sanctions are most often used in women's prisons.

IIIII Social Organization

The social organization of men's prisons is shaped primarily by the gang structures and other groupings male inmates create. In most prisons today, gangs are very powerful and control drugs, other types of contraband, and practically everything else. Inmates must either join a gang or risk victimization. Admittedly, a number of male inmates successfully isolate themselves from the gang structures, and a number of others are rejected by the gangs, but many inmates either belong to a gang or are controlled by the gangs in their prison. Other groupings may be formed in conjunction with formal prison programs—for instance, clubs. These groups are different from gangs but still have the elements of strength through numbers and a formal hierarchy of power. Males bond together sometimes in "homie" relationships based on where they are from, and some friendships form. However, by all accounts prison life for men is an extremely anomic existence. Men rarely get close to one another, and most ties are based on racial or political allegiance. Male inmates share a subculture with a strict hierarchy of power, and rulers and ruled live in uneasy alliance, marked by frequent battles.

Whereas racial gangs are common in male prisons, racial problems do not usually exist in prisons for women. Although a few recent reports have described women banding together in racial groupings and discussing racial tensions (Mahan, 1984), most studies have found that integration is the norm. For instance, one study found that although black women felt that job placement and other staff treatment was racially discriminatory in a prison, there was a high degree of informal racial integration among inmates. According to Kruttschnitt (1983), 55 percent of white inmates had close ties with one or more black women, and 75 percent of black women had one or more close ties with white women (1983: 583). Finally, different mechanisms are used to distribute resources. Whereas men tend to operate businesslike black market systems, complete with entrepreneurs and corporate mergers, women distribute contraband and noncontraband items through family ties and small cliques.

Another aspect of social organization is the existence and power of inmate leaders. In a male prison, leaders are connected with gangs. Leaders may also arise from formal organizations in the prison, but these individuals often have no real power in the inmate subculture. Leadership in a male institution tends to be fragmented; no universal leaders emerge, although some men may gain notoriety through violence and intimidation. Leadership is a complicated concept. In a male prison, leadership may consist primarily of fear and threat—the gang leader may hold his place through fear rather than respect. Another component of leadership is respect. Some male inmates may gain the respect of numbers of prisoners through the force of their personalities or their interactions with administration; these leaders, however, may not hold formal roles or be connected with a particular gang or following.

Giallombardo (1966a, b) postulated that leaders within the female system were to be found only within the kinship system; the male or father figure was the unquestioned leader for that family, and to some extent "he" gained status in the eyes of those outside the family by virtue of "his" position. This implies that women value qualities in a leader that parallel the traditional male role in society.

Other studies of leadership in women's prisons found that leadership as observed in a classroom situation bore no relation to age or race, and education was a more influential factor than male or female roles (van Wormer, 1976, 1979). Other studies found that leaders tended to be young, black, and high interactors, and they were likely to be homosexually active (Simmons, 1975; Moyer, 1980).

Researchers have learned that they must be aware of the effect of the total subculture on who is identified as a leader. For example, in a loose, atomized subculture with few ties, those who would emerge as leaders in a questionnaire would be those identified by a cohesive group, however small. This reason has been suggested to explain why young, black, violent inmates are identified as leaders in prisons for men, since the group Irwin characterized as the state-raised youth would be likely to be the most cohesive force in the prison, and consequently their members would show up as leaders in a questionnaire. That these individuals emerge statistically does not necessarily mean that they are status leaders for the total inmate population. This situation could be true of studies that identify certain types as leaders in female prisons as well. In this case, homosexually active leaders would likely be represented, since the homosexual subculture would likely be the strongest force at work.

Simmons/Moyer described the women leaders as high interactors, young, black, narcotics offenders with prior felony records and prison incarcerations. They are part of "the life" and are oriented toward prison life. They are able to fight and are forceful characters. They may be homosexual stud broads (1975: 5). Moyer defined leaders as those who stand up for others and get what they want; they are also known for their ability to fight (1975, 1980). Moyer found a relationship between interaction and leadership and a somewhat less clear relationship between homosexuality and leadership.

Van Wormer (1976) used an ethological approach to study sex role behavior in several prison classrooms. She examined the relationships between leadership and qualities such as masculinity, homosexual involvement, age, race, and dominance. The author found no significant relationship between leadership and masculinity. Leadership was related to the violence of the crime (using the Mann-Whitney test); it was also related to homosexual involvement. Van Wormer found that education was more important than masculine/feminine (M/F) factors in determining leadership, and pseudofamily involvement bore little relationship to M/F scores. No significant relationship showed up between leadership and age, race, or other variables. This study suffers from methodological problems, however, in that van Wormer used sex stereotypes as the model of masculine and feminine behavior and also used staff reports to measure other items, such as homosexuality.

Heffernan also discussed types of women leaders. The "real woman" was one who told people the truth regardless of consequences, never did anything spiteful, was loyal, and so on. It is clear that leaders do exist in a female prison, but they may emerge for smaller groups and possess traits different from those observed in prisons for men. Although maternal qualities are valued, and many leaders in women's prisons enact a "mother" role, it is unquestionably true that male qualities in a woman are also valued, and female inmates respond to such a person as they might to a male. An interesting if coincidental example of this kind of response occurred in a prison in which this author spent most of one summer. A person who held no less than three of the formal leader slots—namely, head of the inmate grievance committee, representative to the administration from her unit, and president of an inmate club—was a transsexual who had completed several of the series of operations necessary for making her a male. This individual, with facial hair and a deep voice, was literally the only male in a female prison and held most of the formal leadership roles.

Women are also observed to have more difficulty organizing and cooperating with a leader.

> Men are more organized than females. With the leaders they'll stand there and they'll face whatever's necessary. But with the females, they'll start something, I won't call them leaders, instigators really, and then fade into the background and then leave their followers to continue on (Pollock, 1981).

This difficulty may relate to the lower frequency of organized protests, fewer lawsuits, and smaller number of formal inmate organizations characteristic of women's prisons.

The social organization of a women's prison is centered around pseudofamilies, friendships, and homosexual liaisons. The social groupings are different; rather than grouping themselves in gangs and pseudopolitical organizations such as inmate clubs and associations, women group together in familial units, cliques, or dyads. Their advocacy is emotional and personal; their allegiance is to a few rather than to the many.

IIIII Prisonization

Obviously the concept of prisonization means little if one does not accurately understand the subculture to which the inmate adapts. All research on prisonization, unfortunately, has relied on early descriptions of the male inmate code and value system as the subculture to which inmates are supposedly prisonized. Initially, findings indicated that women in prison possessed no "solidarity," meaning that they were unlike male inmates, who bonded together in subcultural groups. Ward and Kassebaum (1964) remarked that there was "little evidence" of social solidarity. They used a questionnaire that presented hypothetical situations, such as an inmate's planned escape; the response of individual inmates as to what they would do indicated the extent to which they held subcultural values. Women evidently did not answer in the same way as male prisoners.

The measurement of solidarity with a prisoner subculture is always measured by terms common to the male inmate code—namely, adherence to such values as violence, toughness, coolness, and antiauthoritarianism. It should not be surprising, then, that many studies have failed to find these themes dominant in the institution for women. The researchers have interpreted this finding to mean that women do not bond together or do not make a subcultural adaptation to prison life. The alternative argument, of course, is that women do form a subculture in a prison, but it is a subculture that meets their particular needs. Values are those values common to women in general and to prison women in particular.

Researchers assume that an inmate code is, by definition, a male inmate code. For instance, Tittle (1969) reports that fewer women in a co-correctional treatment center for imprisoned drug addicts subscribed to such values as "Mind your own business," "Be loyal to other patients," "Be a man," and "Don't rat." These are the typical values of what researchers call the inmate code or prison culture. One should have no difficulty understanding why women would be less likely to subscribe to the value "Be a man." The concept has relevance only in a male institution, although the values of a female institution do not necessarily conform to dominant society either.

Alpert, Noblit, and Wiorkowski (1977) also used hypotheticals to measure prisonization. The hypotheticals were changed only to the extent of changing the name of the main character, so that in the hypothetical "Convict Johnson on work release gets busted and sent back to prison. Another con in the work release center, Dager, breaks into Johnson's room, takes his stereo, and sells it. Dager is a sharp operator, "convict Johnson" becomes "inmate Jean," and "Dager" becomes "Patty." Others are also changed only to the extent of feminizing the names of the inmates involved (Alpert et al., 1977: 33). This hypothetical points to some confusion even regarding the essence of the male inmate code, since the early formulations of the code suggested that real men in prison (right guys) shunned the concept of exploiting one another. This study also emphasizes the difficulty in interpreting the term *prisonization*, since these authors include such factors as attitudes toward lawyers and the justice system—a concept very different from adherence to the values cited earlier. The authors find that women "evidence vestiges of a traditional sex role orientation which is personal, specific, agent oriented and possibly vindictive" (Alpert et al., 1977: 32). However, since it is unclear how the authors are measuring prisonization or what prisonization is supposed to represent, this conclusion has little value.

Jensen and Jones (1976) also used male measures of prisonization with a female prisoner sample. Prisonization was defined as adopting values such as "Do not divulge information," "Do not respect staff," "Do not weaken, submit, or accept," and so on. He found that the career phase of female prisoners (early in the prison sentence, middle phase, or late) was related to adherence to the code (the middle phase showed highest adherence) even though it did not reach a level of significance. Age was the strongest predictor of adherence, and other variables, such as visiting or number of letters received, made no difference. The author found that different types of inmates showed different patterns of adherence. For instance, misdemeanants exhibited the career phase effect whereas felons did not.

Kruttschnitt (1981) used Wheeler's index of conformity to staff role expectations to measure commitment to an inmate code. In a small sample of fifty-seven inmates, she found that women inmates failed to endorse an inmate code of ethics, yet they did not express conformity to staff expectations either. However, conformity increased during the length of the prison term—a finding directly contrary to Wheeler's regarding male inmates. Unfortunately, because this measurement device only targets values from the male inmate code, again we don't know what values women do endorse.

In sum, the research in this area suffers from a lack of willingness to relinquish outdated theories regarding the inmate code. There seems little doubt that the prison of today is different from that of Clemmer's and Syke's time. There may be a modern code of values and prescriptions of behavior, but researchers will never discover it so long as they continue to constrain inmates' beliefs to

agreement or disagreement with the traditional code that characterized the "Big House." The research on women prisoners suffers
the most from this single-mindedness, since women deviate the
farthest from the old value system. There may indeed be a female
inmate code, but it must be found by phenomenological means—
listening to women's views and values rather than attempting to
measure them against an outdated and inappropriate male yardstick.

IIIII Importation and Deprivation

Two competing explanations for the existence of prison subcultures
have been developed. The deprivation model (Sykes, 1958) explains
that the deprivations of prison life, including deprivation of freedom,
safety, sex, privacy, and so on, create the need for a subculture to
meet the needs of the suffering prisoners. The importation model
(Irwin and Cressey, 1962) explains that the characteristics of the
inmates themselves create the subculture. Specifically, street gangs
are brought into prison, and role types are based on previous
criminal history and social class, as well as other individual variables; thus what exists in the prison is what is brought to it from
the outside.

Each of these theories could be used to explain the differences
found between male and female prisons. For instance, the deprivation theory may be applied with the assumption that females in
prison are less deprived; thus their subculture should not be as
strong or possess the elements the male subculture has developed.
A variation of this hypothesis would be that since the deprivations
for women are different, the subculture has developed differently to
meet the needs women feel most acutely. Importation theory may
also be used to explain differences. Sex roles from society are
brought into prison along with criminal roles, and these roles with
their contingent expectations and needs have shaped the different
subcultures.

Researchers have sought to discover which of these theories has
more predictive power in the commitment to a prisoner subculture
in the female prison. In an early article, Tittle (1969) looked at
females and males incarcerated together in a drug treatment program. Assuming that the custodial conditions were similar for both
groups, he set about to discover whether importation or deprivation
factors better explained inmate organization. First, he observed
differences in the two groups' subcultural adaptations to imprisonment. He noted that although the rates of homosexuality were
similar, the meaning of the relationships were different. For women,
homosexual activity represented affection and love; for men, it

represented physical release and economic exchange. Male inmates scored higher on social cohesion and adherence to the inmate code, although the differences were not large in some areas. Women were more likely to form small groups than men. The author then held constant a number of importation features, such as criminal history, intelligence, age, and visitation contact, and found a small but apparent sex difference in the measures of social cohesion and adherence to a code. Thus he concluded that neither deprivation nor other importation factors seemed as important as sex differences in explaining subcultural adaptations.

Zingraff (1980) compared 267 male inmates and 137 female inmates. He used measurements of deprivation (that is, powerlessness) and measurements of importation (that is, social class and involvement in criminal behavior) and examined their influence on prisonization. He found that for males, the deprivation model was a better predictor of prisonization, but for females, both models seemed to influence the women's prisonization (Zingraff, 1980: 284). Hartnagel and Gillan (1980), in a similar study, found that importation factors—age, prior imprisonment, and staff friends—were more influential in the adoption of an inmate code than sex was.

Most studies that use such measures have found that the deprivation theory has little support in female institutions. The explanation offered is that women's institutions are less harsh than male institutions, and consequently there is less need for a subculture to emerge in response to deprivation. Interestingly, none of these studies attempts to adapt the prisonization measures to the female institution. They typically assume the same elements make up deprivation for men and women and then measure women's adherence to the male inmate code.

IIIII Importation Factors

Gender is an importation factor, since it is brought into the prison and shaped by societal forces outside the prison. Thus, even given exactly similar prison circumstances, one might expect women and men to react differently and adapt to the prison environment in a different manner. Gender differences are a controversial subject. However, it seems safe to say that regardless of whether men and women are inherently different, in this society men and women may behave differently and have different value systems because of their socialization. These socialized differences are brought into the prison and shape the subculture. For instance, women spend more time talking and worrying about their children; this concern with the outside world tends to diffuse the importance of prison life.

Women's criminal backgrounds are different from men's. Fewer women inmates have had professional orientations to crime before their prison stay. Fewer of them have extensive criminal histories or histories of violence. Many women are amateurs at crime, and their histories reflect a lack of commitment to the criminal life-style. They may commit less serious crimes, such as forgery or shoplifting, only when they need the money for drugs or because of economic pressures in their life. They may never develop techniques in the way a professional develops his or her craft, criminal or otherwise. Crime tends to be sporadic and tied to economics, drugs, or male figures for many women.

A greater percentage of women are also "square johns," that is, individuals who have no criminal orientation per se but rather subscribe to the value system of society. Women like Jean Harris and the battered women described earlier who kill in passion, frustration, or fear find themselves in prison because of their actions, yet they have no stake in the criminal life-style. Although these types exist in the prison for men as well, they compose a larger percentage in the women's prisons. Of course there are some professional criminals in the women's prison, as well as some women who profess a radical or terrorist philosophy toward the state and capitalist society. However, these types do not predominate, nor do they seem to acquire the converts that appear in prisons for men.

The composition and criminality of the inmate group obviously impacts on the subculture within. Women are more fragmented and more likely to come from different backgrounds, and more of them share a fairly conventional value system; these characteristics influence the nature of the prison subculture and even its very existence. Women do have some commonalities as well. Many of them have had experiences of being exploited and abused. Many have struggled under an economic system that restricts their ability to care for themselves or their children. Many have come from family backgrounds of abuse, neglect, and sexual exploitation. These backgrounds shape the women and affect how they see the world and their needs.

Race is an importation factor. Interestingly, race does not seem to be the cause of animosity in the women's facility as it does in the male facility. Although there are complaints of racism by staff and discrimination against blacks in job assignments, and some women choose to isolate themselves from other races, there is very little evidence of violence caused by racial disharmony. Women tend frequently to develop relationships that cross racial boundaries, and certainly no racial gangs are to be found in the prison for women. Because race is a predominant issue in this society, the differences between male and female inmates in this regard are intriguing. It may be the case that because women do not form large groups, there is a greater possibility for individual understanding and friendship rather than group stereotyping and the creation of boundaries.

IIIII Deprivation Factors

The "pains of imprisonment" felt by women are somewhat different from those felt by men. Although both groups obviously share similar deprivation, they are touched in a different way by the prison experience. For women prison by all accounts is most painful because it cuts off ties to family and loved ones. Sex and companionship are needs of all humans, and women cite their absence as a painful aspect of imprisonment as well. Another pain of imprisonment is the inherent and unceasing boredom of prison life. One day follows the other in pretty much an endless succession. If a woman does not have personal resources to combat her boredom, such as an interest in writing, reading, or handcrafts, she is left to the activities of the prison program to fill her day—an inadequate resource. Another pain felt by women is the forced association and lack of privacy. Women must live together with others they scorn and despise. They must share their living space against their will and must learn to coexist with others with whom they would never associate outside prison. Privacy is nonexistent, since women must shower together and may be observed even when excreting or taking care of private needs.

The most severe pain for women in prison is the severing of family ties and friendships. Women respond to this deprivation by creating ties within the prison to serve as substitutes until they are released. These relationships are no less real than those the woman possessed on the outside, and they sometimes provide the love and concern that she never received from her outside family and relationships. The need for affiliation is met by homosexual liaisons, pseudofamilies, and friendships.

IIIII The Need for Affiliation

One of the first areas that attracted researchers to women's prisons was the pervasive homosexuality that seemed to characterize most adult female institutions. The relationships of women in prison seemed to be defined as either familial or connubial; women formed pseudofamilies, with parental and sibling roles in an extended family system, or they entered lesbian liaisons, sometimes formalized by "marriages," complete with mock ministers and marriage certificates. Less permanent relationships existed in "romantic love affairs" accompanied by love notes, hand-holding, or kissing. Often one party to a relationship plays a masculine role, with stereotypical short hair, masculine clothing, and assumed authoritativeness and dictatorial behavior. However, a prison relationship may also be one in which neither party exhibits a masculine role or any public signs of affection. Although it is true that perhaps too much interest has been displayed by researchers in the homosexuality of women prisoners, the importance the relationships play in a prison for women demands attention. To describe a women's prison without reference to the homosexual relationships found there would be like describing the prison for men without mentioning drugs or violence.

Another issue that needs to be addressed is the nature of prison homosexuality. According to most research and inmate accounts, a very small portion of the women who engage in homosexual relationships in prison are committed to this orientation as a life-style. Prison homosexuality is thus a sociological phenomenon and a subcultural adaptation to a specific situation. Except for a small group who have adopted a homosexual life-style even before prison and a few more who do so during prison, most women are "in the life" during their prison stay and then revert back to a primarily heterosexual life-style upon release. In fact, as will be reported, much of what has been described as prison homosexuality does not even include a sexual relationship. Rather, the women involved receive the affection and attention they need in a dyad with a sexual connotation.

Homosexual activity seems to differ drastically between the sexes. While sex is a commodity for men, it is an expression of attachment for women. As one officer explained:

> The homosexuality that is done in the male facilities is usually masked, and there is a percentage of rapes, but I think a lot more of it is permissive, it is sold and so forth. In the female facilities it's not sold, it's not rape, it's just an agreement between two people that they're going to participate and there is a lot of participation. In this facility of 420 people or 430, I would say that maybe 50 percent of the population tends to deal in homosexual acts (Pollock, 1981).

Homosexuality in men's prisons may be the result of violent assaults or coercion; older inmates (wolves) offer protection to young men (punks) for sexual favors and commissary articles. In women's prisons, homosexuality is consensual, and the majority of females (femmes) vie for the favors of the few who have assumed the male role (butches).

Since the early 1900s, when writers first exposed this form of subculture in the women's institution, the forms of the relationships have seemed to remain fairly stable. One of the first descriptions of female inmate homosexuality was written more than seventy-five years ago. Otis (1913) described "unnatural" relationships between white and black female inmates. Even today, one of the most obvious differences between men and women is that there seems to be little racial disharmony in institutions for women. Indeed, many homosexual relationships cross racial boundaries. Although homosexuality in prisons for men may also cross racial lines, it is more likely to be an expression of domination rather than the consensual liaison found in women's prisons.

Selling (1931) described four types or stages of homosexual involvement, including lesbianism, pseudohomosexuality, mother–daughter relationships, and friendship. He observed that these relationships were a substitute for the natural family group the women had been deprived of by their imprisonment. Although he observed that homosexual involvement progressed in stages, this is no doubt a misconception, since there does not seem to be any progressive nature to the women's involvement in these type of relationships. Women may be in either or both types of relationships and may even play a male role in a pseudofamily system while abstaining from homosexual relations.

Other early works described the love notes of girls in juvenile institutions involved in romantic affairs (Kosofsky and Ellis, 1958) and the nicknames that all girls participating seemed to adopt (Taylor, 1968). Halleck and Herski (1962) used a self-report questionnaire to find that more than half of the females in the sample participated in some form of homosexuality. The percentage differed, however, depending on the activity. While 69 percent were involved in "girl stuff," 71 percent said they had only kissed; 11 percent had said they had been involved in fondling; and only 5 percent had engaged in stimulation of genitals. Nine percent predicted they would continue to be involved (Halleck and Herski, 1962: 913). Some of these studies were done in institutions for adolescents and some in prisons for adults, and it would be wise to differentiate between the two because some differences do seem to show up between the involvements of females at different ages. For instance, juvenile institutions seem to manifest the most active pseudofamily systems.

Several studies have discovered that although large numbers may participate in relatively innocent love relationships confined to holding hands or kissing, fewer women engage in actual lesbian affairs, and these take place more often in institutions for adults rather than in juvenile institutions. This difference may result because different needs are being met by the relationships. Whereas adult women are more likely perhaps to need and seek sexual relationships, juveniles' needs are still predominantly for love, support, and excitement. The "girl stuff" reported in juvenile institutions may meet those needs. This difference may also explain the wide range in the estimates of homosexuality. Ward and Kassebaum reported that although official records indicate only 19 percent of women were involved, more than half the staff felt that 30 to 70 percent of women were involved. Most of the inmate respondents also reported wide ranges, between 30 and 70 percent. Although the authors described homosexuality as kissing and fondling of breasts, manual and/or oral stimulation of the clitoris, and simulation of intercourse, the respondents may have had different definitions of sexual involvement (Ward and Kassebaum, 1965: 167).

There have been several descriptions of the role types in the homosexual subculture of the women's prison. Ward and Kassebaum discussed the "jailhouse turnout," which represented, according to the authors, 90 percent of the women involved in homosexual activity. This individual would return to heterosexuality upon release, unlike the "true homosexual," who engaged in such affairs before her incarceration (Ward and Kassebaum, 1965: 167). The individuals who take on masculine characteristics are called "butch," "stud broad," or "drag butch." These women may have resorted to the masculine role because of the power and privileges it brings in a women's prison, especially if they are not visibly "feminine" to begin with, either because of physical features or size (Ward and Kassebaum, 1965: 168). The butches trade their femininity for power. They receive goods and services from the femmes in a parody of a traditional sexual relationship. The butches maintain their power by "servicing" the femmes sexually. In this way, they maintain control because the femmes are dependent on them for sexual gratification. Toigo (1962) described the "hard daddy" role found in one female institution, which contrasted with the "mom" or "soft mama" (1962: 9). Characteristics of toughness, belligerence, dominance, dress, and different wearing of hair identified the girls who were taking on the masculine role. Use of nicknames also furthered the illusion, with "hard daddies" taking on masculine variations of their given name. The role of the butch in the women's prison is interesting in its illustration of how women see men. These women, who evidently pattern their male personality after the men in their lives, tend to be dominating, aggressive, and unfaithful. Some women who have been the victim in sexual relationships with men on the outside may take on the butch role to be able to possess the power that they never had or felt they had as women in society.

Many officers believe that the adoption of the masculine role is often a protective device designed to insulate the woman from victimization. Her masculine characteristics are indications that she is not to be exploited or attacked.

> A lot of women when they come . . . they may be extremely feminine on the outside, but as a cover in order not to be picked on, they take on the masculine role, even though they have two or three kids on the outside, they have a husband and things like that. But in order not to be picked on once they come inside, they'll take on

the masculine role in order to be left alone by other people (Pollock, 1981).

Others see the adoption of the masculine role as an option after rejection.

> You either gonna be a femme or you gonna be a dyke, o.k.? If you come in here and nobody is attracted to you as a femme, you gotta belong so you do a complete turnaround, you become the masculine role, you got control, you go after who you want (Pollock, 1981).

Giallombardo (1966a, b; 1974) described pseudofamilies and homosexuality in an adult female institution and several juvenile institutions. At Alderson, West Virginia, she described the social roles that are part of homosexuality, including "pinners," "penitentiary turnouts," "lesbians," "femmes," "stud broads," "tricks," "commissary hustlers," "chippies," "kick partners," "cherries," "punks," and "turnabouts" (Giallombardo, 1966b: 277–281). These roles describe the masculine or feminine orientation of the woman (butch, femme, or turnabout who changes roles), the commitment to a homosexual lifestyle (lesbian or turnouts), and the motivation in entering a homosexual relationship—the commissary hustler for goods and the chippie and kick partners for transitory excitement and sexual gratification rather than a lasting relationship. The extent or nature of the women's involvement illustrates the needs that are being met. For some, the prison relationship is no more than an attempt to combat the boredom of prison life. For others, the relationship may be more meaningful and real than any experienced on the outside. For some, an appearance of homosexuality may mask a simple friendship. For some, the relationships may be avenues to acquire desired goods or services.

IIIII Pseudofamilies

A different phenomenon from lesbianism are the pseudofamilies that exist in some prisons. These relationships may or may not involve sex. More of the relationships are familial, including parent–child, sibling–sibling, and even extended family relationships, such as grandparents, aunts, and uncles. Each relationship is a reflection of the stereotypical one in society. "Fathers" are authoritarian and guiding; "mothers" are nurturing and comforting. Siblings fight; parents control.

Adoption of role types has something to do with personal characteristics, but roles are not necessarily demographically accurate. For instance, an older woman may more often play the mother role, but some mature younger women who are respected may also collect "daughters." The mother–daughter relationship is the most common, and some mothers may have many daughters in the institution who look to her for comfort and support. She, in turn, listens to their problems and gives advice. In larger, more elaborate family systems, a mother might have a husband who becomes a father to her daughters (but not necessarily). In some institutions, the family systems have become complex, and the intergenerational ties are very complicated.

Toigo found that some pseudofamilies possessed more status than others in the juvenile institution he studied (1962: 10). Staff legitimated the presence of these family systems by rewarding family leaders for controlling their inmate family members. Indeed, it seems if the staff use the informal subculture to control inmate behavior at all, most often it is to the family that the staff appeal. For instance, a mother may be approached to keep her daughter from "cutting up," if staff guess the woman may be suicidal or depressed but do not have enough reason to put her under observation. The family leaders may also be approached to calm down a consistently troublesome inmate if she is a member of a family. This would parallel staff use of gang leaders to control the inmate population in a prison for men.

Propper (1976: 94) found that more liking was expressed for girls outside the pseudofamily, a finding that seems to contradict Giallombardo's assumption that females dislike the majority of other inmates and thus form families to isolate themselves from others. Although this finding is interesting, more work needs to be done before any assumptions can be made. The finding may have resulted from a quirk in the sample, or it may be that the question tapped a "familiarity breeds contempt" concept—that is, the more an individual knows someone, the more things are bothersome about that person. By sharing a family system, it may be that women experience the worst side of the personalities of other family members, as real siblings do.

Commitments to such family systems differ. Whereas some women take the relationships very seriously, often the family relationships are more of a joke or a game than something influential or important in the woman's life. What may influence her commitment to the family, of course, are the other elements that make up the woman's prison life. When a women nears release or when she has maintained strong and continuing ties with her natural family, especially her children, the pull of the pseudofamily is weak. When a woman has come from a poor environment on the outside, when she is isolated from other ties, when the prison world is her only world, then often the relationships she develops there become more real than any she had on the outside. In a sense, she may be creating the type of family she wished she had had. A woman who came from an abusive, tortured home may seek the mother she never had; the woman who is severed from her children, unable to mother, may displace her need to mother her own children by directing this maternal interest to other women in the prison.

One interesting observation about female inmates' involvement in pseudofamilies and dyadic relationships is their attempt to create ideal relationships that probably do not represent their own experiences in real life. The inmate "mother" may be a better mother to her inmate daughters than she was to her own children before imprisonment. The inmate couple may seek a romantic bond that neither woman ever before experienced, since many in prison have had only poor and exploitative relationships with men. Indeed, because of the limitations of the prison environment and the ever present supervision, the inmate "couple" may be, for the first time in their lives, engaging in a relationship where the bond is one of affection and romance rather than sex.

Fox (1984) found that inmate participation in pseudofamilies changed between the 1970s and the 1980s. He states that during the 1970s a large number of youthful offenders (ages seventeen to twenty-four) were sent to Bedford Hills, and they were more often a part of pseudofamily units than older women were. The administration used the kinship systems to control these "disruptive daughters," since more than half reported involvement. Close to half also reported close personal relationships, sometimes including sex, but often only mimicking the butch–femme relationship (Fox, 1984: 26). However, in the second half of the 1970s, visiting policies and programming became more liberalized. More women became active in social programs; also, men from a nearby facility came in for recreation and, for a short time, dances. Kinship systems, once strong, began to dissipate. By late 1978, only 27 percent of women reported active membership in a kinship unit; all families had fewer than four members; and involvement in close personal relationships also declined (Fox, 1984: 32). In the 1980s, even fewer women reported belonging to such a family system; if they did, their allegiance was not as strong as in earlier days when the prison was less permeable. Today, family programs and furloughs help strengthen real family ties. Women are more politicized in that they maintain and foster ties outside the community and enjoy some attention from community interest groups. This permeability decreases dependence on prison life and deprivation; consequently, the prison family system is less necessary.

It seems clear that the type of institution may play a part in the extent of homosexual liaisons and pseudofamily involvement. Propper (1976; 1982) compared seven juvenile institutions, three of which were co-correctional. She used questionnaires and interviews and collected information on features of the institution, characteristics of the inmates, and the extent of homosexuality and pseudofamily involvement. She found little variability in the amount of homosexuality across the different institutions. Interestingly, the co-correctional institutions did not show decreased levels of pseudofamily or homosexual involvement, although fewer females took on the male role in these institutions. In co-correctional institutions, boys were sometimes recruited to fill the male roles in the pseudofamily systems. Homosexual marriages were rare, and the most common relationships were asexual mother–daughter or sister–sister ties (Propper, 1982: 133). Her findings showed less homosexuality than other studies did; 91 percent reported no homosexual activity. Staff estimates ranged from 7 percent to 14 percent. The background of the inmate influenced homosexual involvement more than the characteristics of the institution did, which supports the importation theory discussed earlier. Propper found that previous histories of foster care and previous homosexuality explained 29 percent of the variance in homosexual involvement. The results of this study must be viewed with caution, however, since the author mentions problems in the administration of questionnaires, including male interviewers and public interviews with staff. Also, according to the author the institutions resembled boarding schools, and their characteristics are thus hardly a good measure of deprivation. As mentioned earlier, one must also be careful in applying findings from juvenile institutions to adult women.

Mitchell (1975) also looked at the relationship between homosexual activity and the type of institution. She used questionnaires and interviews in two prisons, one labeled a treatment institution and the other a custody institution. Mitchell found that inmates in both prisons expressed negative views of one another (1975: 27). Homosexuality, contrary to a deprivation view, was more prevalent in the treatment institution (Mitchell, 1975: 27). Mitchell suggested that this prevalence may be due to more privacy and thus more opportunity in the treatment institution. One might question that assumption, however, since treatment institutions are often characterized by excessive programming and a paternalistic interest in every aspect of the inmate's life. Thus, other factors in the treatment institution or in the background characteristics of the prisoners may have influenced the degree of homosexual involvement.

Another study of deprivation and importation, and the relative efficacy of either to predict or explain homosexuality, found that black women were more likely to be active in the homosexual subculture. The author suggests that the black woman's socialization—to be aggressive and strong—predisposes her to take up the "butch" role. She also found that black women were more likely to have had homosexual relationships before prison. Both findings support the importation theory of subcultural adaptation (Nelson, 1974). It does seem to be true that black women are the dominant participants in the subculture of the prison. They emerge as the leaders and as the most active proponents of the homosexual adaptation. Black women in prison may have a similar role to black men in prison, in that their background and experiences give them more coping skills for prison life. They may have more experience in the institutional environment, coming from foster homes, juvenile institutions, or other state facilities. They are used to being financially independent, even though their backgrounds often exhibit chronic dysfunctional dependent relationships with men. For these reasons, black women more often emerge as the dominant force in an institution and shape the subculture to a great degree.

Early explanations of prison homosexuality were psychological and viewed prison homosexuality as an abnormal effect of early developmental problems. Halleck and Herski (1962), for instance, found psychoanalytic reasons for the juvenile's involvement. The authors reported that none in their study had a "mature sexual adjustment," evidently assuming heterosexuality was the only "mature" sexual orientation. Juveniles' problems may have been attributed to sexual contacts with fathers or brothers (20 percent reported such contacts) or a lack of female identification—mothers were often inadequate, and the girls' image of females was that they were weak, helpless, and vulnerable (Halleck and Herski, 1962: 914). The "masculine" partner was reported to receive vicarious gratification of her own dependency needs through unconscious identification with the dependent "feminine" partner (Halleck and Herski, 1962: 914). The unfaithfulness and flighty character of these liaisons was reported to be a coping mechanism designed to protect the girls from their fears of being abandoned (Halleck and Herski, 1962: 918). These early theories ignored the possibility of homosexuality as a rational and free choice of sexual preference. Obviously, the mental health profession has changed its approach to homosexuality, and it is no longer widely believed to be an abnormal orientation. However, some sociological aspects of prison homosexuality are still important to consider.

An alternative to the standard explanations of homosexuality in prison is the cost-benefit analysis. One might look at the advantages and disadvantages of each role in each of the prisons to tell us something about why the roles occur with the frequency they do. First, the two roles in the male prison are "wolf" and "punk"; the wolf role has the advantages of sexual gratification, access to commissary articles, and power. The disadvantage is that the individual has to physically prove himself at times either to the punk or to someone anxious to usurp the wolf's place. The wolf role is not at all contrary to the standard male sex role, apart from the object of sexual attention. The punk, on the other hand, enjoys very few advantages other than protection. In addition to being the virtual slave of the wolf (evidently this is the male interpretation of the female role), the punk role completely destroys his male image. He is required to share himself financially and sexually with his protector.

In the women's prison, the femme role has the advantage of status in being attached to a "male," some affection, and some sexual gratification; but she is also required to wait on her partner, to share commissary articles, and not to become jealous if "he" decides to take on another partner. The butch role has advantages similar to the wolf in the male prison: "he" is the taker in the relationship by virtue of the male sex role "he" has adopted. The disadvantages of the butch role are that it is contrary to the female identity; the individual is probably acting contrary to her own identity; and the woman may be suppressing her own personality because she must maintain a male front at all times.

It is clear from the superficial analysis given here that the artificial role in the women's prison, the butch, has a great many more advantages to it than the artificial role in the male prison, the punk. Following from this, it is not surprising that the butch role is usually a consensual one, whereas the punk is created only by force or coercion. Even in prisons for men, there are examples of voluntary sex role switches. "Queens" may, by charisma or the protection of powerful friends, freely take on the female role and reap rewards from a courtesan life-style. These men, however, who act as independent females, are rare and must always guard against being cast into a subservient role.

Dobash, Dobash, and Gutteridge (1986) provide a cross-cultural note. They found no evidence of pseudofamilies or homosexuality in Cornton Vale in Scotland or Holloway Prison in England. The women there were socially isolated, and when asked to name friends, few named other inmates and some even named staff members. It may be that the excessive maternality and strictness of the staff at these small prisons prevented the emergence of a homosexual subculture. An alternative hypothesis is that the women came from stronger families on the outside, although this hypothesis doesn't seem to be supported by the women's backgrounds, which were just as fragmented as American women's. Taylor (1968), on the other hand, did find romantic liaisons between girls in an Australian Borstal; thus homosexuality may be a cross-cultural phenomenon after all. Other research is needed to discover female adaptations in other countries.

IIIII Other Needs

In addition to the need for affiliation, women must find a way to cope with the prison environment, which is cold, inconvenient, and unaccommodating. It is not as hostile as the prison for men, but there are dangers. Women report fears upon entry, and they learn to either isolate themselves as best they can or adapt to the prison social life. Whereas the prison for men seems to be a jungle, where the strong survive at the expense of the weak and the only other option is to band together for mutual protection, the women's prison is marked by small pockets of friendship and allegiance. Although individuals must be constantly on guard against exploitation, there is less reason to fear and more opportunity to create bonds of love, even if transitory.

There are reports of violence in women's prisons. Women have been "raped" by other women inmates with bottles and fingers. At times this is done as punishment for perceived infractions of the informal code; at other times it seems to be done for no other reason than because the woman thought she was "better" than other prisoners and "needed to be taught a lesson." In addition to these serious violent incidents, women often attempt exploitation through intimidation. One woman inmate during her first day in general population was approached by an aggressive, "tough" woman prisoner. This woman said, "Give me your ring," and upon the refusal of the newcomer, the exploiter retorted, "Give me your ring, bitch, or I'll cut your finger off!" The newcomer continued to refuse to acquiesce to the demands of the other woman and eventually was left alone, but more often the "fish" may fear the threats sufficiently to submit to exploitation.

On the other hand, much less violence is reported in the women's prison than in prisons for men. Women are also less likely to manufacture or carry weapons. This lack of weapons may be partly due to the lack of opportunity, since women's institutions are not likely to have metal shops or other industry that provides materials for weapons. Women are probably also less skilled in the manufacture of weapons because of their backgrounds and life experiences. Some women do carry weapons, but they are less sophisticated than weapons found in prisons for men and less lethal. During an altercation, women pick up nearby objects—chairs, brooms, irons—to use as makeshift weapons, or they fight without weapons. Violence in a women's prison stems from problems in relationships or perceived thefts more often than any other reason. Thus the violence is rarely impersonal and very infrequently results in serious injury.

Another need prisoners experience in prison is for items that are taken for granted on the outside. Prisoners develop elaborate mechanisms for preserving such small freedoms as having a cup of coffee during evening relaxation or a sandwich at midnight. Another species of contraband, of course, is drugs. The need for drugs may be physical or psychological. Drugs may serve as a release from the frustration and boredom of a prison day or be used to forget the experiences of a lifetime. One consistent finding of all research is that female prisoners have less variety and quantity of contraband, including drugs, than men in prison do. One possible explanation for the women's smaller black market in street drugs is that they have less ability to obtain outside drugs, fewer resources, and no organization, all of which are needed to set up a distribution system. Another explanation, as one officer spelled out, is that women get relatively smaller amounts of street drugs because of their greater success in obtaining prescribed drugs from prison officials.

> I don't see as much drunkenness, for example, among women in prison. . . . An awful lot of people will tell you that psychotropic drugs are used more and they're used probably legally perhaps because the medical staff are more prone to give out Valium, probably the same way, you know, if you went into everybody's pocketbook on this floor you'd find a lot of Valium. Doctors seem to give it to the women and it's a drug that's very easily abused (Pollock, 1981).

No information indicates that a black market operates in women's prisons to the extent that it can be found in institutions for men. Although women may engage in petty theft, and contraband is distributed in informal circles, the degree of organization observed in prisons for men does not seem to be present in women's institutions.

Women, like men, must learn to reconcile themselves to prison life. They can either do "hard time," when personal losses and isolation create emotional distress that continues through the period of imprisonment, or good time, when they can put aside their civilian life until they can do something about it. Good time can be achieved by "doing time," which means passing the days in prison using any activities and distractions available (Mahan, 1984: 369). Some inmates do easier time than others because they immerse themselves in the prison culture. For them, prison becomes their life, and they fully participate in pseudofamilies and homosexual relationships that provide affection, comfort, and support. Some strong women thrive in a prison environment, as do some men. For these exploiters, the prison allows an opportunity to use their aggressiveness to get what they want with little chance of formal retaliation. Only another "tough" inmate will stand up to these women or men, since officers often have no knowledge of their trespasses. Other women remain social isolates, avoiding all but necessary contact with other inmates and leading a solitary existence among the many. For the most part, these women will be left alone, unless they verbalize or show their scorn of other inmates, in which case they may be socially or physically sanctioned.

"The Just Community"

An interesting example of how men and women will create a different social organization even given a similar setting was presented by Sharf and Hickey's "just community" experiment. The authors created a therapeutic community in a women's prison, using the concepts of participation and commitment to increase the moral development of the residents. They had an opportunity to create a similar model in a men's prison and were able to observe differences between the two groups. The women tended to govern using emotional, personal decision making, whereas men were more political. The daily meetings of the women were marked by feelings; men tended to be concerned with tensions and conflicts, frequently exhibiting an adversarial front toward the staff. The female inmates tended to be oriented toward a greater sense of community than the men; they were observed to support one another emotionally. In the male unit there existed a political consciousness strikingly absent among the women; men challenged the justification of the program and pushed the limits of their power. The authors termed the women's unit communitarian and the men's political (Hickey and Scharf, 1980).

IIIII Conclusion

It is important to note that research on prison subcultures is ongoing. One cannot assume that the prison is a static environment. Obviously, as crime patterns, criminals, prisons, and prison administration change, so will the prisoner subculture. It is unfortunate that there is no tradition of research on the female subculture. The research reported in this chapter that only compares women's values and social roles to the male subculture lacks a vital component. Women in prison must not be measured against a male yardstick of prisonization but should be described in their own right. The women's prison today and the subculture found there are obviously not the same as the women inmate's subculture of even a decade ago. For an approximation of what early prisons and prisoners were like, one must resort to biographical and journalistic information, because no tradition of academic research exists.

References

Allen, G. (1978) "On the Women's Side of the Pen." *Humanist* 38, 5: 28–31.

Alpert, G. P., G. Noblit, and J. Wiorkowski. (1977) "Comparative Look at Prisonization: Sex and Prison Culture." *Quarterly Journal of Corrections* 1, 3: 29–34.

Barker, G., and W. Adams. (1962) "Comparison of the Delinquency of Boys and Girls." *Journal of Criminal Law, Criminology and Police Science* 53: 470–475.

Berk, B. (1966) "Organizational Goals and Inmate Organization." *American Journal of Sociology* 71 (March): 522–534.

Bluestone, H., E. P. O'Malley, and S. Connel. (1966) "Homosexuals in Prison." *Corrective Psychiatry and Journal of Social Therapy* 12: 13–24.

Bresler, L., and D. Lewis. (1983) "Black and White Women Prisoners: Differences in Family Ties and Their Programmatic Implications." *The Prison Journal* 63, 2: 116–123.

Bunch, B., L. Foley, and S. Urbina. (1983) "The Psychology of Violent Female Offenders: A Sex-Role Perspective." *The Prison Journal* 63, 2: 66–79.

Burkhardt, K. (1979) *Women in Prison*. Garden City, N.J.: Doubleday.

Catalino, A. (1972) "Boys and Girls in a Co-educational Training School Are Different, Aren't They?" *Canadian Journal of Criminology and Corrections* 14: 120–131.

Chesney-Lind, M., and N. Rodriquez. (1983) "Women Under Lock and Key: A View from the Inside." *The Prison Journal* 63, 2: 47–65.

Climent, C. E., A. Rollins, and C. J. Batinelli. (1977) "Epidemiological Studies of Female Prisoners." *Journal of Nervous and Mental Disease* 164, 1: 25–29.

Cochrane, R. (1971) "The Structure of Value Systems in Male and Female Prisoners." *British Journal of Criminology* 11: 73–79.

Cookson, H. M. (1977) "Survey of Self-Injury in a Closed Prison for Women." *British Journal of Criminology* 17, 4: 332–347.

Culbertson, R., and E. Fortune. (1986) "Incarcerated Women: Self Concept and Argot Roles." *Journal of Offender Counseling, Services and Rehabilitation* 10, 3: 25–49.

Dobash, R., R. Dobash, and S. Gutteridge. (1986) *The Imprisonment of Women*. New York: Basil Blackwell.

Faily, A., and G. A. Roundtree. (1979) "Study of Aggressions and Rule Violations in a Female Prison Population." *Journal of Offender Counseling, Services and Rehabilitation* 4, 1: 81–87.

Faily, A., G. A. Roundtree, and R. K. Miller. (1980) "Study of the Maintenance of Discipline with Regard to Rule Infractions at the Louisiana Correctional Institute for Women." *Corrective and Social Psychiatry and Journal of Behavior Technology Methods and Therapy* 26, 4: 151–155.

Flowers, R. B. (1987) *Women and Criminality: The Woman as Victim, Offender and Practitioner*. Westport, Conn.: Greenwood Press.

Foster, T. (1975) "Make-believe Families: A Response of Women and Girls to the Deprivations of Imprisonment." *International Journal of Criminology and Penology* 3: 71–78.

Fox, J. (1975) "Women in Crisis." In H. Toch, *Men in Crisis*, pp. 181–205. Chicago: Aldine-Atherton.

Fox, J. (1984) "Women's Prison Policy, Prisoner Activism, and the Impact of the Contemporary Feminist Movement: A Case Study." *The Prison Journal* 64, 1: 15–36.

French, L. (1978) "Incarcerated Black Females: The Case of Social Double Jeopardy." *Journal of Black Studies* 8, 3: 321–335.

French, L. (1983) "A Profile of the Incarcerated Black Female Offender." *The Prison Journal* 63, 2: 80–87.

Gagnon, J., and W. Simon. (1968) "The Social Meaning of Prison Homosexuality." *Federal Probation* 32, 1: 23–29.

Garabedian, P. (1964) "Social Roles in a Correctional Community." *Journal of Criminal Law and Criminology* 55 (September): 338–345.

Giallombardo, R. (1966) *Society of Women: A Study of a Women's Prison.* New York: Wiley.

Giallombardo, R. (1966b) "Social Roles in a Prison for Women." *Social Problems* 13: 268–288.

Giallombardo, R. (1974) *The Social World of Imprisoned Girls: A Comparative Study of Institutions for Juvenile Delinquents.* New York: Wiley.

Ginsburg, C. (1980) "Who Are the Women in Prison?" *Corrections Today* 42, 5: 56–59.

Goetting, A. (1985) "Racism, Sexism and Ageism in the Prison Community." *Federal Probation* 44, 3: 10–22.

Goetting, A., and R. Howsen. (1983) "Women in Prison: A Profile." *The Prison Journal* 63, 2: 27–46.

Halleck, S., and M. Herski. (1962) "Homosexual Behavior in a Correctional Institution for Adolescent Girls." *American Journal of Orthopsychiatry* 32: 911–917.

Hammer, M. (1965) "Homosexuality in a Women's Reformatory." *Corrective Psychiatry and Journal of Social Therapy* 11, 3: 168–169.

Hammer, M. (1969) "Hypersexuality in Reformatory Women." *Corrective Psychiatry and Journal of Social Therapy* 15, 4: 20–26.

Hannum, T. E., F. H. Borgen, and R. M., Anderson. (1978) "Self-Concept Changes Associated with Incarceration in Female Prisoners." *Criminal Justice and Behavior* 5, 3: 271–279.

Harper, I. (1952) "The Role of the 'Fringer' in a State Prison for Women." *Social Forces* 31: 53–60.

Harris, J. (1986) *Stranger in Two Worlds.* New York: Macmillan.

Hartnagel, J., and M. E. Gillan. (1980) "Female Prisoners and the Inmate Code." *Pacific Sociological Review* 23, 1: 85–104.

Hayner, N. (1961) "Characteristics of Five Offender Types." *American Sociological Review* 26: 97–98.

Hayner, N., and E. Ash. (1939) "The Prisoner Community as a Social Group." *American Sociological Review* 4: 362.

Heffernan, R. (1972) *Making It In Prison: The Square, the Cool and the Life.* New York: Wiley.

Henriques, Z. W. (1982) *Imprisoned Mothers and Their Children: A Descriptive and Analytical Study.* Lanham, Md.: University Press of America.

Hickey, J., and P. Scharf. (1980) *Toward a Just Correctional System.* San Francisco: Jossey-Bass.

Huntington, J. (1982) "Powerless and Vulnerable: The Social Experiences of Imprisoned Girls." *Juvenile and Family Court Journal* 33, 2: 33–44.

Irwin, J., and D. Cressey. (1962) "Thieves, Convicts and the Inmate Culture." *Social Problems* 10 (Fall): 145–147.

Jensen, G. (1977) "Age and Rule Breaking in Prison: A Test of Sociocultural Interpretations." *Criminology* 14, 4: 555–568.

Jensen, G., and D. Jones. (1976) "Perspectives on Inmate Culture: A Study of Women in Prison." *Social Forces* 54, 3: 590–603.

Kates, E. (1955) "Sexual Problems in Women's Institutions." *Journal of Social Therapy* 1: 187–191.

Kay, B. (1969) "Value Orientations as Reflected in Expressed Attitudes Are Associated with Ascribed Social Sex Roles." *Canadian Journal of Corrections* 11, 3: 193–197.

Koban, L. A. (1983) "Parents in Prison: A Comparative Analysis of the Effects of Incarceration on the Families of Men and Women." *Research in Law, Deviance and Social Control* 5: 171–183.

Kosofsky, S., and A. Ellis. (1958) "Illegal Communication Among Institutionalized Female Delinquents." *Journal of Social Psychiatry* 48: 155–160.

Kruttschnitt, C. (1981) "Prison Codes, Inmate Solidarity and Women: A Reexamination." In M. Warren, *Comparing Female and Male Offenders*, pp. 123–141. Newbury Park: Sage Publications.

Kruttschnitt, C. (1983) "Race Relations and the Female Inmate." *Crime and Delinquency* 29, 4: 577–592.

Larson, J., and J. Nelson. (1984) "Women, Friendship and Adaptation to Prison." *Journal of Criminal Justice* 12, 6: 601–615.

Lindquist, C. (1980) "Prison Discipline and the Female Offender." *Journal of Offender Counseling, Services and Rehabilitation* 4, 4: 305–319.

Lorimer, A., and M. Heads. (1962) "The Significance of Morale in a Female Penal Institution." *Federal Probation* 26: 38–44.

Mahan, S. (1984) "Imposition of Despair: An Ethnography of Women in Prison." *Justice Quarterly* 1, 3: 357–385. Reprinted in *Journal of Crime and Justice* 7: 101–129.

Mandaraka-Sheppard, A. (1986) "The Dynamics of Aggression in Women's Prisons in England." *The Howard Journal of Criminal Justice* 25, 4: 317–319.

Mandaraka-Sheppard, A., and P. Carlen. (1987) "The Dynamics of Aggression in Women's Prisons in England." *The Sociological Review* 35, 1: 225–228.

McKerracher, D. W., D. R. K. Street, and L. S. Segal. (1966) "A Comparison of the Behavior Problems Presented by Male and Female Subnormal Offenders." *British Journal of Psychiatry* 112: 891–899.

Mitchell, A. (1975) *Informal Inmate Social Structure in Prisons for Women: A Comparative Study.* San Francisco: R & E Research Associates.

Moyer, I. (1980) "Leadership in a Women's Prison." *Journal of Criminal Justice* 8, 4: 233–241.

Moyer, I. (1984) "Deceptions and Realities of Life in Women's Prisons." *The Prison Journal* 64, 1: 45–56.

Moyer, I. (1985) *Changing Roles of Women in the Criminal Justice System: Offenders, Victims, and Professionals.* Prospect Heights, Ill.: Waveland Press.

Nelson, C. "A Study of Homosexuality Among Women Inmates at Two State Prisons." Ph.D. diss., Temple University, Philadelphia, 1974.

Neto, V., and L. Bainer. (1983) "Mother and Wife Locked Up: A Day with the Family." *The Prison Journal* 63, 2: 124–141.

Norris, L. (1974) "Comparison of Two Groups in a Southern State Women's Prison: Homosexual Behavior Versus Non-homosexual Behavior." *Psychological Reports* 34: 75–78.

Novick, A. (1960) "The Make-believe Family: Informal Group Structure Among Institutionalized Delinquent Girls." In *Casework Papers from the National Conference on Social Welfare,* pp. 44–59. New York: New York Family Service Association of America.

Otis, M. (1913) "A Perversion Not Commonly Noted." *Journal of Abnormal Psychology* 8: 113–116.

Pelka-Slugocka, M., and L. Slugocka. (1980) "The Impact of Imprisonment on the Family Life of Women Convicts." *International Journal of Offender Therapy and Comparative Criminology* 24, 3: 249–259.

Pollock, J. (1981) From interviews conducted with correctional officers.

Propper, A. (1976) *Importation and Deprivation Perspectives on Homosexuality in Correctional Institutions: An Empirical Test of Their Relative Efficacy.* Ph.D. diss., University of Michigan, Ann Arbor.

Propper, A. (1978) "Lesbianism in Female and Coed Correctional Institutions." *Journal of Homosexuality* 3, 3: 265–274.

Propper, A. (1982) "Make Believe Families and Homosexuality Among Imprisoned Girls." *Criminology* 20, 1: 127–139.

Roundtree, G., B. Mohan, and L. Maheffey. (1980) "Determinants of Female Aggression: A Study of a Prison Population." *International Journal of Offender Therapy and Comparative Criminology* 24, 3: 260–269.

Roundtree, G. A., A. D. Parker, D. W. Edwards, and C. B. Teddlie. (1982) "Survey of the Types of Crimes Committed by Incarcerated Females in Two States Who Reported Being Battered." *Corrective and Social Psychiatry and Journal of Behavior Technology Methods and Therapy* 28, 1: 23–26.

Schrag, C. (1954) "Leadership Among Prison Inmates." *American Sociological Review* 19 (February): 37.

Schrag, C. (1961) "A Preliminary Criminal Typology." *Pacific Sociological Review* 4 (Spring): 11.

Schweber, C. (1984) "Beauty Marks and Blemishes: The Coed Prison as a Microcosm of Integrated Society." *The Prison Journal* 64, 1: 3–15.

Selling, L. (1931) "The Pseudo-Family." *American Journal of Sociology* 37: 247–253.

Shaffer, E., C. Pettigrew, C. Gary, D. Blouin, and D. Edwards. (1983) "Multivariate Classification of Female Offender MMPI Profiles." *Journal of Crime and Justice* 6: 57–65.

Shoemaker, D., and G. Hillery. (1980) "Violence and Commitment in Custodial Settings." *Criminology* 18, 1: 94–102.

Sieverdes, C., and B. Bartollas (1980) "Institutional Adjustment Among Female Delinquents." In A. Cohn and B. Ward, *Improving Management* in *Criminal Justice*, pp. 91–105. Newbury Park, Calif.: Sage Publications.

Simmons, I. (1975) *Interaction and Leadership Among Female Prisoners.* Ph.D. diss., University of Missouri, Columbia, Missouri.

Snortum, J. R., T. E. Hannum, and D. H. Mills. (1970) "The Relationship of Self-Concept and Parent Image to Rule Violations in a Women's Prison." *Journal of Clinical Psychology* 26: 284–287.

Sultan, F., G. Long, S. Kiefer, D. Schrum, J. Selby, and L. Calhoun. (1984) "The Female Offender's Adjustment to Prison Life: A Comparison of Psychodidactic and Traditional Supportive Approaches to Treatment." *Journal of Offender Counseling, Services and Rehabilitation* 9, 1–2: 49–56.

Sutker, P. B., and C. E. Moan. (1973) "A Psychosocial Description of Penitentiary Inmates." *Archives of General Psychiatry* 29: 663–667.

Sykes, G. (1956) "Men, Merchants and Toughs: A Study of Reactions to Imprisonment." *Social Problems* 4 (October): 130–138.

Sykes, G. (1958) *The Society of Captives.* Princeton, N.J.: Princeton University Press.

Taylor, A. J. W. (1968) "The Significance of 'Darls' or 'Special Relationships' for Borstal Girls." *British Journal of Criminology* 5: 406–418.

Taylor, A. J. W. (1968) "A Search Among Borstal Girls for the Psychological and Special Significance of Their Tattoos." *British Journal of Criminology* 8: 170–185.

Tittle, C. (1969) "Inmate Organization: Sex Differentiation and the Influence of Criminal Subcultures." *American Sociological Review* 34: 492–505.

Tittle, C. (1973) "Institutional Living and Self Esteem." *Social Problems* 20, 4: 65–77.

Toigo, R. (1962) "Illegitimate and Legitimate Cultures in a Training School for Girls." *Rip Van Winkle Clinic Proceedings* 13: 3–29.

van Wormer, K. (1976) *Sex Role Behavior in a Women's Prison: An Ethological Analysis.* San Francisco: R & E Research Associates.

van Wormer, K. (1979) "Study of Leadership Roles in an Alabama Prison for Women." *Human Relations* 32, 9: 793–801.

Velimesis, M. L. (1981) "Sex Roles and Mental Health of Women in Prison." *Professional Psychology* 12, 1: 128–135.

Ward, D., and G. Kassebaum. (1964) "Homosexuality: A Mode of Adaptation in a Prison for Women." *Social Problems* 12: 159–177.

Ward, D., and G. Kassebaum. (1965) *Women's Prison: Sex and Social Structure.* Chicago: Aldine-Atherton.

Wilson, T. W. (1986) "Gender Differences in the Inmate Code." *Canadian Journal of Criminology* 28, 4: 397–405.

Zalba, A. (1964) *Women Prisoners and Their Families.* Los Angeles: Delmar Press.

Zingraff, M. (1980) "Inmate Assimilation: A Comparison of Male and Female Delinquents." *Criminal Justice and Behavior* 7, 3: 275–292.

8 ||||||||||||||||||||||||||||||||||||||||||||||||||||||||||
Legal Issues of Incarcerated Women

The decade of the 1970s brought about many changes in courts' recognition of prisoners' legal rights. After *Holt versus Sarver*, 309 F. Supp. 362 (E.D. Ark. 1970), which challenged the conditions of the Tucker and Cummins prison farms in Arkansas and illustrated the sometimes brutal and horrifying conditions of prison, the courts were unable to continue their hands-off approach to prisoner suits. A steady stream of prisoner cases established rights in the areas of religion, censorship, discipline procedures, access to courts, and medical treatment. Basically, courts always balanced the individual inmate's particular interest against the state's interest in security, safety, and order. Sometimes, when the individual right being litigated was considered paramount and the state could demonstrate no substantial governmental interest in interfering with that right, inmates won—for example, courts recognized the inmate's right to practice religion in a way that did not disrupt or endanger the institution. Sometimes, when the inmate interest might arguably threaten institutional security, the state won. The biggest change, however, was the development of the view that prisoners did not "check their constitutional rights at the prison door." The view that prisoners had all the rights of free people except those inconsistent with their status as prisoners contrasted sharply with the earlier view that prisoners had only those rights given them by prison administrators. More than any single element, this change in perception led to a different burden of proof and a different outcome for many of the cases decided by the Warren Court in the 1960s and 1970s.

Without exception, all the groundbreaking cases in the prisoners' rights area were brought by male inmates: *Wolff versus McDonnell*, 418 U.S. 359 (1975), which dealt with the inmates' due process rights in disciplinary hearings; *Estelle versus Gamble*, 429 U.S. 97 (1976), which established that the deliberate withholding of medical care could constitute unconstitutionally cruel and unusual punishment; and *Procunier versus Martinez*, 416 U.S. 396 (1974), which established inmates' rights to some due process protections against censorship. Recent cases that deal with the "totality of circumstances" argument also involve male inmates. The conditions challenged by male prisoners in these cases are also present in prisons for women, of course, but women have been much less likely to bring suits or seek protection from the courts, although this hesitation has been decreasing in the 1980s.

Activity concerning legal rights for women offenders first was directed to the differential treatment of women under the law. Vestiges of earlier sexist legal systems were still present in sentencing and child-custody laws until court challenges. The law's double standard has placed women in a protected but restricted position. In the not too distant past, women were barred from some rights men enjoyed, such as voting, owning property, and even working. But the law also protected women; the defense for the restrictions just listed was that if women had a somewhat restricted life-style, they were also protected by the law from the draft and onerous work conditions, and they were financially protected by means of some divorce laws. Obviously, many would argue that greater legal equality would be well worth sacrificing these so-called protections, especially since the law never protected women from worse problems, such as abusive husbands and poverty. Most of these sexist laws have been overturned, but their rationale is still found in areas touching the female offender.

Sentencing laws were originally written differently for men and women in several states. As has been discussed in previous chapters, the laws establishing reformatories for women were premised on a notion that women were uniquely amenable to that type of treatment. Laws covering sentencing of women were also written consistently with this view to ensure that women offenders ended up in these reformatories and served enough time to be "reformed." Ordinarily this meant that women were given indeterminate sentences for crimes similar to those that would result in determinate sentences for men. They may also have been given reformatory sentences for misdemeanors or public-order offenses that, if committed by men, would result in fines or no correctional sanction at all. The same conceptions created institutions that offered very few services of benefit to a woman upon release. These historical misconceptions of the needs of women offenders have resulted today in institutions that fail to meet women's needs in the area of vocational and educational progamming and medical services.

Only recently have advocates brought suits challenging conditions in prisons for females. Typically, these challenges revolve around the lack of services and programs found in women's prisons. One argument has been that equalization of services is required by the Constitution. A second argument has been that some differential treatment is needed by a female population—for instance, in medical care. Here, rather than an equalization in services, females may need different and greater services than male inmates—namely, gynecological and obstetric care. The segregation of women inmates has rarely been challenged. Although some have attacked segregated facilities as the root of many problems, and a stigma in itself since it perpetuates the concept that women are different and must be treated differently from men, most advocates for female prisoners do not aspire to integration but rather to parity in programming and services (Herbert, 1985: 1181). This "separate but equal" goal obviously is different from what courts would allow when dealing with discriminatory treatment on the basis of race.

One of the most obvious differences in the comparison of female and male prisoners is the lack of litigation on the part of women inmates. Gabel (1982) surveyed several women's prisons to determine why women engage in less litigation than men do. They found that, although women have definite legal needs and concerns, they are less likely to have resources available to meet their needs. Administrators were found to underestimate and misinterpret women's legal needs, impacting on resource provision. Women cited jail credit or good time and child custody issues as most important. Other issues were prison programs, appeals, and disciplinary issues. The survey staff found that although the prisons had legal services and law books, many prisoners were unaware of them or unaware of how to obtain the service.

> We found each system to be consistently lacking in some important aspect of its resources. If institutions had sophisticated legal materials, no introductory or explanatory guides were available to

facilitate their use. On the other hand, if institutions provided only introductory legal books inmates were unable to do in-depth research often necessary in pursuing cases. Where personnel were provided, inmates either did not know they existed or were unable to reach them (Gabel, 1982: 201).

The survey found that the women who were likely to utilize legal services were usually better educated and had held jobs on the outside. Communication among the inmates was also found to influence the amount of litigation. Women who serve long sentences are more likely to be litigious. Finally, the amount of resources available influenced the degree to which women filed suits (Gabel, 1982: 206–207).

Aylward and Thomas (1984) compared a men's prison and a women's prison that had roughly comparable population size and inmate composition. They found that although the institutions had an identical number of vocational programs, only 26 percent of the women participated, compared to 50 percent of the men. Both institutions had law libraries and law clerks, and the authors hypothesized that because of overcrowding in the women's prison, litigation should have been prevalent; however, it was found that women were much less likely to bring suits. The study looked at summary decisions of all federal civil rights complaints filed in the Illinois Northern Division under 42 U.S.C. section 1983 between August 1977 and December 1983. Although women inmates were 3 percent of the population, they represented only .6 percent of the total cases brought in the state (Aylward and Thomas, 1984: 263). The types of cases brought by the inmates were also different. In Dwight, the women's institution, the cases tended to be about conditions and internal due process, whereas in Sheridan, the male institution, the men also brought complaints concerning their original case and violence in the institution (Aylward and Thomas, 1984: 264). The authors were surprised that so few suits were filed by women despite dramatic events in the prison, such as a salmonella outbreak and a sex-for-favors scandal on the part of top-level administrators (Aylward and Thomas, 1984: 266). The authors could not attribute the lower degree of legal activity of the women to a better grievance procedure, since Dwight's procedure was supposed to be less effective; nor could they attribute it to less cause for litigation at the women's institution. What they did suggest as the explanation for the women's absence of litigation was that women were "less aggressive" than men; they were more apathetic concerning attempts to try to change their environment; they had lower political consciousness; and they had no prisoner role models who were successful "jailhouse lawyers" (Aylward and Thomas, 1984: 270). Interestingly, the women were more successful in the suits they did bring. Whereas 77 percent of the women's suits were successful, only 56 percent of the men's suits were; these statistics compare to a statewide average of 62 percent (Aylward and Thomas, 1984: 267).

Fox (1984) suggests that as younger, more assertive females are incarcerated, there will be more criticism and legal action on the part of women inmates. He observed that volunteers also stimulated greater criticism and dissatisfaction over prison policies and rules because they supported the prisoners (Fox, 1984: 27). In Bedford Hills Correctional Institution for Women in New York, several female activist lawyers encouraged women in the 1970s to file lawsuits. The volume of these suits increased steadily between 1972 and 1978; issues included medical care, disciplinary procedures, violation of personal privacy rights, arbitrary transfers to mental hygiene facilities, and liability for personal injuries (Fox, 1984: 28). Inmates objected to older officers who treated them like children and also to newer management attempts to bring some of the order and strictness from the prisons for men into Bedford Hills. These objections also found their way into court suits (Fox, 1984: 30–32).

Basically, two sources are used for women's challenges to prison conditions and treatment. The first is the equal protection clause of the Fourteenth Amendment, passed in 1868, which guarantees equal protection from state and federal laws for everyone. The difficulty of using this clause is that, so far, sex has not been ruled a "suspect class" by the Supreme Court as race has, and thus differential treatment of the sexes does not receive strict scrutiny in the determination of whether the state's action bears a rational relationship to a legitimate state purpose. However, since *Reed versus Reed*, 404 U.S. 71 (1971), courts have placed sex in a middle ground, between giving it no scrutiny at all and giving it "strict scrutiny." Thus, differences based on sex warrant an intermediate level of evaluation, and the state must show an important interest and a substantial relationship between the different treatment and the state interest. The person objecting to the differential treatment has the burden of proof to show that the law or practice was without a rational basis or was unrelated to the achievement of a valid state purpose. Courts may uphold state action in this situation, since there is a presumption of constitutionality. Thus, the state may manage to explain discriminatory or differential treatment on grounds such as that women have different needs or that the state has a legitimate reason for keeping them out of programs for men.

The second source women inmates might use in their challenges to prison conditions is the Eighth Amendment, passed in 1791, which prohibits cruel and unusual punishment. The important element of this argument is the definition of "cruel and unusual punishment" and whether the challenged condition is sufficient to meet the stringent tests the courts have established to prove unconstitutionality. The use of the Eighth Amendment has been tremendously expanded over the years. Originally used to invalidate prison practices such as whipping and other forms of physical discipline, "evolving standards of decency" now condemn other practices, such as solitary confinement for long periods of time, lack of recreation, lack of medical care, and separation from family. The "totality of circumstances" test is the most recent form of the use of the Eighth Amendment in prisoner suits and has been used to invalidate whole prison systems as unconstitutional. In this use of the Eighth Amendment, the court looks at the total environment of the prison to determine whether the living conditions violate the cruel and unusual punishment standards. Such problems as overcrowding, lack of programs, brutality, and inadequate sanitation are combined together and considered as a whole. The situation still must meet the other tests of the Eighth Amendment, such as "shocking to the conscience" and "cruel and unusual."

These tests are much more stringent than simple carelessness or negligence in meeting the needs of the inmate. For instance, although poor medical care may be sufficient to uphold a negligence suit against a prison doctor, poor medical services would not be enough to meet a test for unconstitutional treatment. The lack of medical treatment must be complete and such that "deliberate indifference" was shown, leading to the conclusion that the withholding of such treatment was meant to induce unconstitutional pain and suffering. Similar stringent tests must be met to uphold a constitutional challenge for conditions or treatment.

Title VII of the 1964 Civil Rights Act prohibits discrimination in employment on the basis of sex, and some attempts have been made to use this source to secure more equal access for female prisoners to the training and employment opportunities given male prisoners. State constitutions may provide another source for suits protesting unequal treatment of women prisoners, since often state constitutions provide broader protections than does the federal constitution. For instance, in *Inmates of Sybil Brand Institution for Women versus County of Los Angeles*, 130 Cal. App. 3d 89, 181 Cal. Rptr. 599 (1982), a California court held that the California constitution required strict scrutiny whenever a fundamental right was violated by a prison regulation. This ruling made it easier to prove unconstitutionality in the procedures and programs for women inmates. In this case, even under strict scrutiny, the court upheld the prison's regulations as advancing the state interest of security. Causes of action may also exist under the Equal Pay Act, Title IX, and other federal laws. Some of these may not be helpful; for instance, prisoners have been specifically cited as nonemployees for purposes of the Equal Pay Act by a Department of Labor source and some state statutes (Lown and Snow, 1980: 206). Since the use of these other laws has as yet been relatively unexplored, it is unclear to what extent courts would be willing to expand their use for the purpose of challenging unequal conditions in women's prisons.

IIIII Disparate Sentencing

Some of the first targets for court challenge were the sentencing laws of several states, which allowed for different sentences for female offenders. These sentencing laws were premised on the different nature of the female offender—she was thought to be more amenable to rehabilitation and thus as able to benefit from an indeterminate sentence, whereas the male was sentenced primarily for the purpose of punishment.

In early years, the courts were content to justify the different sentencing practices by pointing to sex differences. For instance, in *State versus Heitman*, 105 Kan. 139, 181 P. 630 (1919), the Kansas Supreme Court refused to invalidate a statute that imposed fixed sentences on males but gave females indeterminate sentences, on the rationale that the two sexes were different physically and psychologically (Rubick, 1975: 305). However, in recent years courts have been unwilling to accept this argument, and states have been unable to justify such laws on the basis of differences between the sexes.

Another example of disparate sentencing was the Muncy Act in Pennsylvania, which required the sentencing judge to issue a general sentence to women convicted of offenses punishable by more than one year of imprisonment, to give a three-year sentence if the maximum permitted by law was three years or less, and to sentence the woman to the maximum allowable where the permissible term was longer than three years. The sentencing judge, therefore, had no discretion to issue less than the maximum sentence or to provide a minimum sentence with eligibility for parole, as could be done for male offenders (Bershad, 1985: 399). Because of the Muncy Act, most women were sent to the reformatory at Muncy for offenses that, if committed by a male, would result in a county jail term. In *Commonwealth versus Daniel*, 430 Pa. 642, 243 A.2d 400 (1968), the Muncy Act was overturned. The court held that there was no rational basis for distinguishing men and women in sentencing.

In *State versus Chambers*, 63 N.J. 287, 296, 307 A.2d 78, 82 (1973), the Supreme Court of New Jersey evaluated that state's similar sentencing law and found that there were no differences between men and women "in capacity for intellectual achievement, self-perception, self-control, or the ability to change attitude and behavior, adjust to social norms and accept responsibility." Thus the law was held to be invalid (Bershad, 1985: 400). A federal district court declared the Connecticut indeterminate sentencing statute to be unconstitutional for much the same reason, in *United States ex rel. Robinson versus York*, 281 F. Supp. 8 (D. Conn. 1968) (Bershad, 1985: 400).

Another aspect of differential sentencing appeared in the laws concerning supervision of juveniles, which allowed for longer periods of jurisdiction over females, arguably because they were less mature or independent than males and would benefit from continued contact with the juvenile justice system. New York's Persons in Need of Supervision law was struck down as unconstitutional by the New York Court of Appeals in 1972 because it permitted juvenile court jurisdiction over females, who were considered "persons in need of supervision," for two years longer than males (*Patricia A. versus City of New York*, 335 N.Y.S. 2d 33 (1972)). Some observers have noted that female juveniles tend to be treated more harshly by the system while adult women may be treated more leniently. This disparity is probably related to the perceptions of female criminality discussed in previous chapters. Since female juveniles are capable of being impregnated, the law paternalistically sought to save the female from her promiscuity and so enabled juvenile justice workers to hold her longer and for less reason.

Today, these disparate sentencing laws no longer exist. Any attempt to reinstitute such laws would meet strong resistance from legal advocates, who could use such tools as the Fourteenth Amendment. Obviously, the discretion still present in the sentencing laws may create disparate treatment between men and women. Earlier chapters examined the role of "chivalry" in the system. Some evidence has indicated that women have been less likely to receive prison sentences for some crimes. In other cases, however, judges may actually be more harsh with a female offender. However, courts today are clear that unequal treatment under the law is no longer allowed unless the state can show a clear and substantial interest and a relationship between this interest and differential treatment based on sex.

lllll Programming and Medical Services

Theoretically, the suits won by male inmates in the areas of medical services and program opportunities should have benefited women prisoners as well. This has not been the case, however, since the courts' decisions were often limited to conditions in specific prisons or made no reference to the women's prisons in the state (Leonard, 1983: 45). As reported in previous chapters, the vocational and educational programs available to males far exceed those available to females. Typically, women's programs are small in number and usually sex stereotyped. Thus, whereas men may have access to programs in welding, electronics, construction, tailoring, computers, and plumbing, and to college programs, women may have cosmetology, and child-care, keypunch, and nurse's aide programs, and often high school is the only education available to women. State prison officials offer various explanations for the paucity of programs in women's institutions: women may lack the background necessary for some technical programs; their small numbers make any program expensive; and they may not be interested in programs in some of the more lucrative but nontraditional fields. Finally, women on average have shorter sentences than men, making some programs impossible for them to complete (Bershad, 1985: 412).

Although courts have held that prisoners do not have a constitutional right to vocational or educational programs per se, the disparity in access to programs between men and women may be unconstitutional. It was not until the mid-1970s that women addressed these conditions in their own litigation efforts. Since then, some court opinions have supported women's challenges to unequal programming or at least their requests for more opportunities for programs that could benefit them upon release. As in disparate sentencing challenges, the source of women's challenges has been the equal protection clause of the Fourteenth Amendment.

In *Barefield versus Leach*, No. 10282 (D. N.M., 1974), New Mexico was found to have failed to provide parity in vocational programming and wage-paying work within the institution. An important feature of this case was the court's definition of the equal protection standard. According to this court, the state can only justify a lack of parity in treatment or opportunities when its actions have a fair and substantial relationship to the purpose of the inmate's incarceration. When the state is guided by the inmate's sex in its determinations, the standard of review is strict in determining the rational relationship. Further, the small numbers of women and the consequent economic difficulties of providing them with vocational programs cannot justify disparate treatment. According to the court, "If the State of New Mexico is going to operate a penitentiary for women, it must operate one that measures up to constitutional standards" (*Barefield versus Leach*, No. 10282 (D.N.M. 1974), at 41). This is reminiscent of the court's views in *Holt versus Sarver*, 309 F. Supp. 362, 385 (E.D. Ark. 1970) when discussing the unsanitary and dangerous conditions that male inmates were forced to live in: "If Arkansas is going to operate a Penitentiary System, it is going to have to be a system that is countenanced by the Constitution of the United States." In *Grosso versus Lally*, No. 4-74-447 (D. Md. 1977), the Maryland Division of Corrections also agreed to a consent decree that provided for both qualitative and quantitative parity in programs, conditions, and opportunities for women inmates.

The most well known case concerning the equal protection claim and prison programming was *Glover versus Johnson*, 478 F. Supp. 1075 ((E.D. Mich.) 1979), a Michigan case. At the time the suit was filed, males had access to twenty-two vocational training programs while women had access to only three. The female's programs were low-paying and sex stereotyped. Male prisoners could earn bachelor and associate degrees, whereas women were able to take only post–high school classes that did not lead to a degree. Men but not women had access to an apprenticeship program, work release, and prison industries. Women were paid lower wages than men for the same jobs. Women had no opportunity to earn incentive good time. The law library for women contained only a few outdated books. Some of the state female prisoners were housed in Kalamazoo County Jail until a new women's facility could be built; while there they spent approximately twenty-two hours a day in their cells. They were not allowed hardbound books or personal items in their cells. They lived in four-to-six person cells, sleeping on mattresses on steel slabs.

Several sources were used in the suit against Michigan. Obviously, many of the differences in treatment fell under the equal protection clause of the Fourteenth Amendment, but the First Amendment was also used to challenge some of the conditions regulating postage stamps and attendance at religious services. The Eighth Amendment was used to challenge some of the conditions at the Kalamazoo County Jail, and Title IX of the Education Amendments of 1972 was used to challenge differential access to educational opportunities (Lown and Snow, 1980: 201–202).

The court held that programs for women prisoners were sex stereotyped and that women were denied equal access to beneficial vocational and educational programs. The test used was the middle standard—a test more rigorous than the "rational relationship" test but less rigorous than "strict scrutiny." The court ordered more educational courses for the women, an apprenticeship program, a work-release program, and an expanded legal training program. It also ordered the state to stop using the county jail as an overflow facility, since women there deserved the same programs as other state prisoners (Lown and Snow, 1980: 205; Leonard, 1983: 48).

Because women constitute such a small percentage of all inmates, the state has an understandable argument in its refusal to initiate programs that are relatively expensive because of the small number of women who would participate. Although courts have been somewhat sympathetic to this argument in the past, recently courts have taken a hard-line approach to states' attempts to use budgetary considerations to justify denying certain groups of prisoners programs to help them prepare for release.

Work-release programs, which allow prisoners to obtain outside employment while serving a sentence, are a valuable rehabilitative tool and beneficial to the individual inmate, yet women are often denied opportunities to participate in such programs (Krause, 1974: 1453). Work-release administrators have cited three arguments to justify exclusion: first, women are "unsuited" to work release; second, women's smaller numbers create a great deal of administrative difficulty; and, third, housing for women in work release is nonexistent (Krause, 1974: 1458). Courts have not been sympathetic to such arguments and have ordered correctional systems to implement work-release programs for women. Economics and administrative convenience have been denied as valid state purposes for denying programs to any particular group of inmates if the designation is made on the basis of sex. If work-release programs are tools of rehabilitation, they should be applied equally to females and males. No support can be given for the proposition that female inmates are less in need of economic self-sufficiency than males or would benefit less from a work-release program.

In one California case, all women offenders were sent to one facility while males were sent to any of a number of facilities, one of which was minimum-security and offered the men access to a work-release program. The court held this practice to be violative of the California constitution and the equal protection clause of the Fourteenth Amendment (*Molar versus Gates*, 98 Cal. App. 3d 1, 159 Cal. Rptr. 239 (1979)) (Bershad, 1985: 417).

In addition to a difference in access to vocational and educational programs, women often suffer from a lack of recreational programs. Especially in county jails where women are often housed in a segregated block, incarcerated women may not receive the recreational opportunities afforded male prisoners, despite the psychological and medical benefits such physical exercise provides. Even in prisons, women typically are not provided the range of and equipment for recreation that males receive. State correctional officials explain these disparities by pointing to the lower participation rates of women in physical activities and cost factors. Suits challenging these deficiencies are based on the Eighth and Fourteenth Amendments as well as state constitutional protections. Typically, courts have ruled as they have in vocational programming cases that unless the state can prove a legitimate reason for the different treatment, parity must be achieved (Bershad, 1985: 418).

Lack of medical services for inmates may be unconstitutional if it is severe enough to meet the court's test of "deliberate indifference." In *Estelle versus Gamble*, 429 U.S. 97 (1976), the U.S. Supreme Court held that when medical care was deliberately withheld and when it caused needless suffering and pain, it could constitute cruel and unusual punishment, thus violating the Eighth Amendment. Most prisons for men have a full-time staff of doctors and dentists, whereas women often have to travel out of the prison for treatment. Women inmates have been shown to possess a disproportional degree of medical problems; however, medical services for women are often poor and inadequate. Women's special needs in the area of gynecological and obstetric treatment are often unmet by prison medical services. In order to highlight the disparate and poor medical treatment of women inmates, several class action suits have been brought by female inmates.

One successful class action suit brought by women at the Bedford Hills Correctional Facility in New York established that medical care at Bedford Hills was inadequate and violated the Eighth Amendment (*Todaro versus Ward*, 431 F. Supp. 1129 (S.D.N.Y. 1977), aff'd No. 77-2095 (2d Cir. 1977)). Although the medical staff and the facilities themselves were deemed adequate, prisoners were often denied access to medical help through arbitrary procedures (Leonard, 1983: 49). Deficiencies in the availability of physicians, repeated failures to perform laboratory tests, long delays in the return of laboratory reports, a grossly inadequate system for keeping medical records, and a lack of adequate supervision of patients in the sick wing were some of the findings of the court (Bershad, 1985: 422). Also, the court found that health screenings were delayed, there was a defective chest x-ray machine, and gynecological concerns were ignored (Chapman, 1980: 158). The court noted that one woman was denied treatment for a month for an infection that could have resulted in sterility. The court acknowledged that Bedford Hills was no worse than other institutions but refused to agree that this meant its policies were constitutional (Leonard, 1983: 50). The court ordered better access, better nurse screening, prompt access to a doctor during sick call, better follow-up care, and periodic self-audits. The Second Circuit Court of Appeals affirmed the district court's decision.

One major problem in health care for women prisoners is the absence of pregnancy counseling or services. The National Prison Project of the American Civil Liberties Union claims that pregnant women come under strong pressure from prison officials to abort their fetuses. In *Morales versus Turman*, 383 F. Supp. 53 (E.D. Tex. 1974), a pregnant woman testified that prison officials instructed her to take ten unidentified pills and exercise. Inmates warned her that this had caused other women to miscarry, but she obeyed and later aborted (Leonard, 1983: 50). The court found that pregnant women were denied access to medical care and noted that one woman who had miscarried in prison was denied medical treatment for two days (Leonard, 1983: 50; Bershad, 1985: 424).

On the other hand, at least one inmate won a suit that challenged the prison's refusal to allow her an abortion because the prison would not pay for the guards needed to bring her to the hospital during the procedure. The court agreed that the prison's refusal violated her constitutional rights (*Lett versus Withworth*, No. C-1-77-246 (S.D.Oh. 1976)). Other incidents where states refused to fund abortion on demand by pregnant women incarcerated in state prisons have also found their way into the courts, and courts have not recognized the right of incarcerated women to demand an abortion unless they could pay for it themselves (Bershad, 1985: 424).

Many prison systems have grossly inadequate facilities for treating pregnant women. Approximately eight babies were born each year in one particular Alabama prison under conditions that threatened the lives of both mother and child, since there were no facilities to deal with possible complications. Leonard reports that many prisons have no facilities for giving birth, and women are transported to nearby hospitals. After giving birth, they are immediately separated from their babies and returned to the prison; sometimes they are subjected to vaginal searches despite their condition and risk of infection (Leonard, 1983: 51). Prison food, made up primarily of starches, and lack of exercise is not conducive to a safe and healthy pregnancy. Deficiencies in nutrition and lack of prenatal counseling may lead to premature births, prenatal mortality, birth defects, and mental retardation. Bershad (1985: 425) reports that many prisons provide no special diets or vitamin supplements for pregnant inmates.

The needs of women inmates in this area go beyond parity. Women in prison possess all the needs of women everywhere, and often their needs are more severe. In the areas of pregnancy services, gynecological care, treatment for sexually transmitted diseases, and complications brought on by drug use, women inmates arguably need more services than male inmates. Unfortunately, until prodded, often state prisons for women are unwilling or unable financially to provide such services.

IIIII Other Issues

The propriety of transferring women prisoners out of the state was first challenged in 1972 in *Park versus Thomson*, 356 F. Supp. 783 (D. Hawaii 1976). The Court found that the transfer and its attendant infringement of rights made conditions of confinement more onerous for female prisoners and thus was unconstitutional (Fabian, 1980: 182). Even when a state has an institution for women, it is often farther away from her home than the prison where men might be sentenced. However, in *Pitts versus Meese*, 684 F. Supp. 303 (D.D.C. 1987), the court refused to accept an equal protection argument against the practice of sending District of Columbia female offenders to Alderson, a federal facility much farther away than the facility that male offenders were sent to. The court said that no prisoner has a right to be in any particular prison and may be transferred within the state or out of the state according to the needs of the institution. This case indicates that at least in this regard, women litigants may not soon win much improvement.

Classification is impossible with women offenders, and misdemeanants and felons, younger and older offenders, and those with serious mental or drug problems and less serious offenders are housed together. The lack of classification for female offenders, resulting in forced incarceration with all types of offenders, often results in unintentional punishment (Rippon and Hassell, 1981: 457). In *Commonwealth versus Stauffer*, 214 Pa. Super. 113, 241 A.2d 718 (1969), a woman was housed in the state's prison for women although her crime was such that a man incarcerated for the same offense would have been in a county jail. She brought suit, and the court agreed that it was unconstitutional to treat women more severely than men by incarcerating them with hardened offenders.

Chapman (1980: 157) discussed the fact that until recently, three California counties had no facilities for women other than a maximum-security prison; there were so few women who might have been incarcerated at a county jail that the counties had no cells for them, and they were sent to the state prison. Women were then denied programs because of where they were housed. These practices, although understandable, may be unsupportable given recent court opinions and the unwillingness of courts to recognize economics as a valid state argument for denying women equal protection. It may be necessary for counties to develop innovative procedures in order to ensure that women are not treated more severely due to budgetary constraints and placement problems.

As women correctional officers have entered male prisons, so too have male correctional officers entered prisons for women. Both entries have initiated suits by prisoners alleging that opposite-sex officers violate their privacy rights. The major case concerning female officers, *Dothard versus Rawlinson*, 433 U.S. 321 (1977), was decided in favor of the state of Alabama, which sought to prevent Diane Rawlinson from working in the state prison for men, on the grounds of legitimate state interest in protecting women from the "jungle atmosphere" of the prison. Thus, the privacy rights of the prisoners were not a basis for the court's determination. In *Gunther versus Iowa State Men's Reformatory*, 612 F.2d 1079 (8th Cir. 1980), the privacy rights of male prisoners were noted, but the court determined that those rights could be protected by assigning female officers only to certain positions.

The opposing argument to privacy rights of prisoners was the equal employment rights of female officers. Since promotion is based on experience in a number of settings, and promotional opportunities are limited if women are restricted to the sometimes single facility for women in the state, it was essential for women to be allowed into male prisons to advance their careers. No such interest exists for male correctional officers who wish to work in women's institutions. Assignment to a women's institution is not necessary and may even impede promotional opportunities. In any case, males have always been in institutions for women. Even after the separate institutions for women were established, male supervisors and line staff have been common in institutions for women, although typically their job assignments have been limited. Their numbers may be increasing today, however, as unions object to restrictive assignment policies. The presence of males in an institution for women may raise greater privacy issues than does the presence of female officers in prisons for men. Whether sexist or not, some courts have recognized that women are socialized to have greater privacy needs than men in our society, and there are more potential dangers in having men observe women in their living units than are raised by women officers supervising men.

When male correctional officers were introduced into the living units at Bedford Hills, the women sued, alleging that the presence of male officers violated their right to privacy when supervising areas where the women should have been able to expect some bodily privacy, such as in the shower or in their cells during evening hours. Although the lower court agreed that privacy interests were at stake and restricted males to certain assignments that did not infringe on the women's privacy, this decision was reversed in part by the Second Circuit Court of Appeals. It was determined that arrangements could be made to allow free use of male officers and also protect the women's privacy; for instance, the Court explained that the women's complaints regarding nightgowns becoming disarranged during sleep and the possibility of being observed by male officers could be solved by issuing pajamas. Shower areas could be protected by frosted glass (*Forts versus Ward,* 434 F. Supp. 946 (S.D.N.Y.), rev'd and remanded, 566 F.2d 849 (2d Cir. 1977), 471 F. Supp. 1095 (S.D.N.Y. 1979), aff'd in part and rev'd in part, 621 F.2d 1210 (2d Cir. 1980)). The state reached an agreement whereby male officers would not be placed alone in living units and would announce their presence before proceeding into the living-unit hallways.

Some cases have challenged different punishment systems for women and men. In *Canterino versus Wilson,* 546 F. Supp. 174 (W.D. Ky. 1982), women prisoners challenged a behavior modification program that was mandatory for all women prisoners and nonexistent for male prisoners. Under this system, women were restricted from the exercise of normal privileges and punished differently from males for lesser offenses. The court held that the system unconstitutionally discriminated against women. The system was based on gender and was "unrelated to any important governmental objective," thus violating the equal protection clause of the Fourteenth Amendment under the intermediate scrutiny standard (Bershad, 1985: 405). Prisoners in this case also challenged the practice whereby women were allowed only half the visiting time that men received and were limited to fifteen-minute phone calls while men had unlimited access to telephones during free time. The court agreed that these policies constituted unconstitutional violations of equal rights (Bershad, 1985: 407).

Although *Bounds versus Smith,* 430 U.S. 817 (1977), established the right of inmates to have meaningful access to the courts through the presence of law libraries and clerks or other devices to ensure access, the provisions made for female inmates have fallen far short of those provided to male inmates. In *Glover versus Johnson,* 478 F. Supp. 1075, 1095 (E.D. Mich., 1979), the court required Michigan to provide a paralegal training program for women prisoners, not because of equal access but because it was necessary to ensure constitutional access to the courts, since women were shown to be less skilled in research and writing legal materials (Bershad, 1985: 427). Another court held that Kentucky needed to improve the women's law library and legal programs to make them equivalent to those available to male prisoners; thus, the rationale there was equal protection (*Canterino versus Wilson,* 546 F. Supp. 174 (W.D. Ky. 1982)).

IIIII Child Custody and Separation Issues

Prisoner-mothers have generally not prevailed in their attempts to keep possession of newborns in prison. Although a few states have enabling laws for such a contingency, courts typically interpret such laws as discretionary and allow prison officials to decide whether or not an imprisoned mother may keep her baby. More often than not, prison officials do not allow the child to remain inside prison walls for "the benefit of the child," and mothers who attempt to sue to keep custody of their baby lose (*Cardell versus Enomoto,* No. 701-094, Sup. Ct. Calif., San Francisco Co. 1976). Florida has repealed its statute allowing prisoner-mothers to keep their babies; New York still has its statute, but prison officials may use their discretion (Schupak, 1986).

In California, the statute allowing women prisoners to keep their babies was repealed and a law was passed in its place allowing community placement for mothers with babies. Other states have similar laws or laws allowing immediate parole upon birth. However, these laws are sometimes restrictive in terms of offense and previous criminal history, and thus they do not help many women offenders who give birth while incarcerated; nor do they help inmates who already have children.

As reported in previous chapters, inmate-mothers are often the sole supports of their infant children, and while the mothers are imprisoned, the children are often cared for by the women's relatives. However, if the state takes control of the children, retaining or reestablishing custody is sometimes difficult. Although most states do not cite imprisonment in and of itself as a cause for terminating parental rights, a few states do, and others interpret imprisonment as a type of abandonment, justifying termination in that way (Bershad, 1985: 409). These concerns ordinarily do not exist for male prisoners since their children are typically cared for by the mother in an intact home environment while the father is imprisoned. Child-custody issues typically do not arise with male prisoners either, because the family is awaiting his release or because he does not seek to maintain custody as often as the imprisoned woman does.

The child-care agency may put tremendous pressure on the woman to put the child up for adoption. The state's orientation in these cases is to do what is best for the child, and many courts will put that priority ahead of parental rights. Thus, the woman may have her parental rights terminated involuntarily solely because of her incarceration. In one case, an imprisoned woman lost her parental rights six months before release, even though the child had been in six foster homes over a period of four and one-half years. The court decided against the woman based on the fact that she was not going to be released "immediately" (*Los Angeles County Department of Adoptions versus Hutchinson*, No. 2 Civil 48729, unreported decision (Cal. Super. Ct. 1977)).

Another disadvantage women have in retrieving their children from the state is that the criterion to determine whether parental custody is in the best interests of the child is the parent's ability to support the child. If the woman does not receive vocational programs that enable her to support herself and her children, it becomes difficult to prove that she deserves the children upon release (Bershad, 1985: 411).

Poor communication between the inmate-mother and the child-care agency and lack of legal advocacy exacerbate these problems. The decisions of courts presented with a conflict between the rights of the parent and the interests of the child are mixed. Some courts will terminate parental rights quickly; others will do so only when the nature of the crime indicates that the child would be in peril if kept in the mother's custody. Inmate-mothers seek to avoid problems with custody by placing the child in the care of family members, but sometimes this is impossible. As has been noted before, child custody is one of the most important legal issues of incarcerated women and, unfortunately, the area in which they may receive the least aid.

||||| Conclusion

One problem of legal activity by prisoners is that some gains achieved in equal protection may be offset by courts' perception that parity is the only constitutional solution. Women may thus lose some of the special advantages they have had. As Ardeti (1973) pointed out, the sexual segregation of our prisons leads to some advantages as well as disadvantages for the female inmates. Although women have fewer programs and vocational programming for them is sex stereotyped, they do ordinarily enjoy more privacy in separate rooms rather than dormitories (Ardeti, 1973: 1238, 1242). They also receive more protection from staff because of better ratios of officers to inmates (Ardeti, 1973: 1240). Advocates must be careful to steer carefully between Scylla and Charybdis in attacking unequal treatment without sacrificing the mandate to meet the special needs of women inmates.

Women inmates are not men. Some needs of women are identical to those of men; thus women deserve and must receive parity in opportunity. Such needs include vocational and educational opportunities, sanitation, correspondence, legal access, and other services necessary in an institutional environment. Some of women's needs are different from those of men. They have greater and different medical needs: women need gynecological and obstetric services, and they may need to have more dollars per person spent on their medical services than is spent on those for male inmates because of physical differences between the two sexes. In this area, parity would not be sufficient, and it is necessary to recognize the need for "unequal" treatment.

In other areas, the arguments are not as clear. Should women receive different sentencing, such as community placement, because of childbirth, or would that be "unequal treatment" without a rational basis? Should greater privacy rights of women be recognized, so that they are more often than not housed in rooms rather than dormitories and have greater protections from surveillance from opposite-sex officers than do male inmates? Should women enjoy greater access to children through visiting and child-care programs, or is that a violation of men's equal protection rights? These questions must be addressed now that advocates have used equal protection arguments to achieve parity in other areas of women's prisons.

It has been noted by some that parity is the lowest minimum goal, since men's institutions are woefully inadequate themselves. Correctional departments, already faced with huge problems and court orders requiring expenditures that legislatures are not funding, are hard pressed to improve women's prisons without cuts in men's prisons. A conceivable solution is a decline in services for all, since the parity argument cannot address the absolute level of services, only differences in existing service levels.

Some solutions may be to further integrate correctional facilities and thus to open up opportunities for both sexes while reducing costs. Community corrections for both sexes may also solve some problems with access, as long as access to such programs is equal. How these issues are resolved will determine in large measure the future of correctional services.

References

Alpert, G. P. (1980) *Legal Rights of Prisoners*. Newbury Park, Calif.: Sage Publications.

Ardeti, R. (1973) "The Sexual Segregation of American Prisons." *Yale Law Journal* 82, 6: 1229–1273.

Aylward, A., and J. Thomas. (1984) "Quiescence in Women's Prisons Litigation: Some Exploratory Issues." *Justice Quarterly* 1, 2: 253–276.

Bershad, L. (1985) "Discriminatory Treatment of the Female Offender in the Criminal Justice System." *Boston College Law Review* 26, 2: 389–438.

Chapman, J. (1980) *Economic Realities and Female Crime*. Lexington, Mass.: Lexington Books.

Fabian, S. (1980) "Women Prisoners: Challenge of the Future." In G. Alpert *Legal Rights of Prisoners*, pp. 129–171. Newbury Park, Calif.: Sage Publications.

Fox, J. (1984) "Women's Prison Policy, Prisoner Activism, and the Impact of the Contemporary Feminist Movement: A Case Study." *The Prison Journal* 64, 1: 15–36.

Gabel, K. (1982) *Legal Issues of Female Inmates*. Northampton, Mass.: Smith College School for Social Work.

Haft, M. G. (1974) "Women in Prison: Discrminatory Practices and Some Legal Solutions." *Clearinghouse Review* 8: 1–6.

Herbert, R. (1985) "Women's Prisons: An Equal Protection Evaluation." *Yale Law Journal* 94, 5: 1182–1206.

Krause, K. (1974) "Denial of Work Release Programs to Women: A Violation of Equal Protection." *Southern California Law Review* 47: 1453–1490.

Leonard, E. B. (1983) "Judicial Decisions and Prison Reform: The Impact of Litigation on Women Prisoners." *Social Problems* 31, 1: 45–58.

Lown, R., and C. Snow. (1980) "Women: The Forgotten Prisoners: *Glover versus Johnson*." In G. Alpert, *Legal Rights of Prisoners*, pp. 195–216. Newbury Park, Calif.: Sage Publications.

Rafter, N. (1985) *Partial Justice: State Prisons and Their Inmates, 1800–1935*. Boston: Northeastern University Press.

Rippon, M., and R. A. Hassell. (1981) "Women, Prison and the Eighth Amendment." *North Carolina Central Law Journal* 12, 2: 434–460.

Rubick, R. B. (1975) "The Sexually Integrated Prison: A Legal and Policy Evaluation." *American Journal of Criminal Law* 3, 3: 301–330.

Schupak, J. (1986) "Women and Children First: An Examination of the Unique Needs of Women in Prison." *Golden Gate University Law Review* 16: 455–474.

9 Future Directions

Women and men are different; so too are women and men in prison. Partly because of their imported differences, and partly because of societal expectations, prisons for men and women are different on many dimensions. In this book, we have seen how the history, rationale, and philosophy of women's institutions developed differently from those for men. The women's institution was created to protect the women inmates from the abuses that occurred in institutions for men where men supervised them. The goal of women's institutions was to teach the woman inmate to behave "more like a lady." What it meant to be a "lady" during the late 1800s, however, was distinctly different from the life experience of most women inmates, then or now. Women were expected to become domestic and demure and to learn the gentle arts of sewing, cooking, housekeeping, and child rearing. It was hoped that the criminal woman, after becoming more refined would be able to attract a husband who would keep her out of crime. The reality for these women, however, was poverty. They typically escaped from their own family early by marriage, running away, or being kicked out after an illegitimate pregnancy. They lived by prostitution and petty crime, at times exploiting men, more often being exploited by them. Their lives were often marred by sexual and physical abuse. In the same manner that they themselves had been victimized, they often passed abuse down to their children by neglecting and abandoning them, either to get money or to squeeze some pleasure from their bleak lives by "carousing."

Even during the time when wayward women were placed in reformatories, the majority of minority women and many older women who were considered irredeemable were housed in institutions that did not professs much treatment of any kind. There the women continued to be used for their labor and their sex—too weak to be true criminals, too deviant to be worthy of consideration. Today, there is still a disproportionate number of minority women in prison. As is true of men's institutions, the most obvious fact when one enters a women's prison is that it is largely an institution run by whites to house blacks. Of course today, because of affirmative action and a lack of other career choices, in some states disproportionate numbers of blacks guard as well as live inside the prison.

Women in the correctional field have always been an afterthought—an addendum to a world almost completely male. Women have suffered the fate of all minority groups. Their needs have been ignored or misunderstood, and they have been relegated to restricted roles and functions—for instance, sewing and washing for the entire prison system or being sexually exploited by male correctional officials. Because of disinterest, institutions for females remained remarkably unchanged through the decades, whereas there was a great deal of activity in the prisons for men. During the 1950s; 1960s, and 1970s, prisons for men were under enormous pressure to change, in terms of treatment and vocational programs and general living conditions, including brutality toward inmates. The pressure came from the courts but also from scrutiny by the academic community and the public. On the other hand, very little litigation concerned women's prisons, and researchers showed very little interest in them. Consequently, well into the 1960s the same psychiatric explanations for female crime and behaviors in prison were being used that had been current a hundred years earlier. Only in the 1970s did interest in the female offender or the prison for women begin to be shown. During the 1980s there has been more activism, and litigation now is pushing back the sex discrimination that has characterized prison programming and treatment.

However, the current advocacy and interest in women offenders and prisons suffers from the lack of a good research tradition. It also suffers from competing paradigms. For instance, feminists may object to any approach that presents differences between men and women, since their position is that differences are either nonexistent or trivial. Others, including this author, will counter that there are real differences between the two groups. These differences may be, and probably are, almost entirely due to socialization or interactional factors, but they are real nonetheless and must be dealt with. Behaviors of men and women in prison are different, and so are their needs; and women may respond better to different procedures and regulations from those found in prisons for men.

As discussed in the last chapter, parity may not be an appropriate goal, since women inmates have distinct needs, different from those of men. Although it is useful to compare prisons for men and women on such criteria as number of programs, staff–inmate ratio, and rules and privileges, it is important to remember that to aspire to the level present in facilities for men is not a very high aspiration. Also, some programs may be more appropriate in a facility for men. For instance, women show a definite disinterest in many types of recreational programs. There is no reason to assume they would take advantage of all the programs offered in institutions for men. This is not to say, of course, that women should do without. Rather, an attempt must be made to specify the unique needs of women offenders and then meet them.

Vocational program parity in terms of numbers and even types of programs is something many advocates are seeking; however, it seems to be more appropriate, given the lower security risk women pose and their lower rates of recidivism, to push for work-release and community programs for women. Health program parity is certainly not appropriate, since women have different and arguably greater needs in this area. Prison administrators must realize that women need prenatal care and medical service throughout pregnancy. This kind of care is even more important for women who have used drugs and have other health problems. The services women's prisons provide in this area are woefully inadequate and must be improved, not only for the sake of the woman inmate but also, and perhaps more important, for the unborn child. Legal programs are relatively underutilized in women's prisons, yet their legal needs are extreme. Women need legal assistance in custody issues and other civil matters and seem less prepared and in need of greater assistance than males in this regard.

Other competing paradigms have to do with who is the focus of research. Studies that present the inmate's world almost automatically portray officers and staff in the same light that inmates do, specifically as cold, uncaring bureaucrats or, worse, sadists who enjoy the torment they inflict on the inmate population. Obviously the inmate perceives the officer group in a stereotyped way and can be excused for bias; however, a researcher who adopts this view of the officer without question has no excuse. On the other hand, the officer perspective is fraught with the opposite inclination—to view the woman inmate as childish, temperamental, hysterical, and possessing all the worst traits of criminals and women combined.

An objective picture of the prison world tries to mesh these two views together. There may be a little bit of truth to each side; individuals do sometimes fit stereotypes. However, a more accurate representation would detail how the perceptions create the reality, at least for the group that holds the expectations. For instance, if a woman officer expects inmates to act like children, she will undoubtedly treat them as children. When a woman inmate is told to comb her hair or clean her room or is otherwise spoken to in a manner that ignores the fact that she is an adult, she may respond by an obscenity or refusal that seems to the observer irrational and petulant. She does so as a defense against the infantilization; but the behavior is taken as proof that inmates really do act like children, and thus the cycle is perpetuated.

In the same manner, inmates resent being dependent on officers for the most minute details of daily living. It is difficult for an adult to ask for toilet paper, and so inmates mask the dependency by ordering and demanding that officers meet their needs immediately. Often such orders are accompanied by obscenities, to indicate that the inmate despises the need to ask and despises the officer for having the power to refuse. Because officers resent this type of treatment by inmates, they may use the little bit of power they have to retaliate. Inmates may find that request slips did not get processed; inmate belongings get lost; visitors are made to wait because their names did not appear on the visiting list; and sanitary napkins are rationed to one a day. These petty tyrannies only reinforce the perception of inmates that officers are all sadists, and again the cycle is perpetuated.

Currently, we have enormous numbers of women living in prison. True, their numbers are still minuscule compared to the numbers of men in prison, but there is no doubt that the number of women being sent to prison is increasing. Further, evidence indicates that the increase is not due to increased crime among women. Rather it seems to be due to sentencing practices and the greater willingness to send women to prison. No doubt partly a result of determinate sentencing, this tendency is disturbing since there is no indication that prison is necessary for many women criminals. Of course, there is also a real question whether prison is necessary for many male inmates, but that issue must be addressed independently.

Historically, and even today to a lesser extent, courts have shown a tendency to use imprisonment as a last resort for women.

Their dependent marital status, the presence of dependent children, and other factors seem to affect the likelihood of a prison sentence. For women who fit the societal roles of wife and mother, courts were more willing to use alternative means of sentencing. No evidence indicates that these alternative sentencing measures resulted in more crime. Women do not violate probation in larger numbers than men. In fact, by all accounts recidivism is lower for females, whatever the sentence. In some states, before a prison was built, this practice was even more apparent. Only women who committed murder and other very serious crimes were incarcerated, because the state had to utilize county jails or contract with another state to house their female offenders. Again, however, the fact that states did not imprison women to any great extent did not create a crime wave among the female population. Despite this history, almost all states now have built prisons for women. Many states are currently considering building new prisons or adding on to old ones. In every state that built a new prison for women, it was filled within a year or so. States that had a couple of dozen women prisoners before a prison was built suddenly had a couple of hundred after a prison was available. No doubt as cells for women increase in number, the women who are deemed to need institutionalization will also increase in number in direct correlation.

This development is unfortunate and probably unnecessary. For the most part, women commit minor property crimes. Their imprisonment destroys a family unit and subjects their children to extreme dislocation and anxiety. Many women never regain a maternal relationship with children who are left with others to care for them; sometimes the mother loses the children entirely when the state takes custody. The fact of imprisonment, and the separation it entails, necessitates the family programs found in some prisons, which attempt to maintain mother–child ties. A prison can never provide a program, however, that makes up for the fact that the mother is separated from the child—sometimes for months, sometimes for years. This separation may have cyclical implications, since there is evidence that children are prone to delinquency and crime when their mother is in prison.

Some women in prison are there because the state was unable to protect them from abusive husbands. These battered women have been doubly victimized—first, by having to endure the abuse in a marriage because society does not provide economic or legal solutions to battering; and second, because when she kills her husband as a desperate act of self-defense, society feels justified in punishing her for "taking the law into her own hands."

Of course, some women in prison are committed to criminal life-styles. For these women, crime is a job, and they have extensive criminal histories. The professional woman criminal seems to be a rarity, and most do not profess such an orientation. There has been very little research on career criminals among women offenders, however, so it is unclear what types of female career criminals exist and the nature of their activities and motivations. It is clear that women criminals are not becoming more violent; their numbers in robbery and other violent crimes continues to remain stable. Women continue to predominantly commit such crimes as shoplifting, forgery, check fraud, larceny, and to a lesser extent burglary.

There is still no real answer to the question of why women commit so much less crime than men. Women's lesser involvement in crime seems to be related to their socialization, but it may also be an effect of possibly inherent differences in men and women, especially in the importance they place on relationships and family. These differences should be further explored and encouraged, if they serve to reduce criminal activities.

Increasing numbers of women are becoming involved in drug violations and other crimes due to drug use. This trend will probably continue, and jails and prisons will have to deal with the medical problems of addicted women inmates—the problems will be more acute, obviously, if the women are pregnant. Drugs will probably continue to have an effect on the numbers and types of crime women commit, and treatment programs must adapt accordingly. Although treatment programs exist in most prisons, the numbers of women that must be accomodated continue to grow.

In fact, all programs in women's prisons will need to be expanded if the trend of sentencing more and more women to prison continues. Women, if they must be imprisoned, should not waste the time spent there but rather be able to benefit from adequate vocational programs that may prepare them to take care of themselves and their children without resort to drugs or other types of crime. Vocational programs in the clerical areas are the most well received by women inmates, but prisons should continue to expand their offerings in nontraditional areas, such as the skilled trades. As long as society continues to undervalue "women's work," such as the clerical and service trades, women inmates are not well served by training programs designed to place them in such occupations. Computers, carpentry, mechanical training, and other programs prepare a woman for occupations that pay almost double what she might make as a secretary or cafeteria worker.

There will continue to be cross-sex supervision; thus, the problems that arise when male officers supervise women inmates must be addressed. It is unlikely that courts will uphold privacy rights for women prisoners, since they have not done so in suits by male prisoners fighting the entry of women officers into the living units of men's prisons. Thus, the provisions made for male officers in living units for females continue to be ad hoc and unworkable. Some suggestions have been to provide architectural designs to provide some amount of privacy, such as frosted glass in the shower and curtains in front of toilets. Some prisons use such designs; along with other alternatives, they should be explored by all institutional administrations that expect to use males in locations where privacy is a problem.

Training in correctional academies should recognize that women's institutions are part of the corrections system and should pay attention to the special training needs of officers destined for such facilities. More research needs to be done to determine why greater behavioral problems are perceived in prisons for women; if these perceived problems are a real issue, then training may help reduce the problem. It is possible that the supervision of women creates the problem, because women inmates are treated like children; if so, officers need to be trained out of this practice. The trend now seems to be to get women's institutions "in line," which means treating women "like inmates." If this means to treat them like adults, that is a step forward. It is more likely, however, that it means treating them like men in prison, which means that women may lose the more personal nature of staff–inmate interaction typically found in women's institutions. For instance, staff are trained to treat all inmates alike. While such treatment is helpful in that it reduces favoritism and encourages fairness, all inmates are not alike. In fact, some women as well as men at times literally scream to be recognized for their individuality by "cutting up," fighting, or mistreating officers and inmates with loud and abusive behavior. It is more beneficial to inmates, but perhaps more stressful for officers, to recognize each inmate as an individual with unique needs and motivations. For example, it takes more skill to recognize that one woman is sincere in her need to see a counselor, while another is merely manipulating the system to avoid work or boredom. It takes skill to recognize when a woman is suffering from acute depression and needs to be put under observation. It takes skill to recognize that the rude and abusive behavior of some women inmates is a reaction to the fact of imprisonment and not to be taken personally.

One cannot put more demands on the correctional officer staff without some provisions for greater rewards. Professionalization has been the theme for the last decade, but this trend needs encouragement. For instance, all correctional officers should be rewarded and assisted if they desire higher education or membership and attendance at national or regional professional conferences. Actually, two trends are developing among correctional staff today; the first is professionalization, which tends to emphasize education and enforced standards of conduct; the second is unionization, which emphasizes material rewards and security concerns. Both of these movements are important for correctional staff, but unionization may be more shortsighted, in that ordinarily demands center on wage increases rather than job enrichment. As long as the role of correctional officer is one that demands or expects no intelligence or skill, there will be people in these positions that display none. Their lack of skill undercuts the performance of those who aspire to do more than count inmates and turn keys and frustrates their attempts to enlarge their role. At this time, people who do aspire to a larger role are typically leaving the correctional officer position as soon as they acquire the necessary qualifications for other positions. This result is unfortunate, and some attempts should be made to keep these individuals in the positions that have the most contact with inmates.

The unique subculture of the women inmates has been of great interest to researchers and continues to be intriguing in its relative absence of violence or a black market and in the affectional ties that prevail. No doubt results of the socialization of women in society and their needs for affiliation and support, the pseudofamilies and dyad relationships in prison often provide women with greater support and love than they have ever received on the outside. These relationships, women report, help make prison bearable. Yet prison officials typically discourage such connections among women, and some states deny visitation from friends who have been released. It is true that some relationships in prison are exploitive, but it is unfortunate that beneficial prison relationships are not more widely recognized as productive and rehabilitative.

Improvements should continue in women's prisons, but efforts should also be made to greatly expand the alternatives to prison for women. The number of halfway-house beds for women is drastically disproportional to the number available for men, even given the smaller numbers of women in the system. This disproportion seems to stem from a belief that women have a place to go after release, either with family or back to a husband. Unfortunately, many women do not have such a place to go, and women are in great need of a transition from prison to the outside. The woman offender needs time to get herself settled into a position where she can afford to take her children back. Sometimes, however, because of custody problems, she must take responsibility for her children immediately—rarely a good alternative, since women may need time to reestablish ties and certainly need time to build up some economic reserves.

The greatest need of women offenders is for correctional alternatives that recognize the presence of children in their lives. For instance, halfway houses that would accept women and children would be a vast improvement over what is currently available. A few facilities scattered across the country house women offenders and their children, but they are the exception. A halfway house centered around women's needs and the needs of their children would provide parenting classes and day-care. Day-care would give the woman the security of knowing her children were safe while she was at work. The children could benefit from programs that would address their special problems—namely, the anxiety of reuniting with a mother who might have been absent for a long time, perhaps even for the lifetime of a young child. Birth control should be encouraged. Some women offenders started having children very early and continue to have children without regard to who will care for them. These child-mothers never had a childhood of their own; they are criticized for being bad mothers and running around when in fact they are too young to take on the responsibilities of motherhood.

Rather than large facilities, halfway houses should be homes, small enough to blend in with the neighborhood and not stigmatize the women or children who live within them. Because women are typically not feared, as male criminals are, the problems of community acceptance should be less severe. Women can provide support for one another in their attempts to lead a life free from drugs, crime, and negative associations with men. Perhaps there should even be a range of custody grades; the lowest-security homes would not need staff but could operate as group homes, providing three or four women and their children with a house to live in and resident day-care until they were able to afford to live on their own.

These facilities could also be used for women instead of a prison term. In fact, any attempts to keep women in the community instead of prison should be welcomed, as long as accompanying measures go toward preventing the factors that cause women to commit crime. Placement in a residential community setting allows control but does not destroy beneficial family ties. Especially if the woman is able to keep her children with her, correctional professionals may be able to help provide a setting where she can learn to be a good mother if she wasn't before, to stay off drugs if she couldn't on her own, and to support herself without resort to criminality. Of course most women will continue to seek relationships with men. In a setting where self-discovery is possible, women may help one another break the pattern of disastrous relationships with abusive, drug-addicted, or criminal men. Some women must learn to be more independent from men; others could learn to be less fearful and suspicious of them; still others need to learn to be less exploitive of men. Not all women are victims—some do the victimizing.

Finally, today we no longer should be concerned with training women inmates to be "ladies," as was attempted in the early institutions; but it is still important to recognize that these inmates are women. Corrections should punish wrongdoing, but it is even more important to help women offenders be strong, productive, and healthy so they can encourage their children (if they have them) to be the same.

Index